AF884936

# The Truth Of The Modern Recession

**Winner of the 2010 Indie Book Finalist Award**

# The Truth Of The Modern Recession

## Root Causes and Reliable Solutions

**Dr. Alec Feinberg**

**WE-Economy Press**

**Copyright © 2009 by WE-Economy Press, Revised (July 2010)**

Library of Congress Control Number: 2009943627

ISBN-13: 978-0-615-31529-4

ISBN-10: 0-615-31529-1

Also available in larger easy read print size (ISBN-13: 978-0-615-34274-0, ISBN-10:0-615-34274-4, Library of Congress Control Number: 2009943627)

All rights reserved. No part of this book may be reproduced, in any form or any means without permission in writing by the publisher. You are permitted to quote brief passages of this book for research, scholarship, critique, broadcast, and review in a magazine, newspaper, broadcast, website, or government appraisal, as generally defined under the concept of fair use. Any factual public domain material or government reproduced studies, in this book may, of course, be used without permission. Please also see Disclaimer and Legal Statements in the back of this book.

For Copyright requests contact the author at
**www.modernrecession.com**

# Preface

The reader should expect to learn more on the Modern Recession from this book than from any other source. It is easy to understand, comprehensive, and well supported by facts. Areas investigated include: free trade and its deficit, separation of wealth, the housing bubble, tax issues, lobbyist problems, the national debt, etc. A proper root cause analysis has provided a logical assessment of the real issues. For example, the reader may be interested to learn: 1) Separation of wealth has increased 28% since 1980 (about 1% per year) and is a leading reason for tight money in the recession. 2) This has lead to a hoarding crisis. 3) The top 1% to 5% of the wealthiest individuals in the 35% bracket (some who make $1 billion or more in a year) only pay about a 20% tax. 4) The free trade deficit has accumulated to over $7.5 trillion, and is the main reason why the U.S. economy and our national debt are increasingly owned by foreigners. 5) Related outsourcing has led to a 33% decrease in manufacturing job losses in the last 10 years. 6) Foreclosures, government deregulation, and unsubstantiated marketplace rumors ignited a U.S. financial collapse toppling Lehman Brothers and 229 failed and 733 bailed-out banks. 7) All these issues have taken a toll on the national debt. 8) Even the trade deficit has tax related losses that appear well correlated to the national debt. These are substantial losses that cause us to question trade deficit ethical issues and a related clear violation of constitutional law! 9) A purpose of government is proper decision making, yet U.S. economists and legislatures do not use proper problem solving techniques. Our nation is in the hands of individuals who are ether strongly influenced by lobbyists or jump right to the solution without root cause analysis. All these are interrelated facts that contribute to our unreliable economy and are a Truth of the Modern Recession. Therefore, the modern recession will linger until real economic change occurs.

*"Change will not come if we wait for some other person or some other time. We are the ones we've been waiting for. We are the change that we seek."*

—BARACK OBAMA, speech, February 5, 2008

## TABLE OF CONTENTS

# Economic Drought

*What if*
*The wind could no longer howl*
*Clouds slowed to a standstill*
*The rains turned to sprinkles*
*Mountain streams stopped flowing*
*Waterfalls only trickled*

*Your life blood lost circulation?*

*What if*
*The buck really did stop here*
*And here was at your fingertips*
*And you were a CEO, movie Star, famous athlete…*
*A congressman, A senator*

*And collectively*
*You all ran for cover*

*Surely then*
*Lightning will not strike*
*But its thunder will be heard round the world.*

*–Alec Feinberg –*

# ■ 1.0 ■

# INTRODUCTION TO A RELIABLE APPROACH FOR OUR ECONOMY

Although our Modern Recession is a terrible time for so many individuals who suffer financial problems, it is in fact the best time to look at our economy's true failure modes from a reliability perspective. This is because the economy is under stress and recessions don't lie about our problems. If you try and find mechanical problems with a car, for example, by testing it under ideal conditions (on a smooth road on a nice cool day), this will not be a good stress test to find any design problems that might fail over time. A car needs to be tested under stress (a bumpy road on a stormy rainy day). Similarly, looking at problems in our economy under stress, i.e., during a recession, does give us a chance to find our real root cause issues. Therefore, the one good thing about our recession is that it does put our economic engine through a major stress test, resulting in the surfacing of our economy's design failures. We now have the opportunity to contemplate and address the reasons for these failures and to formulate solutions that will help improve our economy and quality of life. If we fail to look at the real root of each problem now and address it, we will miss the boat and jeopardize future generations.

What is needed is a new perspective; this unique approach we will term, "Reliability Macroeconomics" for the layperson or the economist (also referred to in this book more simply as "Reliability Economics"). However, do not let the word "economics" turn you off. This book focuses on the economy, not on the math of economics. The term simply helps describe our common sense corporate model approach for problem solving and investigating, and for recommending improvement in order to provide a reliable economy.

Our approach is to use industry-wide accepted standard problem solving tools that lead us to the actual root cause issues on the Modern Recession. Such tools will be very helpful for the reader, legislatures, and even economists. Currently, our congress people and economists do not use such tools and the consequences can be significant. These tools aid in proper investigative methods to uncovering key issues. Reading on, you will find that each detail is logically supported by sound information from our economy. As you might imagine, our U.S. and global financial crises consist of unaddressed problems that turn out to be key issues of unreliability. Underlying these issues is the common chord that America has become a nation of "haves" and "have-nots". We present strong research data. For example, looking at the trend over the last twenty-six years, you will see shocking evidence (similar to Figure 1.1) that the wealthy are now totally dominating our income-tax revenue. Here we note that the top 5% of our population are now paying 61% of U.S. income taxes, up from about 37% in 1980. On the other end of the population, the bottom 50% have, coincidentally, moved in the opposite direction, with total tax revenue falling from 7% in 1980 down to 3% in 2007. This dichotomy, a 28% separation of wealth change (averaging 1% increase per year), is relevant to the unreliability of our economy through tight money problems in our recession, and will be discussed in the following chapters. Yet the trend is clearly visible and has been for years, indicating a lack of planning for a reliable economy.

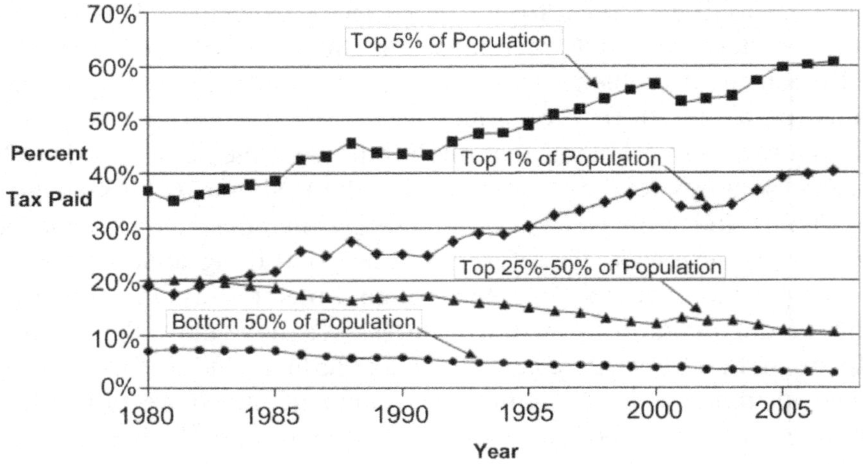


**Figure 1.1** Plot of federal individual income tax data from 1980 to 2006 with selected percentage contribution from the U.S. population[1].

An interesting misconception in the literature or web—and equally misleading from this figure—is that it appears the wealthy (top 5%) pay their fair share of taxes, yet logical analysis will indicate otherwise (see Chapter 4 for detail assessment). In particular, one cannot ignore the observation that the wealthy must also be taking up most of the earnings resources. This figure has been researched from our federal income tax data, and is one of our central findings that must be understood as a major issue of our economy.

Since this and other unattended key problems are not being addressed, yet will be shown to be root causes, we end up having a poor-performing economy,

[1] Analysis of July 8, 2008 data, Tax Foundation, www.taxfoundation.org/news/show/250.html

and are misinformed on key issues by our government leaders and their economists. The results are inappropriate corrective actions, including questionable governmental bailout choices, job losses, and what we feel are unnecessary increases in our national debt. Lastly, increases in the separation of wealth are often correlated to social problems such as higher crime rates, increase in drug abuse, etc. It remains unfortunate that the government does not use traditional problem solving tools and issue root cause analysis on many of their decisions including spending our TARP (Troubled Asset Relief Program) monies. Most of our congress people fall into the trap of identifying solutions without first understanding the root causes. Prior to any spending or policy change, there should be a full team analysis, performed and issued on a public website, to explain where and why our monies are being spent. Reliability tools can provide such a format without interfering with the traditional political system.

*The Truth of the Modern Recession is that we have an unreliable economy because of problematic economic policies.* These failing policies stem from misguided political practices due to a lack of reliability economics. This includes a need for problem solving tools for the layperson, legislatures, and economists that could help prevent such failures in the first place. This book illustrates how reliability economics can help make policies more reliable.

You may not understand the significance of what reliability can do and how it has affected your life. The next time you drive a car, board a plane, or even drop your cell phone, realize that your piece of mind is in part due to the science of reliability. Now multiply that by millions of people in the world and think of the cost and lives saved. For example, since 1950, automotive and airplanes have improved in reliability by 10 times with longer life and higher safety. Now compare this, with a lack of reliability economics for our economy. In just the last 10 years, we have witnessed substantial increases in the national debt (doubled), manufacturing job losses (40% lost), free trade deficit (tripled), separation of wealth (up 8%), unemployment (doubled), and other increases in business failure rate, housing failure rate, lobbyist influences, and so forth. In part, this is a statement of failure for macroeconomics. The main issue is that economists and legislatures do not use proper problem solving techniques, and our nation is in the hands of individuals who fail to understand basic reliability principles. There is a large gap; a reliability assurance group is needed. It is likely that you may not agree with all suggested economic changes presented in this book. However, you will gain broad and valuable insight into U.S. issues using basic problem solving methods, and realize the need for reliability tools to help safeguard our economy.

The reliability approach applied here to investigate such facts is similar to that applied in industry. Companies spend millions of dollars each year making dependable products using reliability methods. It makes sense to borrow their methods to investigate and suggest ways to design-in a reliable economy. The key method used is a well-known technique called Failure Modes and Effects

Analysis (FMEA). A tool that helps everyone to understand and participate in finding issues. It is similar to that applied in industry. It is actually helpful for the layperson in terms of understanding how the economy works, and allows for formal investigations. It takes advantage of a team approach, and could be a logical way to force bipartisan politics to reach agreement on root causes and solutions. This technique is easy to understand and is widely accepted for problem solving in industry to help make dependable products. It could easily supplement decision making improvements in government without interfering in the traditional voting system on bills, yet can be influential. It should be a requirement for legislatures to learn and use just as it is for engineers in industry. Lack of using this problem solving tool has led to inadequate policies by our economist, legislatures, and are in fact, a key essential root cause truth of the modern recession. However, a full reliability approach would require three basic activities, adapted from industry, for reliability of the economy:[2]

- Design for reliability economics
- Perform reliability economic verification testing
- Perform root cause fiscal analyses

Currently, there are no formal practical corporate reliability methods applied to the economy. We will see that the implementation of these methods would make enormous sense, just as it does in industry. First, we seek to ensure that we have identified the root cause issues, and then we will look to make improvements, focusing on designing-in reliable solutions for the economy (as opposed to short term solutions). Finally, we need feedback through verification testing. Testing takes time, especially when we are dealing with the economy, and should be done in phases throughout any significant design change to the economy. For example, if Alan Greenspan had performed stress-related testing of bank deregulations over time, he would likely have observed the subprime mortgage abuses by lenders and the irresponsible banking irregularities occurring; had he done so, perhaps he would not have allowed this widespread policy that has led to our housing crisis. Thus allowance for testing can and should be built into any proposed legislation.

We know that during this time of stress, many failures have surfaced. Our economy's engine uses too much wasteful oil, is inefficient on gas, has too many parts not made in America, and our economy's designers/advisors have, over time, failed to build-in reliability. We have gone into debt trying to fix the economy's engine with needed improvements. We simply cannot turn our backs on reliability macroeconomics. In part, that is what the national debt does; it is a measure of fiscal irresponsibility and unreliability. We also describe reliability economics issues with our free trade deficit and related tax losses, substantial

[2] *Design for Reliability*, CRC Press, Edited by A. Feinberg, Dana Crowe

losses that even cause us to question surrounding ethical trade deficit issues and a constitutional law violation (see Sec. 9.7 and 9.8). You will find, upon learning reliability methods applied to the economy, that they are easy to understand, help the layman understand the economy quickly, are unavoidably logical, and do not lie. Reliability economics provides an organized approach with a mindset for building-in reliability into the economy. This includes such keys to success as being proactive, not reactive. That is, we simply cannot afford to be reactive any longer, putting out fires in the economy as they occur. We need to be proactive and design reliability into our economics so that these fires do not occur in the first place. We provide more details on implementing a supplementary reliability economics corporate government model approach in Chapter 11. However, in an effort to keep the reader's interest, we only provide the basics in this introduction.

Problem solving requires a team effort. Relying on the perspective of our congressmen, who are mainly lawyers—or by our economists, who also have narrow perspective on finance—is a limited way to find solutions for multiple complex issues. If the lawyers and economists were enough, we would not have the results which have transpired. There is a physics joke that has some truth to it:

> A biologist, a chemist, and a physicist were all looking at a sick horse. The biologist said, "It is obvious, the horse has some sort of biological imbalance." The chemist replied, "No, it is a chemical imbalance." Finally, the physicist said, "Well, to a first approximation, the horse is a sphere!"

As you will find out, the idea of reliability provides reasonable, powerful methods for understanding how a complex system will work when exposed to harsh economic conditions (including misuse such as economic greed for example). Such tools should be applied to our economy. We seek to predict and ensure the future. We want our economy to demonstrate "reliability growth." Such growth in reliability is measured by a reduced rate of product failure over time. In a similar manner, we need to have measurable and meaningful reliability indexes for the economy consisting of our unemployment rate, home and business failure rates, and so forth. Such measures, when tracked frequently, can help warn us prior to a crisis so that corrective actions can be applied in a timely manner. This is analogous to quality field-data tracking of a product, which is done all the time by industry.

If we are provided unbiased facts and logical analyses that stem from real root causes, and if the fixes are aimed at efficient reliability in the economy, with tests planned over time to verify that improvements are working; we will then end up with a trustworthy economy. After all, we want an economy whose engine runs dependably over time without failures. That's what we mean by Reliability Economics.

# ■ 2.0 ■

# TIGHT MONEY

## 2.1: Investigating the Root Causes of Tight Money

We know that money is tight. This is not just an expression; it is the reality of the Modern Recession. Tight money is partly to blame for the financial crisis. If people cannot pay their loans, and thereby default on their mortgages and credit cards, it creates havoc in the financial world. We know there were bad loans and problems with government deregulation that play a key role in the recession, but we cannot assume this leads us to the root cause. For the moment let's simply ask the logical question, "Where have the dollars gone?" After all, this is a clear symptom that cannot be ignored. It may seem simplistic, with numerous answers, but let's take the time to do a root cause analysis. This is, after all, an economic reliability issue, since it is hindering the long-term performance of our economic growth. If we just quickly assume the faltering economy is due to job loss, such as work being shipped overseas, that does not actually address the question or go far enough. The actual question is, "Where has the money gone?" One must ask the right question before we can find a solution. The initial key issue is then simplified to:

**Money Is Tight.**

In order to analyze why money is tight, we use the easy-to-understand reliability method called Failure Modes and Effects Analysis (FMEA) to help with problem solving. An overview of this method is provided in Appendix 2A. In this method, we start with the key issue, and ask the question, "***What can go wrong?*** We then define its potential failure mode(s), the potential effect of the failure mode, and theorize on what the possible root causes are to the key issue. After that, we define what would be a potential economic design control and corrective action. Typically, we would use a diverse core team to do this analysis. The team should consist of a team leader (reliability economists), subject matter experts, and a champion owner of the process or design. Logically for an economic policy the team should include democrats and republicans for a bipartisan solution, and subject experts. However, here we have to rely on historical causes from our research for the FMEA. Table 2.1 is an example of how we would assess this key issue. All the root causes need to be substantiated with facts. This, however, provides an initial launch to our investigation. FMEA is one method used in industry to analyze root causes of failure modes and corrective actions. Why not use it for our economy? It also serves as good chapter overview for the reader mainly interested in the Modern Recession root causes. The full corporate model is explained in Chapter 11.

**Table 2.1** Failure Modes and Effects Analysis on Tight Money

| Key Issue | Potential Failure Mode | Potential Effect of Failure | Root Cause(s) | Root Cause Rating | Design Control | Possible Corrective Action |
|---|---|---|---|---|---|---|
| Money Is Tight | Reduced money in circulation | Business and personnel financial failure | 1) Individual hoarding 2) Decline in GDP 3) Job loss 4) Business hoarding 5) Housing crisis | 1) 8 2) 8 3) 8 4) 7 5) 6 | 1, 2) FMEA on tax structure 3, 4) Assess hoarding issues 5) Govern-ment Regula-tions | 1,3,4,5) Change tax structure 1,4) Anti-hoarding legislation for individuals and corpora-tions |
| Tax Struc-ture | Loss of needed government revenue | Poor monetary circulation Governm ental debt | To be identified | To be Deter-mined | Analyze tax structure | To be identified |

In summary, the basis of problem solving is then: 1) obtain a core team, 2) define the problem statement and convert it to a key issues ("Money is Tight"), 3) I.D. the failure modes, 4) and their effects, 5) for each failure mode brainstorm its root cause, 6) assess the risks with ratings, 7) suggest design controls and, 8) corrective actions. Analysis should be based on facts/data and not ideology. *Congress members should not fall into the trap of identifying solutions without first properly understanding the root cause problems.*

From our table, we see five possible root causes to the "tight money issue": hoarding (individual and business), decline in the Gross Domestic Product (GDP), job loss, and the housing crisis. The research leading to these conclusions is now necessary to substantiate the claims. We have also identified feasible design controls related to each root cause. These are FMEA on tax structure, and assess hoarding issues, and government regulations. Since we cannot address every root cause in this book, we have ranked them in order of importance using the column called Root Cause Rating. We score each root cause using a number from 1 to 10, with 10 indicating the most severe value (See Appendix 2A, Table

2A-1). Typically the scoring would be performed by an investigative team. Here the root causes of highest rating in Table 2.1 are 8, and these 8's correspond to:

**Hoarding, Decline in GDP, and Job Loss.**

In working our table, we have actually come up with another possible key issue, namely our tax structure. That is, if the corrective action on "Money is Tight" is a change in the tax structure, as indicated in the table, this infers that there is a problem with it. Therefore, the second identified key issue is:

**The Tax Structure.**

We will look at this in Chapter 4, but first we need to focus still on tight money and its root causes that have initially been identified. We will focus first on hoarding, and decline in the GDP, and look to substantiate these with facts.

*"According to the New York Times, swine flu can be transmitted on money. You know what that means.... We're all safe. No one's got any."*

—Jay Leno, May 2009

Perhaps Mr. Leno should have added, "*Except me, of course*!"

**Remark:** Jay Leno's Net worth is a reported $32 million![3]

**2.2: Understanding Economic Hoarding and the Velocity of Money**

First we will use an analogy to understand our notion that hoarding could cause tight money, then later substantiate the issue for this recession with facts (since some economists actually might disagree with this premise). Initially, we'll look at an extreme analogy and then refine it. For the moment, consider that someone invents a way to attract rain with a new breakthrough device called a magnetic "rainometer" that has the ability to gather rain to one region of the world. What will happen? Somehow the magnetic rainometer doesn't allow evaporation back into the atmosphere for the rest of the world. As one might expect with this evil device, very soon a drought will be created everywhere else. In this situation, world governments would have to mix hydrogen and oxygen to create moisture. However, such moisture or rain created by world leaders would soon be futile, as it would again be collected by the magnetic rainometer. Now the inventor can control the water flow, its price, and the valve to turn it on or off anywhere in the world.

This is simply an analogy to help illustrate a problem; we have theorized that we are in the midst of an economic drought. It is logical to believe that the

---

[3] www.knowyournetworth.com/jay_leno.html

wealthy have created a kind of magnetic "moneyometer." We prefer shopping at Wal-Mart to buy low-priced items; we enjoy supporting high-salaried celebrities by going to their movies or sports events; we mainly buy Microsoft's computer products, and so forth. The government will mix ink with paper and create bailout after bailout. However, like the rainometer, their effort will be futile; the bailout money will eventually be collected by the magnetic "moneyometer." The wealthy have the economic "moneyometer" to attract our dollars and hoard them. The government actually has the combat weapon: it's called taxes. However, we have also surmised that the government doesn't have a reasonable tax structure to help keep money in circulation.

We currently have a theory, that this magnetic "moneyometer" makes our system problematic, because not enough U.S. dollars go back into circulation during a recession. Banks are reluctant to lend money. Our economic engine is sputtering along now. It is inefficient, and the flow of its fuel, namely money, is having problems circulating through our engine to all parts of our economy. We have poor economic reliability and performance, which also leads to job losses.

Money hoarding is a bit more complex than just the accumulation of wealth. It is related to the lack of circulation of dollars through our economic engine, as we have noted. Eduard Daladier, the Prime Minister of France, said the following during a London Conference in 1934:

> In our economic system, money has the same function as blood for the body of human beings. In order to fulfill all the different functions of life, circulation of the blood must be ensured without interruption. With money it is the same—it necessarily needs to circulate in order to realize full employment.

And herein is the major problem with our now global economy. Accumulation of great wealth can be devastating, especially in the time of a recession, principally when a small portion of the population (< 5%) apparently earns most of our revenues according to Figure 1.1. A person having great wealth can choose what to do with his money. This choice affects the manner and speed with which dollars enter back into proper circulation. Most individuals and corporations that accumulate great assets think more about preserving their funds than investing. In reality, they can simply live off of their savings. Investing can lead to helping money circulate and stimulating job creation and retention. (We discuss job-friendly investing in Chapter 8). It is no sin to save money, but hoarding (as we define below) is another matter.

In a time of a recession, individual bank savings and money market accounts (see Chapter 3 on money market accounts) end up effectively as "mattress accounts." A mattress account is a common analogy referring to money stuffed away in a mattress—hoarded and out of circulation.

This is because many banks and money markets hoard cash so money doesn't circulate. Banks are very reluctant to take even minimal risks on loans in a recession (see Chapter 3). Money markets primarily invest in banks (see Chapter 3). This is our first piece of evidence.

> **Remark 2.1:** According to *Forbes* (February 2009)—"Bank excess reserves (unloaned dollars) went from $2 billion in August 2008 to $267 billion in October 2008. As of the middle of January 2009, they had mushroomed to $843 billion."[4]

It is hard to blame banks for being reluctant to lend when, for instance, the housing crisis hit a record high in quarter one of 2009.

> **Remark 2.2:** "According to the *Associated Press*, mortgage delinquencies hit a record high in quarter one of 2009 where 12 percent of homeowners were behind on their mortgage payments or in foreclosure as the housing crisis spread to borrowers with good credit. And the wave of foreclosures isn't expected to crest until the end of next year, the Mortgage Bankers Association said Thursday." [5]

Therefore, we see that the housing crisis is one root cause of tight money, as it creates an atmosphere for bank hoarding. However, there are other aspects to hoarding that need to be investigated to realize the primary root of our problems. Remember, we are seeking a reliable economy and real root causes and solutions, not quick fixes. Let's look more at some hoarding facts.

A good measure of our money supply is provided by a quantity in economics called **M1**. This is currency in circulation plus deposits (checking deposits, officially called demand deposits, and other deposits that work like checking deposits). The other key quantity is **M2**. This is M1 plus savings deposits, time deposits less than $100,000, and money market deposit accounts for individuals.

> **Remark 2.3:** "It would appear the institutions and individuals are hoarding cash and cash equivalents. The percent change for M1 over the last 3 months (June 2008 to September 2008) has spiked to 19.5%. The six and twelve month percentage change is 11.4% and 6.4% respectively. Clearly this hoarding behavior is quite sudden and recent. M2 for example

---

[4] www.forbes.com/2009/02/03/banking-federal-reserve-business-wall-street-0203_loans.html

[5] www.sfgate.com/cgibin/article.cgi?f=/n/a/2009/05/28/financial/f070037D89.DTL

isn't increasing nearly as fast at 6.8%, 4.0% and 6.2% over the last three, six and twelve months."[6]

**Remark 2.4:** "Paulson is desperately throwing our money at banks in a futile attempt to convince them to lend. Instead, those banks are either hoarding the cash or acquiring more assets. In other words: Paulson is helping the banks that were 'too big to fail' grow even bigger with taxpayer backing. Swell."[7]

Therefore it becomes difficult to seek capital preservation for wealthy individuals through banks or money markets without hoarding. Great wealth frequently promotes hoarding that increases dramatically in a recession. Accumulation of great wealth creates an economic medical condition that, like an overweight person who is prone to blood clots and lack of circulation, dramatically affects all the vital functions of our economy. This lack of circulation, the slowing of the "velocity of money," is a key factor of our economic reliability's lifeblood.

**Table 2.2** Key Definitions of Economic Hoarding

| Hoarding Concept | Definition |
|---|---|
| Storage | The portion of accumulated wealth that is taken out of proper economic circulation. |
| Velocity (speed) | A decrease in the speed or velocity of money back into our economy typically equates to a hoarding effect. Other main factors that affect velocity are job growth or loss and quantity of goods and services (Gross Domestic Product) |
| Storage vs. Velocity | Hoarding is inversely proportional to velocity of money. |

Table 2.2 defines two key definitions of economic hoarding. The storage concept is familiar to most people. It is the portion of accumulated wealth that is taken out of proper economic circulation. The velocity definition is somewhat more helpful as a measure of the speed for which money exchanges hands, similar to circulation of blood in our body. Another interesting aspect of the velocity of money is that it is somewhat useful as an indicator of consumer confidence.

---

[6] Money Stock Measures. www.federalreserve.gov/releases/h6/current). See also www.istockanalyst.com/article/viewarticle/articleid/2741143

[7] *American Commentator*, Michelle Malkin, December 3, 2008

**Remark 2.5:** "The velocity of money is probably closely linked to the confidence in the economy. If the confidence of the economy goes down so does typically also the velocity of money. Even if I have money to spend, I am less confident in the future of the economy. So it is rational for me to hold back a little even if the government should send me a check. I'll just stash it away." [8]

A more mathematical definition for the velocity of money is the average speed with which a dollar is spent given a certain amount of money, say, in a period of a month. The loss or decline of money circulation equates to degrees of hoarding. Velocity of money is a key economic factor. Higher velocity values reflect a relatively more free-spending society, with each dollar cycling through the economy more quickly. Lower values, on the other hand, indicate a relatively "stingy" society, in which each dollar circulates through the economy more slowly. Velocity of Money (V) is calculated as the Nominal Gross Domestic Product (NGDP) divided by the monetary base—money supply (M), or for those who like equations, a simple form is

$$V = NGDP/M$$

The importance of the velocity of money is clearly demonstrated in figure 2.1, which shows its rate of decline over the past 30 years.[9]

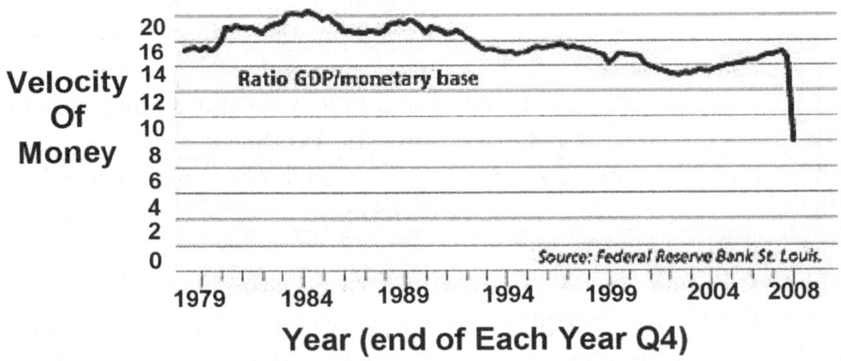


**Figure 2.1** Velocity of money over time (Data from Federal Reserve Bank).

---

[8] www.wilmott.com/blogs/collector/index.cfm/2009/2/15/The-Velocity-of-Money-and-Time-Stamped-Money, *The Velocity of Money and Time Stamped Money*, By : Espen Haug

[9] www.fivecentnickel.com/2009/03/19/velocity-the-speed-of-money/

From a reliability economics perspective, we notice a downward trend of 10 to 20% from 1984 to 2008. This is another warning trend. Then, of course, more recently, we had the dramatic drop of the velocity of money at the end of 2008 by almost 40%. That is, taking 15 as the initial value versus 9 as the final drop-off in the chart, the decrease is 6 out of 15 or 40%. This may be interpreted as follows: the rate at which money exchanged hands slowed down to almost half as often as earlier in the year. This was due to a decrease in bank lending and consumer spending, a reduced GDP, and the increase in the money supply (hoarding factor). Of course, much of the reduction in consumer spending was due to both job loss and consumer sentiment. We can roughly estimate how much of this was due to GDP versus the increase in monetary base where the velocity of money equation (above) shows that it could be either or both factors that contribute. The figure 2.2 shows the GDP in the years 2000 to 2009.

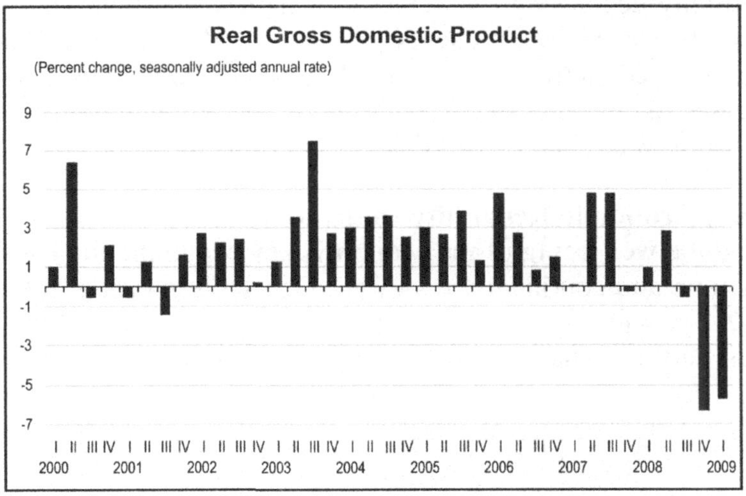


**Figure 2.2** Percent change in the Gross Domestic Product over key years[10].

Figure 2.2 shows the GDP percent change over the period 2000 to 2009.

**Analysis 2.1:** From Figure 2.2, we can see that the GDP drop-off from the end of 2008 to early in 2009 compared to 2007, for example, ranges between 7 and 12%. If we take it to be about 10% for simplicity, than the monetary supply (which is divided into the GDP according to the equation) would have had to increase by a factor of 2.2, or more than doubled. To see this: 1) take the GDP value in 2007 as 100%; this then

[10] www.bea.gov/briefrm/gdp.htm, US Bureau of economic analysis

decreased to 90% for the 10% decline; 2) then divide 2.2 into 90% to end up with a velocity of about 40% change. The conclusion is that the reduction in the velocity of money is primarily due to monetary saving (or hoarding factor) rather than a decrease in the GDP. The 2.2 factor indicated that hoarding more than doubled in the critical time of the recessionary period from the end of 2008 to the beginning of 2009.

Another key correlation is between Figure 1.1 and 2.1. Comparing the years 1984 to 2006, the velocity of money dropped 25%. This compares to the dichotomy in separation of wealth between the top 5% and the bottom 50% that coincidently spread 25% in those years. Poor velocity of money (from this and Analysis 2.1), are key reasons for a persistent recession. More money in the hands of the wealthy, a smaller population of about 5%, equates to lower consumer spending naturally decreasing the velocity of money and hoarding indicator. As consumer spending decreases it causes job losses and vice versa. That is, as jobs are lost, unemployed individuals cannot buy many goods and services, which further decreases the velocity of money, thus compounding the problem. After all, if you are unemployed, velocity of money is painfully slow through your hands!

**2.3: Some Key Economic Reliability Indicators**

To understand the well-being of the economy, key economic indicators should be tracked over time and continually reviewed. One such indicator is the job failure rate. Figure 2.3 provides strong feedback that as early as the middle of 2007, our economy was starting to have issues as the percentage of jobs lost per year was on the rise.

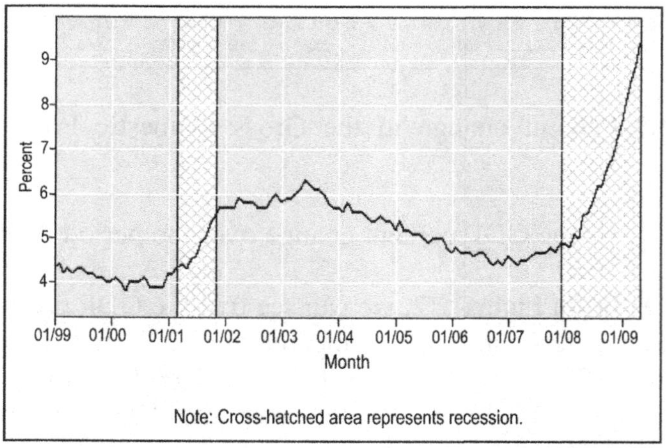


**Figure 2.3** Unemployment rate (seasonally adjusted) in percent per year (from the Bureau of Labor Statistics).

Both the unemployment rate and how fast it changes are key indicators. Appendix 2B.1 discusses how these indicators could be modeled using reliability statistics. There are many reasons for job reduction. It is certainly a root cause of tight money. Another economic reliability indicator is the housing market failure rate. Figures 2.4 and 2.5 provide a strong indication of this issue starting in 2006.

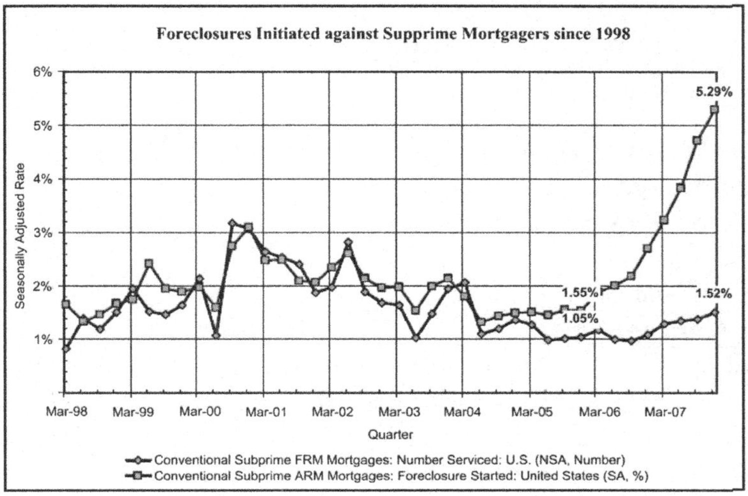


**Figure 2.4** Foreclosures initiated against subprime mortgages.

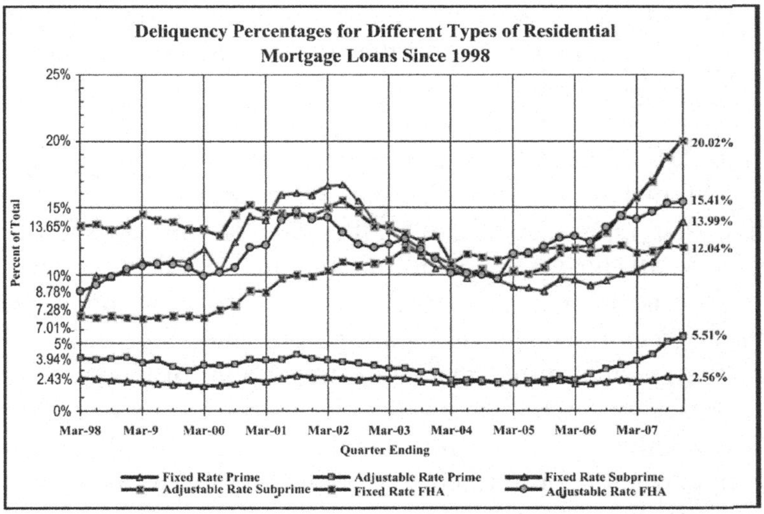


**Figure 2.5** Delinquency on residential mortgages over time[11].

[11] The U.S. Housing Bubble and the Global Financial Crisis: Housing and Housing-Related Finance, Joint Economic Committee, U.S. Congress, May 2008.

**2.4: Collective Mass-Hoarding**

Economic sentiment that turns to fear in a recessionary period creates an environment for collective mass-hoarding. A mattress account is sometimes actually…in a mattress!

> **Remark 2.6:** "An Israeli woman who bought her elderly mother a new mattress threw out the old one, unaware that it had $1 million hidden inside it." [12]

As mass hoarding accumulates, prices eventually drop as money tightens. Investments in the economy drop, stock markets fall as the hoarding cycle develops, and job losses deepen the cycle.

**Table 2.3** Mass Hoarding

| Collective Concept | Definition |
|---|---|
| Mass Hoarding | This is a collective effect of wealthy individuals, businesses, and the general population hoarding cash. This is primarily due to economic sentiment such as a fear of a falling economy as well as a loss of government control to maintain cash flow. |
| Effect of Mass Hoarding | Mass hoarding causes money to tighten, so there is less money in circulation. This slows the velocity of money, and the dollar increases in value as prices drop. |

When money tightens, goods typically become cheaper to encourage buying—this is known as deflation. The dollar essentially increases in value from the perspective that more goods can be bought for the same dollar. This, of course, is one small positive aspect of hoarding that is a good thing for consumers. It also means that, essentially, money is not—in the strictest sense—conserved, since prices fluctuate. In deflation, since the value of a dollar is worth more, it is as if the economy has increased the amount of money somewhat; not enough, of course, to offset a severe recession. However, it provides an opportunity for wealthy individuals to take advantage of their dollar value as well. It can create opportunity for further separation of wealth between the average individual and the truly wealthy. In a deflationary period, the well-known expression "Cash is King," is often used for companies trying to survive and actually prosper in a deflationary period.

---

[12] www.timesonline.co.uk/tol/news/world/middle_east/article6469706.ece, June, 2009

In Chapter 3, we present more facts to illustrate that we are in the midst of a hoarding crisis perpetuated by the wealthy, and this crisis is so huge that no one really understands it and its consequences. It is difficult to comprehend a problem that apparently no economist has yet to put a finger on. This is a totally naked issue, standing before us as if it is invisible, yet we are all aware of it, and it is silent. Every day, consumer shopping contributes to the accumulation of assets for the wealthy in dominated market areas (i.e. supporting movies, professional sports, shopping at Wal-Mart or purchasing Microsoft software—a company with $40 billion on the sideline, from former CEO, Bill Gates (another ~ $40 billion of known accumulated wealth, etc.). The main problem is:

**Accumulation of wealth can be an explosive problem in a recessionary period, as it promotes hoarding.**

Individuals who are so extraordinarily rich that they could not possibly spend their money in numerous lifetimes still wish to preserve capital. They do not properly invest their money but instead go into the protective mode during a recession when we most need their money to be reasonably invested (see job-friendly investing discussion in Chapter 8). Some, such as Warren Buffett (one of the world's wealthiest men), with his holding company Berkshire Hathaway,[13] do keep their money invested in the stock market.

## 2.5: Side Note on Tight Money and This Book's Approach

The reader should note that we are focusing on wealth accumulation/hoarding problems leading to velocity of money slowing as a primary root cause to tight money with selected design controls and corrective actions. Although the corrective actions to increase the velocity of money that we discuss should be key in helping an economic recovery, such solutions by themselves are not enough. The reader should note that tight money (leading to deflation) has other influences. Structural improvements to our economy are required in addition. A number of these will be discussed in this book including proposed solutions for: free trade and job outsourcing (Chapter 9) problems, tax structure (Chapter 4) faults, financial crisis failures, and national debt (Chapter 7) crucial issues. However, there are additional economic improvements that are outside the scope of this book such as monetary policy (interest rates), government regulations, government construction programs, small business initiatives, and other types of business development that are considered necessary. Our approach is to focus on a number of main issues whose root causes and design controls/corrective actions are not being addressed as identified in the FMEA tables.

[13] www.cnbc.com/id/22130601/ reported investments as of March 2008 51.4 billion.

**2.6: Summary**

In this chapter we introduced the method of Failure Modes and Effects Analysis (FMEA) to investigate the key issue of "tight money." The failure mode for this was identified as reduced money in circulation. The top two identified root causes were theorized as being hoarding and job loss. This provides an initial launch of our investigation that needed to be substantiated with facts. We also theorized that possible corrective actions were 1) change in the tax structure and 2) anti-hoarding legislation. These concepts are discussed in the next chapter.

An analogy was presented wherein money circulation has the same function as lifeblood in our body. In order to fulfill all the different functions of life, circulation of the blood must be ensured without interruption. With money it is the same—it needs to circulate in order to realize full job employment.

Facts were presented showing that in a time of a recession, individual bank savings and money market accounts end up hoarded, blocking circulation. This is because many banks and money markets hoard cash, so money doesn't circulate. Banks are very reluctant to take even minimal risks on loans in a recession.

The concept of velocity of money was introduced, providing a measure of the rate at which money exchanges hands (i.e. circulates). Hoarding is inversely proportional to the velocity of money. More exactly, Velocity of money (V) is calculated as the nominal GDP (NGDP) divided by the money supply (M): V=NGDP/M. Using this and some key facts, Analysis 2.1 indicates that the reason for slow velocity of money early in 2009 was primarily the hoarding factor rather than the decrease in NGDP. We see that lower velocity of money values indicate a relatively "stingy" society in which each dollar circulates through the economy more slowly. The result in 2009 has led to high rates of unemployment and business failures.

Reliability economics has some obvious economic indicators. Two important ones are the unemployment and the housing market failure rates. These can and should be analyzed using reliability statistical methods. One example analysis is provided in Appendix 2B-1.

Mass hoarding was defined as a collective effect of wealthy individuals, businesses, and the general population hoarding cash. This tendency is primarily due to economic sentiments such as fear of a falling economy as well as a loss of government control to maintain cash flow. Economic sentiment that turns to fear in a recessionary period creates an environment for collective mass-hoarding. Prices eventually drop as money tightens, causing deflation.

In a time of recession, individual bank savings and money market accounts end up as mattress accounts. This is because banks hoard cash, so money doesn't circulate. Hoarding equates to that portion of accumulated wealth that is taken out of proper economic circulation. Velocity of money is the rate at which money exchanges hands. Hoarding is inversely proportional to the velocity of money. Poor velocity of money will cause job losses.

**Appendix 2A-1: Overview on the Method of Reliability Economic Failure Modes and Effects Analysis (FMEA)**

**FMEA General Overview – Arizona Illegal Immigration Example**
FMEA is used in industry to understand a product's potential failure mode(s). To do this, it is typical to look at the components in the product, typically one-by-one, or by singling out the most likely to be problematic, and asking the questions for each component: "***What can go wrong? What are the potential failure modes?***" Let see how the Corporate FMEA Economic model might work in government by assessing the controversial ***Arizona immigration problem*** as an example. The key issue is illegal immigration. A bipartisan team of experts would get together and look at this key issue. They would identify potential failure modes such as American workers get replaced by illegal immigrants. The effect is higher U.S. unemployment. There may be a few potential root causes such as: poor border patrol, companies willing to hire illegal immigrants, and so forth. Then, they determine design controls such as: assessing the ability to check the status of every suspicious person or, consider investigating companies that hire illegal immigrants. Then, based on the analysis, corrective action(s) are suggested such as: penalize any company found to hire illegal immigrants and this would both discourage illegal immigration and improve U.S. employment. Other corrective actions such as the one passed might seem then less logical. Since a bipartisan team was used, honest assessment would be forcibly inherent with decisions based on research rather than ideological and/or corporate influences as part of the results.

**FMEA Method and Other Problem Solving Tools**

The basis of the FMEA problem solving method is to 1) obtain a core team, 2) use the format of Table 2-1, 3) define the problem statement and convert it to a key issue ("Money is Tight"), 4) ask the question what can go wrong and I.D. the potential failure modes, 5) and their effects, 6) for each failure mode brainstorm its root causes, 7) assess the risks with ratings, 8) suggest design controls and, 9) corrective actions. Some of the reasons for an ineffective problem solving results can include, an incomplete problem definition, unknown causal relationships, a focus on solutions rather than real root causes first, ineffective use of time, and an analysis based on ideology and not the facts and or data. (Note that most of our congressmen fall into the trap of identifying solutions without first understanding the root causes.) After the FMEA is performed, the design controls are then researched or worked in order to validate the final proposed corrective actions to resolve or mitigate the problem.

In the process of identifying root causes, a number of other problem solving tools may be useful. These are briefly mentioned and include: an Affinity Diagrams used to organize a brainstorming session and list root causes in categories, a Fishbone Diagram (see the next Chapter), a Cause and Effect Matrix to help score the root causes, a Cause and Effect Tree to diagram the cause and effect relationships, and a Fault Tree Analysis (similar to the Cause and Effect Tree) as an alternate method to assess the causes and effects in a diagrammatic form. Although these methods are helpful, they are somewhat a matter of preference. The problem solving method of choice in this book is FMEA since it includes more details other than basic causes and effects such as identifying failure modes, design controls, and corrective action all in a readable table format.

**Scoring**

Often in an FMEA there is scoring. In industry, it can be very elaborate. Typically each failure mode is scored with different types of scoring methods. Here, we simplify, scoring only root causes in order of importance. To do this we will need a scoring method. Table 2A-1 provides scoring that is used in this book from 1 to 10.

**Table 2A-1** Scoring Used for FMEA Root Cause Items

| Effect | Criteria: Severity of Effect on the Economy | Ranking |
|---|---|---|
| Highest Threat to Economy | Very high root cause reliability threat to economy with system failure (national level). | 10 |
| National Failure Some Control | Very serious root cause reliability threat to economy with system failure (national level), loss of control. | 9 |
| Very High | High failure rate, with loss of primary economy function | 8 |
| High | Poor but operable failure in economy with reduced level of performance. Dissatisfied populace. | 7 |
| Moderate | Noticeable effect on economy performance. Populace dissatisfied. | 6 |
| Low | Noticeable effect on economy performance. Populace experiences some dissatisfaction. | 5 |
| Very Low | Economy failure rates noticed by most people. | 4 |
| Minor | Poor regulations. Economy problems noticed by average individuals. | 3 |
| Very Minor | Topical reliability items that do not conform. Economy problems noticed by discriminating individuals. | 2 |
| None | No Effect | 1 |

**Multi-Disciplinary Core Team**

An FMEA is typically not done by one person. Typically, we would use a diverse core team to do this analysis. The team should consist of a team leader (reliability economists), subject matter experts, and a champion owner of the design or policy. Such a team should include democrats, republicans, reliability economists, and other subject experts in the area of interest so that everyone signs-up to identify before-hand the failure modes, their root causes, and provide inputs for design controls and corrective actions. It would not only force more of a bipartisan situation, but is also the first step to assuring a reliability mindset. In this book, we have to use historical facts/data from our research to try and compensate for our inability to work with such a team.

**Top-down Versus Bottom-up Approach**

In an FMEA there are two common views to look at potential failure modes, a top-down and a bottom-up approach. For example, in the housing crisis, from a top-down view, a root cause is government deregulation. From a bottom-up approach, a root cause may be job losses leading to high mortgage failures rates. Obviously, before design controls and corrective actions can be suggested, both a top-down and bottom-up investigation should be applied to find all failure modes.

**Appendix 2B-1: Weibull Reliability Analysis of the Unemployment Rate**

This appendix is provided for the reader who is interested in how reliability statistics can be applied to model key economic indicators. Specifically, we will model the unemployment rate. It could also be used in a similar manner for the housing market or business failure rate. We encourage readers not interested in the statistics to look at the summary.

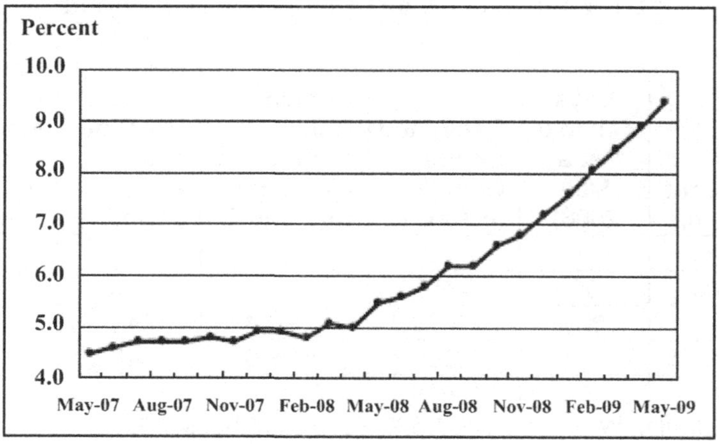


**Figure 2B-1** Unemployment rate (Source: U.S. Dept. of Labor).

Table 2B-1 provides values taken off of Figure 2B-1, issued by the U.S. Department of Labor in June 2009. Here we model the failure rate over the last year using what is called the Weibull Reliability Model. The Weibull Mathematical Model is the most widely used method for product failure rate–analysis. It is clearly the best model to illustrate application of reliability modeling to economics issues. The model, while not provided here, can be found in most reliability books. Table 2B-1 illustrates how to set up the information from the Department of Labor to perform a Weibull prediction. Column 2 is the actual percentage of unemployed. In column 3, we transpose the data to start at time 0 on May 1, 2008. The total number of estimated civilian workforce averages in this time period at about 154,620 million people, according to the U.S. Department of Labor. The number unemployed as of May 1, 2008, is about 7,731 million. We subtract this number to start time zero on May 1, 2008, for Weibull modeling. The number of unemployed individuals turns out in this example as the same, at each percent about 1546 unemployed (column 6, obtained by multiplying the percent unemployed for each period of the 1% change break points that we used for simplicity).

The results of the Weibull fit in to columns 3 and 6 (shown in Figure 2B-2) indicate a Weibull beta of 1.023 and a characteristic life of 8,697 days. Like a normal distribution that is characterized by a mean and a sigma, the Weibull distribution is characterized by a beta and a characteristic life (time to 63% failure) from which prediction can now be made. The Weibull is helpful because the beta is easy to interpret. A beta close to 1 indicates a constant failure rate, a number greater that 1 is an increasing failure rate while a number lower than 1 would be a decreasing failure rate.

**Table 2B-1** Table of Unemployment Rate Over a One-Year Period

| Date | Percent Unemp. | Days (Time 0 Set at May 2008) | Estimated Unemp. Number * In 1000s | Shifted Num Unemp. To May 1 2008 for Time 0 | Number New Unemp. Per Date over each period | Shifted Percent to May 2008 (add 5% for actual value) |
|---|---|---|---|---|---|---|
| 05/01/08 | 5% | 0 | 7731 | 0 | 0 | 0% |
| 08/01/08 | 6% | 90 | 9277.2 | 1546.2 | 1546 | 1% |
| 12/15/08 | 7% | 229 | 10823.4 | 3092.4 | 1546.2 | 2% |
| 02/01/09 | 8% | 274 | 12369.6 | 4638.6 | 1546.2 | 3% |
| 05/01/09 | 9% | 364 | 13915.8 | 6184.8 | 1546.2 | 4% |

*Estimated Total Civilian Work Force 154,620 People (in thousands)

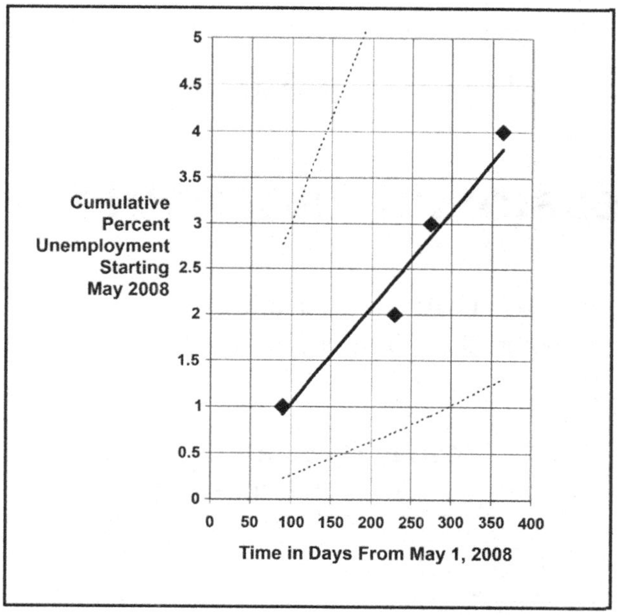


**Figure 2B-2** Weibull reliability data fit analysis for cumulative percent unemployed starting in May 1, 2008. Add 5% to obtain actual rate. Dotted lines show 60% confidence bounds. (Weibull Analysis Tool from DfRSoft.com)

**2B-2: Appendix Conclusion**

We see that in the period of one year from May 2008 that we have maintained a constant unemployment failure rate (i.e. beta approximately 1). Using the beta and the characteristic life we can make predictions. Typically, one would update the model every month. Given that the parameters of the model are unchanged over the next year or two, we would predict a severe situation. The model projects that in another year the unemployment rate will be up to 12.6 (= 7.6 from the model and 5% added for the May shift), and that in two more years (without change) we will be up to 16.3% (11.3% from the model and 5% added for the may shift put at 0). However, we anticipate that the rate of failure will decrease as the recession winds down. This would be reflected in the model as it is updated each month.

# ■ 3.0 ■

# RECESSIONARY HOARDING ANALYSIS

We continue with our FMEA investigation of Chapter 2 by focusing on the root cause, hoarding, and breaking it up in terms of business and individual hoarding.

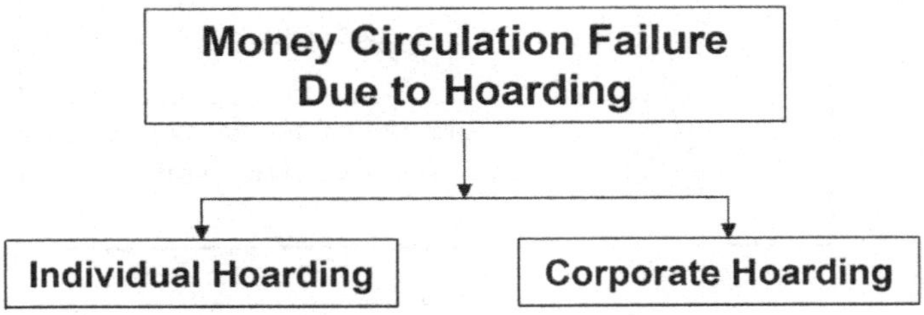


**Figure 3.1** Two primary types of hoarding that effect money flow.

To analyze these further, we will use another useful tool in reliability (also used by quality engineers) called a "Fishbone" or Cause and Effect Diagram. (Here it can supplement our FMEA assessment) which is commonly used to identify and list all the "causes" that are "effecting" a key failure issue. The term fishbone originated by the way information is arranged visually—like a fish skeleton. Similar to a FMEA, it is best to have a multi-disciplinary group to work out the analysis. Here again, we use historical information from our research.

**3.1: Individual Hoarding**
Figure 3.2 provides identified central factors to individual hoarding using a fishbone overview.

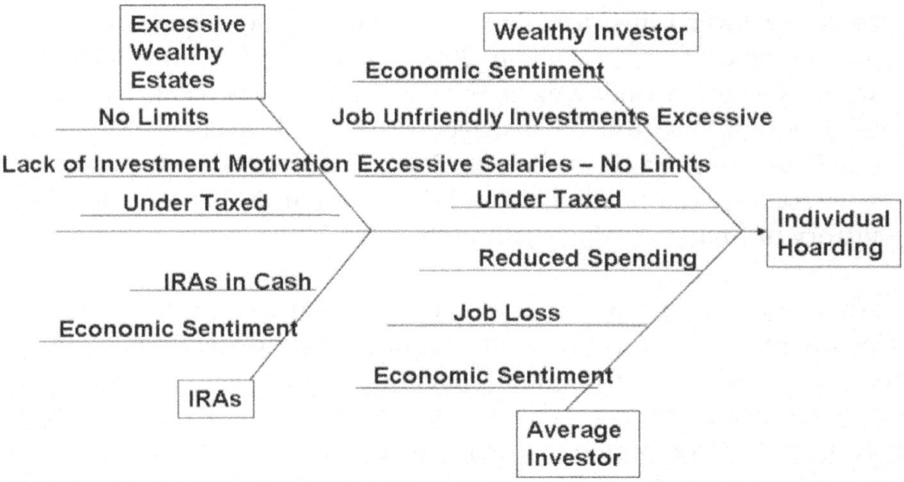


**Figure 3.2** Fishbone or Cause & Effect diagram for individual hoarding issue.

We will primarily focus on the upper portion of the fishbone, the path for the main causes: wealthy investor and for excessively wealthy estates. These are common sense items. Under each main cause are sub-causes. We note that for both the wealthy and the average investor, economic sentiment plays a key role in triggering hoarding. This is fairly well-known. However, we need to understand why it is now that we suspect wealthy investors seem to be playing such a major factor in the recession.

### 3.1.1: Why Suddenly Now Do We Have Individual Hoarding Issues?

Today, more than ever before, we have many wealthy individuals who make disproportionate salaries. We currently can do nothing but idly stand by and watch one **hedge-fund[14] manager make $3.7 billion in one year**, by apparently betting on the recent U.S. housing crisis, with others not far behind him in yearly salary.

> **Remark 3.1:** "LONDON (Reuters)—Bets on a U.S. housing crisis earned hedge fund manager John Paulson $3.7 billion in 2007, ahead of industry legend George Soros and 2006's highest-paid manager James Simons, according to Alpha Magazine. Paulson, whose bet that investment grade mortgage bonds would be subject to default in record numbers came good in the subprime meltdown last summer, was one of five managers earning more than $1 billion, Alpha said in a note on Wednesday. His earnings were more than double those of 2006's top earner—mathematics

[14] An investment company that uses high-risk techniques, such as borrowing money and selling short, in an effort to make extraordinary capital gains.

professor-turned-investor James Simons, who founded Renaissance Technologies Corp.—who in 2007 earned $2.8 billion. George Soros, whose Quantum Endowment Fund returned 32 percent last year, earned $2.9 billion. The top 25 managers earned, on average, $877 million in 2007, up from $532 million in 2006. This "may well prove to be the greatest display of individual wealth creation in any year in the modern history of finance," Alpha said in the note." [15]

Although it is disturbing how an individual can profit from a housing crisis, equally problematic is the ability of many individuals to make that kind of a yearly salary. What is even more shocking is that such individuals paid no higher federal tax percentage than someone in the 35% bracket that makes $372,950. In fact, it is reported that many hedge fund investments (including this one) were only subjected to 15% tax! This tax aspect is also discussed in Chapter 4.

These are privileged assets. This money is suddenly at risk. The U.S. has no control over this money's future and how it may or may not be re-invested, nor whether it will end up recirculating back into the economy through job-friendly investments.

*"It is time to put in place tough, new common-sense rules of the road so that our financial market rewards drive and innovation, and punishes short-cuts and abuse."*

—BARACK OBAMA, Address to Joint Session of Congress, February 24, 2009

But why now? Haven't the wealthy always "been there and done that" (i.e. hoarded money)? Let's look at some facts that demonstrate how things are different now than ever before.

**Remark 3.2:** "It was reported in June 1998 that on average Chief Executive Officer (CEO) salaries had increased to 326 times the pay of factory workers compared to 1980 CEOs made 42 times as much as factory workers and only 4 times as much in 1960." [16]

However, top hedge-fund managers now make greater than $2 billion (see below). That is 100,000 times a factory worker's salary (of $20,000) or equal to 100,000 jobs!

---

[15] www.earthtimes.org/articles/show/199378,hedge-fund-manager-paulson-earns-37-billion.html

[16] www.thirdworldtraveler.com/Society/CEO_Greed.html

> **Remark 3.3:** "Highest paid hedge fund managers (what they made in 2008 for a 1 year salary): James Simons, $2.5 billion (Renaissance Tech), John Paulson, $2 billion (Paulson & Company), John Arnold, $1.5 billion (Centaurus Energy), George Soros, $1.1 billion (Soros Fund), Raymond Dalio, $780 million (Bridgewater Assoc.), Bruce Kovner, $640 million (Caxton Assoc.), Dave Shaw, $275 million (DE Shaw & Co.), Stanley Druckenmiller, $260 million (Duquesne Capital) and so on."[17] In 2009, the top 25 hedge fund managers averaged $1 Billion each![18]

Here are some examples of current top-CEO salaries.

> **Remark 3.4:** "CEO salaries in 2007 (top 3 men and women): Steve Schwarzman, Blackstone Group (BX) $350.7 million, Pete Peterson, Blackstone Group (BX), $174.3 million, Frank Fertitta III, Station Casinos (STN) $146.6 million, Sharilyn Gasaway, Alltel (AT), $38.6 million, Safra Catz, Oracle (ORCL) $34.1 million, Diane Greene Vmware (VMW), $16.4 million."[19]

Athletic salaries are now in many cases higher than CEO salaries.

> **Remark 3.5:** "Highest paid athletes in 2007 according to Sports Illustrated: Tiger Woods: $111 million, Phil Mickelson: $57 million, Oscar De La Hoya: $55 million, Shaquille O'Neal: $35 million, Kobe Bryant: $34 million, Lebron James: $30 million, Derek Jeter: $29 million, Alex Rodriguez: $28 million. As of 2008 the lifetime earnings of the top five baseball players are: $198.4 million for Alex Rodriguez, $188.2 million for Barry Bonds, $167.6 million for Randy Johnson, $162.3 million for Manny Ramírez, and $161.2 million for Derek Jeter."[20]

Celebrities' yearly incomes are now unimaginable.

> **Remark 3.6:** "Oprah Winfrey's earnings (2007) were a staggering $275 million. *Forbes* announced (2007) the top five actors and actresses collectively made $487 million! (Will Smith: $80 million, Johnny Depp: $72 million, Eddie Murphy: $55 million, Mike Myers: $55 million, Leonardo DiCaprio: $45 million, Cameron Diaz: $50 million, Keira

---

[17] *New York Times*, March 2009
[18] New York Times, April 1, 2010.
[19] http://money.cnn.com/galleries/2008/fortune/0809/gallery.women_men_highest_pay.fortune/index.html
[20] http://en.wikipedia.org/wiki/List_of_highest_paid_baseball_players

Knightley: $32 million, Jennifer Aniston: $27 million, Reese Witherspoon: $25 million, Gwyneth Paltrow: $ 25 million.)" [21]

The Top Ten TV Earners in 2004 (U.K./U.S.) are:

**Remark 3.7:** "Simon Cowell: $34.2 million, 2. John Mahoney (*Frasier* sitcom): $33.4 million, 3. Anne Robinson: $19 million, 4. Jane Leeves: $14.9 million, 5. The Osbournes: $13.3 million, 6. Graham Norton: $12.92 million, 7. Jerry Springer: $11.4 million, 8. Jamie Oliver: $9.12 million, 9. Chris Tarrant: $8.83 million, 10. Peter Kay: $8.55 million." [22]

**Remark 3.8:** "Simon Cowell: $144 million for the 2008–2009 season (5 months' work), up from $34.2 million in 2004."[23]

Salaries of CEOs, celebrities, movie stars, and athletes have obviously skyrocketed. Many individuals own billions of dollars of U.S. assets (Also see our website, www.SolutionsWithoutUSDebt.com for many economic hoarding facts). Note, that much of this money is exported to foreigners. More money for the wealthy implies a decrease in the quantity of U.S. money supply in circulation when hoarded. Remember, it is the general population that is America's largest consumer, keeping money circulating; not the wealthy few who couldn't possibly spend their dollars in a lifetime. This results in an economic drought that correlates to failures in the stock market, job loss, inability to make mortgage payments, bank failures, increasing stockpiles of real goods available to be sold, loss of industry, and less money on average in our economy. As the speed of money circulating decreases, money tightens and will eventually equate to a loss of value on homes due to deflation and on goods being sold.

But how do we know for sure that this is worse now than ever before. Looking at Figure 1.1, it is clear. Table 3.1 provides the actual data that was used to generate Figure 1.1. It provides our population's percent share of income tax paid from 1980 to 2006. Note the last 3 columns present the number of individuals (in 1000's) that filed tax returns in the key groups. The trend is clear: the top 1% and 5% have increased incomes that as of 2006 made up 39.9% and 60.1% of tax revenues collected, with the number of individuals who filed at 1,357,000 and 6,786,000 respectively. In contrast, the bottom 50% make up only 3% of all revenues collected and consist of 67,860,000 individuals who paid taxes. This trend, shown in Figure 1.1, was a disaster waiting to happen, and is

[21] www.inthefablane.com/life/celebrity/archive.php?month=7&year=2008, Forbes Magazine., www.people.com/people/article/0,,20214402,00.html

[22]www.contactmusic.com/new/xmlfeed.nsf/mndwebpages/cowell%20named%20britain.s%20top %20tv%20earner

[23] http://ducatimonsterforum.org/index.php?action=printpage;topic=26040.0

one clear root of our financial crisis. This division of wealth is far worse than the housing bubble. Consumer spending by the general population is down because wealthy U.S. individuals are taking up most of the earnings resources in the country.

**Table 3.1** Population Percent Share of Income Tax from 1980–2006 [24]

| Year | Top 1% | Top 5% | Top 26-50% | Bottom 50% | Top 5% Filings* | 1% Filing* | 50% Filings* |
|---|---|---|---|---|---|---|---|
| 1980 | 19.1% | 36.8% | 19.9% | 7.1% | 4,662 | 932 | 46,619 |
| 1981 | 17.6% | 35.1% | 20.3% | 7.5% | 4,729 | 946 | 47,293 |
| 1982 | 19.0% | 36.1% | 20.2% | 7.4% | 4,721 | 944 | 47,213 |
| 1983 | 20.3% | 37.3% | 19.7% | 7.2% | 4,767 | 953 | 47,665 |
| 1984 | 21.1% | 38.0% | 19.2% | 7.4% | 4,922 | 984 | 49,219 |
| 1985 | 21.8% | 38.8% | 18.8% | 7.2% | 5,031 | 1,006 | 50,313 |
| 1986** | 25.8% | 42.6% | 17.5% | 6.5% | 5,104 | 1,021 | 51,044 |
| 1987 | 24.8% | 43.3% | 17.0% | 6.1% | 5,308 | 1,062 | 53,077 |
| 1988 | 27.6% | 45.6% | 16.4% | 5.7% | 5,444 | 1,089 | 54,436 |
| 1989 | 25.2% | 43.9% | 17.0% | 5.8% | 5,566 | 1,113 | 55,656 |
| 1990 | 25.1% | 43.6% | 17.2% | 5.8% | 5,641 | 1,128 | 56,406 |
| 1991 | 24.8% | 43.4% | 17.2% | 5.5% | 5,690 | 1,138 | 56,902 |
| 1992 | 27.5% | 45.9% | 16.5% | 5.1% | 5,633 | 1,127 | 56,326 |
| 1993 | 29.0% | 47.4% | 15.9% | 4.8% | 5,684 | 1,137 | 56,841 |
| 1994 | 28.9% | 47.5% | 15.7% | 4.8% | 5,749 | 1,150 | 57,495 |
| 1995 | 30.3% | 48.9% | 15.0% | 4.6% | 5,864 | 1,173 | 58,637 |
| 1996 | 32.3% | 51.0% | 14.4% | 4.3% | 5,972 | 1,194 | 59,721 |
| 1997 | 33.2% | 51.9% | 14.1% | 4.3% | 6,075 | 1,215 | 60,752 |
| 1998 | 34.8% | 53.8% | 13.1% | 4.2% | 6,189 | 1,238 | 61,888 |
| 1999 | 36.2% | 55.5% | 12.5% | 4.0% | 6,300 | 1,260 | 63,004 |
| 2000 | 37.4% | 56.5% | 12.1% | 3.9% | 6,411 | 1,282 | 64,114 |
| 2001 | 33.9% | 53.3% | 13.1% | 4.0% | 6,441 | 1,288 | 64,409 |
| 2002 | 33.7% | 53.8% | 12.6% | 3.5% | 6,416 | 1,283 | 64,162 |
| 2003 | 34.3% | 54.4% | 12.7% | 3.5% | 6,430 | 1,286 | 64,305 |
| 2004 | 36.9% | 57.1% | 11.9% | 3.3% | 6,519 | 1,304 | 65,186 |
| 2005 | 39.4% | 59.7% | 10.9% | 3.1% | 6,631 | 1,326 | 66,306 |
| 2006 | 39.9% | 60.1% | 10.8% | 3.0% | 6,786 | 1,357 | 67,860 |
| 2007 | 40.4% | 60.6% | 10.5% | 2.9% | 7,054 | 1,411 | 70,535 |

* Filings in 1000s

** Tax Reform Act of 1986 changed the definition of Adjusted Gross Income, so data after and below 1986 is not strictly comparable

The trend has been very clear; it should have never been ignored. If economists had a reliability approach to our economy, studying economic change

[24] www.taxfoundation.org/news/show/250.html

over time and making reliability policy improvements, things may have been different today. However, currently there are no formal reliability economists, since the discipline did not exist (until this book).

We have to realize that every dollar is important rather than take the attitude that there is an endless dollar supply for wealthy individuals to accumulate in their estate. In general, Figure 1.1 represents loss of opportunity for the average worker. Ignoring the trend in this chart means we have allowed an economy to grow that caters to the wealthy. We are truly a society of "haves" and "have-nots." The drastic reduction in the velocity of money for this Modern Recession is a consequence of this build up of accumulated wealth compounded with hoarding by a small portion of the population, and it finally broke like a bridge under stress (see Figure 2.1). The cost of unreliable economics has enormous impact on the quality of the average workers' lives. On the other end of the scale are individuals with thousands of lifetimes of wealth.

The reality is that if one were to burn a dollar, it is permanently lost in our economy. Each dollar is important. A lost dollar is no longer available to buy a product. And in turn, a storeowner who would have received that dollar can no longer pass it on to pay off his overhead items, bills, and employees. This is part of the reason why you may get laid off in the future or are out of work right now. Great estate wealth and hoarded assets actually decrease our tax revenue and promote job losses, especially in a recession. Such individuals can quickly pull out of the stock market, hurting companies, or may be in charge of outsourcing to feed the bottom line. On the good side, less money in circulation does cause deflation, as we mentioned in our last chapter. There are benefits to money tightening, but not enough to overcome the loss in speed of money exchanging hands.

It is relatively easy to look at a number of our wealthiest individuals to start to understand the issues. It is interesting that our CEOs today talk about the economy without any real awareness of their contribution to the consumer spending problem. For example, Warren Buffett (about $37 billion fully invested—it is not known how fully invested he is) often comments on the money channel (CNBC) about the recession, calling it our modern economic war. A possible individual hoarding crisis is never discussed. Of course, Warren Buffett (compared to some wealthy individuals) is one investor that has substantial funds circulating in the economy (through Berkshire Hathaway), thus helping job retention. Eventually, his money is earmarked to be given away through the Gates Foundation, and will have to go back into the economy somehow through charity. (Except that much of the Gates foundation targets oversea health concerns.) Additionally, these facts on the current wealth-hoarding crisis have been ignored by the media. TV and money-oriented talk radio shows are not acknowledging the issue. For example, Jim Cramer, former hedge-fund manager and now *Mad Money* TV host (*Business Week* reports his net worth between $50 to $100 million), while criticizing the government, does not ever speculate that this separation of wealth and hoarding issue is a problem!

However, our facts illuminate this crisis. We have already shown in Analysis 2.1 that monetary hoarding is, in fact, an initial issue leading to the dramatic drop in velocity of money, thereby touching off the recession. It is not logical to ignore hedge-fund manager salaries such as $3.7 billion without proper taxation (as discussed in the next chapter). It takes a severe toll on our economy. What percent goes back into the economy as compared to a mattress account? There are moral and fiscal issues that come with great acquired assets that, in turn, affect society – which is everyone of us.

Table 3.2 is a list of the top 20 wealthiest people in the world, whose tremendous accumulation of wealth logically must be affecting the velocity (speed) of money exchanging hands. In finance, everyone is connected.

**Table 3.2** Top 20 Billionaires in 2009 and Their Assets Over Three Years[25]

| Name | Company | Assets in Billions of Dollars | | |
|---|---|---|---|---|
| | | **2009** | **2008** | **2007** |
| Bill Gates | Microsoft | 40 | 58 | 56 |
| Warren Buffett | Berkshire Hathaway | 37 | 62 | 52 |
| Lawrence Ellison | Oracle | 22.5 | 25 | 21.5 |
| Jim Walton | Wal-Mart | 17.8 | 19.2 | 16.8 |
| Alice Walton | Wal-Mart | 17.6 | 19.2 | 16.7 |
| Christy Walton | Wal-Mart | 17.6 | 19.2 | 16.7 |
| S. Robson Walton | Wal-Mart | 17.6 | 19.2 | 16.7 |
| Michael Bloomberg | Bloomberg L.P. | 16 | 11.5 | 5.3 |
| Charles Koch | Koch Indus. | 14 | 17 | 12 |
| David Koch | Koch Indus. | 14 | 17 | 12 |
| Michael Dell | Dell | 12.3 | 16.4 | 15.8 |
| Donald Bren | Irwin | 12 | 13 | 8.5 |
| Sergey Brin | Google | 12 | 18.7 | 16.6 |
| Larry Page | Google | 12 | 18.6 | 16.6 |
| Steven Ballmer | Microsoft | 11 | 15 | 15 |
| George Soros | Soros Fund | 11 | 9 | 8.5 |
| Paul Allen | Microsoft | 10.5 | 16 | 18 |
| Jacqueline Mars | Mars | 9 | 14 | 10.5 |
| John Mars | Mars | 9 | 14 | 10.5 |
| Abigail Johnson | Fidelity | 10 | 15 | 13 |

These figures are unimaginable even for the modern era. Marco Cagetti (University of Virginia) and Mariacristina De Nardi (Federal Reserve Bank of

[25] http://en.wikipedia.org/wiki/List_of_the_100_wealthiest_people

Chicago), in August of 2005, published a report on wealth inequality, data, and models.

> **Remark 3.9:** "In the United States wealth is highly concentrated and very un-equally distributed: the richest 1% hold one third of the total wealth in the economy." [26]

Although it is hard to find updated 2009 studies, this separation of wealth has most likely grown since 2005 as illustrated from our tax study in Figure 1.1 and in Table 3.1. It has perhaps spiraled out of control. It is certainly difficult to understand how such studies are ignored by economists in power.

If any of these top billionaires (in Table 3.2) died in 2010, due to the repeal of the death tax, these huge sums of U.S. dollars would fully go into their estate to be distributed, most likely, to family members. There are ways that this money should instead be invested into our economy so that we all may benefit. We will describe appropriate investments for the truly wealthy that would help the velocity of money circulating (See Chapter 8 on job-friendly investing).

Family members like the Waltons also get to inherit their businesses along with large non-business assets. The inherited amount depends on the estate tax structure at the time of death, as we have mentioned above and will discuss in detail in Chapter 4. These opportunities equate to lost opportunities for the average American. Estate inheritors may actually end up paying little or no estate tax, with the added opportunity to increase assets through family business growth.

Families can pass their business on through inheritance and also through their connections. This is a case of the rich getting richer on the family level. An excellent example is the movie industry. How often does an unknown actor break through the front line and make it into the movies? Movie stars promote their own family members into the acting business. Such children grow up to be celebrities and also get to inherit their parent's great wealth. This represents a dramatic loss of opportunity for the average unconnected actor. It also creates generations of money which accumulates like a compound interest rate for fortunate families. It is a form of "family hoarding" of wealth.

The wealthy can end up causing a great number of lost opportunities and degrade the common idea that you can be anything you want to be in America. However, if the wealthy are taxed correctly (see Chapter 4), and their money is invested properly, both can lead to job creation and opportunities for average Americans.

---

[26] www.chicagofed.org/publications/workingpapers/wp2005_10.pdf

**3.2: Corporate/Spiral Hoarding**

Companies that do not have dollars set aside and can't get money from banks pose risks of not paying their bills. They are viewed as risky business affiliates. Other companies will choose not to purchase products from them. In an economic downturn, "Cash is King." If a supplier shows a good balance sheet with money in the form of cash, they are viewed as a valuable supplier: a company not only with a good business plan, but one that had money to maintain a high level of innovation and quality. On the other hand, competing companies who are desperate for business will find their weakness worsened by the lack of cash on their balance sheet. They are at risk to lose business. Thus, in a downturn, there are many reasons for companies to have money in cash. This is also a great position in a deflationary period. Opportunities for takeovers and mergers are created as well. A time to knock off your competition! However, it means that when companies put cash on the sideline (hoarding dollars in a recession), they will also seek to find ways to cut their budgets, which include job cuts; thereby creating a further spiral downward of our economy. Money exchanging hands slows down due to layoffs from company hoarding. The buying power of the mass population is decreased, which prompts further economic downturn in the cycle. The results of this spiral hoarding is a lose-lose proposition, resulting in many failing businesses and increased separation of wealth. This creates an unhealthy atmosphere that does not serve the common good as it keeps the cash circle to a select few in this country and is effectively hoarding cash away from the general population increased the difficulty of finding jobs. Even when this Modern Recession ends, we may see a jobless recovery. Thus, in a recession, we have a hoarding spiral in which corporations play a vital role that is roughly summarized by a scenario of the type below:

***competition → forced outsourcing → layoffs → successful product → corporate excess wealth → executive bonuses → separation of wealth→ velocity of money slows → recession starts → companies lose value → more job layoffs → Cash is King, corporations sideline money → more job losses → consumer spending decreases further → banks hoard → individual hoarding increases → money tightens (deflation) → businesses fail → more layoffs → government intervenes → more national debt → recessionary products find success (Wal-Mart, movie industry) → surviving corporate excess wealth → cycle repeats.***

This is a rough cyclical analysis of the issue where corporations seek to maintain excess cash to weather the Modern Recession. We see that the corporate sector plays an even more vital role that can stifle our economy through hoarding. Here are four key corporate sectors, including the stock market:

- Financial—Banks
- Large Businesses
- Money Markets
- Stock Market

Our main concerns are banks, money markets, and large businesses. However, one cannot ignore the stock market, as businesses depend on stock investments. Falling stocks can trigger a hoarding cycle. These are the largest areas where velocity of money is simply slowed in an economic downturn. Performing a fishbone analysis, as was done earlier for individual hoarding on the corporate issue, we have come up with the following diagram.

**Figure 3.3** Fishbone diagram for corporate hoarding issue.

Here the leading "corporate hoarding" fishbone issues are noted by large businesses parking (uninvested) money, banks' inability to lend, money markets pulling out of the financial sector, and economic sentiment where investors hoard cash, causing stocks to fall. All of these factors affect the bottom line: high job-loss, mortgage failure rate, housing deflation (creating increased mortgage failure rate), business-to-business reduction, loss of business orders creating high layoffs, big business bailouts leading to an increase in the national debt, and job outsourcing. These fishbone issues now need factual evidence to support our reasoning.

**3.2.1: Bank Hoarding Facts**

In a typical healthy period, banks may be at a near zero level or in the $1 or $2 billion range collectively in the U.S. for unloaned and uninvested monies. However, by January of 2009, bank hoarding skyrocketed.

> **Remark 3.10:** *Forbes* in February of 2009 reported—"Excess reserves went from $2 billion in August to $267 billion in October. As of the middle of January, they had mushroomed to $843 billion." [27]

Bank hoarding in a time of a recession, while common, is highly controversial.

> **Remark 3.11:** "Bank Hoarding Could Lead to 'Revolution,' Says Dodd, 10/27/08
> —The *Times*' Joe Nocera listened in on a private JPMorgan conference call some weeks ago in which an executive quite clearly stated that the $25 billion given to them by the federal government explicitly to loosen up their lending markets would in no way be used to *actually loosen up lending*. It's quite horrifying, actually. It pissed Senator Dodd right off, too: 'If it turns out that they are hoarding, you'll have a revolution on your hands. People will be so livid and furious that their tax money is going to line their pockets instead of doing the right thing. There will be hell to pay.'"[28]

Bank hoarding creates havoc in our economy. Businesses and consumers are unable to get access to money via credit, so they can't spend it. In addition, there is the "multiplier effect" of money. The fractional-reserve banking system allows money to multiply on top of itself. When banks receive deposits, they are only required to keep 10% of that money on reserve. They are free to lend the other 90% out to other individuals and institutions. So if someone deposits $100,000 at a bank, the bank is then able to take that $100,000 and lend $90,000 of it out to someone else while keeping $10,000 ($100,000 x 0.1 = $10,000) of it on reserve. In essence, the bank magically turns $100,000 into $190,000 on their balance sheet. However, in a recession there is a catch. The 10% of money banks are required to keep in cash actually can cause hoarding and foreclosures! When people default on their mortgage loans, the bank's book assets drop in value. Then the bank needs to make up the devaluation with more cash to maintain the 10% requirement. This will cause banks to call up loans to stay solvent. This

---

[27] www.forbes.com/2009/02/03/banking-federal-reserve-business-wall-street-0203_loans.html

[28] http://nymag.com/daily/intel/2008/10/chris_dodd_if_banks_keep_hoard.html, by Jessica Pressler

makes it hard for banks to keep lending during a recession, and they may also foreclose on businesses. When too much failure occurs at once, as indicated in Remark 2.2, only TARP money can help, which they may need to maintain the 10% cash requirement. In this way, many banks become non-functional without TARP monies, increases in foreclosure occur, house prices depreciate, business foreclosures accelerate, the employment sector bleeds jobs, and the cycle continues with added mortgage failures. It is truly a difficult fire to put out. It is much more cost-effective to be proactive with bank loan regulations by encouraging job creation and improving our tax system. This will be discussed in the next chapter.

> *"We know that government can't solve all our problems – and it shouldn't try. But it should work for us, not against us. It should ensure opportunity not just for those with the most money and influence, but for every American willing to work."*
>
> —BARACK OBAMA, speech, September 10, 2008

**3.2.2: Large-Business Hoarding Facts**

Top executives and money managers in corporate America follow the general notion, as discussed, that "Cash is King," and will sideline money when they can in preparation for any economic downturn. This sounds like reasonable judgment, but maintaining an extreme amount of sidelined money is fiscally irresponsible at a time when jobs are being lost in such magnitudes and we are in the midst of a housing crisis. There are many creative ways that a company can spend excess dollars to improve their competitive advantage and at the same time promote job growth.

For example, in February 2009, when the recession was in full swing, Intel's President and CEO Paul Otellini announced the following:

> **Remark 3.12:** "WASHINGTON, D.C., February 10, 2009—Intel President and CEO Paul Otellini today announced the company would spend $7 billion over the next two years to build advanced manufacturing facilities in the United States. The investment funds deployment of Intel's industry-leading 32 nanometer (nm) manufacturing technology that will be used to build faster, smaller chips that consume less energy….'We're investing in America to keep Intel and our nation at the forefront of innovation,' Otellini said…"[29]

[29] www.intel.com/pressroom/archive/releases/20090210corp.htm

Such spending amounts to a large portion of Intel's assets. We see that this is already starting to show on their balance sheet.

> **Remark 3.13: Intel**—As of April 2009 reported $10.6 billion, way down from April 1, 2008, showing assets of $13.7 billion (amount represents cash and short term investments)[30]

The fact that Intel has made this kind of commitment in the midst of a major recession is noteworthy especially since at the time they had about $8 billion in cash. This is the kind of investment that has trickle down economic impact and has saved many jobs, including the company I work for. Many companies, however, in either a non-recessionary or a recessionary period seek shelter for their cash.

> **Remark 3.14: Exxon Mobil**—(September, 2008): "$39 billion in cash amounts to 15 percent of assets, almost six times the average of the company's 10 biggest peers, according to data compiled by Bloomberg." [31]

Exxon has a history of maintaining large assets. It has had at least $32 billion since 2005. However, in March of 2009, Exxon announced it was finally spending some of its huge reserves!

> **Remark 3.15: "Exxon Mobil** is pumping up its spending to fuel growth. On Thursday, the company said it would increase its capital spending by double-digit percentages in 2009 with long-term growth opportunities to meet global demand.... It will spend about $29.0 billion this year, up 11.1% from $26.1 billion in 2008, and at the high end of its annual target for $25.0 billion to $30.0 billion based on its five-year spending plan....'...In a world where there's a credit squeeze, the idea of strategically aligning yourself with someone who has tremendous access to capital makes a lot of sense,' said energy expert Amy Jaffe of Rice University's James A. Baker III Institute for Public Policy."[32]

We can see this coming off their balance sheet.

---

[30] http://data.cnbc.com/quotes/INTC/tab/7

[31] http://royaldutchshellplc.com/2008/09/22/exxons-cash-hoard-fuels-biggest-stock-price-drop-in-27-years/

[32] www.forbes.com/2009/03/05/exxon-mobil-capital-markets-equity_oil_tillerson.html

**Remark 3.16: Exxon-Mobil**—As of April 2009, reported $25.6 billion, way down from April 1, 2008, showing assets of $41.4 billion (amount is for cash and short-term investments.[33]

Exxon and especially Intel have finally broken their trend, not keeping their mountain of money hidden under a massive mattress account during the recession. This is in contrast to a number of companies that have maintained their sideline cash:

**Remark 3.17: Cisco**—As of April 2009, reported $33.5 billion, up from April 1, 2008, showing assets of $24.4 billion (amount is for cash and short-term investments).[34]

**Remark 3.18:** The *New York Times* noted in February 2009—"Cisco Systems likes to point out it has more cash on hand than any other technology company."[35]

**Remark 3.19: Microsoft**—As of April 2009, reported $25.3 billion, a bit down from April 1, 2008, showing assets of $26.3 billion (amount is for cash and short-term investments).[36]

**Remark 3.20: Apple, Inc.**—As of April 2009, reported $25.0 billion, up from April 1, 2008, showing assets of $19.4 billion (amount is for cash and short-term investments).[37]

**Remark 3.21: Google**—As of April 2009, reported $17.8 billion, way up from April 1, 2008, showing assets of $12.1 billion (amount is for cash and short-term investments).[38]

**Remark 3.22: Yahoo, Inc.**—As of April 2009, reported $3.5 billion, way up from April 1, 2008, showing assets of $2.6 billion (amount is for cash and short term investments).[39]

---

[33] http://data.cnbc.com/quotes/xom/tab/7
[34] http://data.cnbc.com/quotes/csco/tab/7
[35] http://bits.blogs.nytimes.com/2009/02/09/ciscos-cash-hoard-swells-alongside-acquistion-rumors/
[36] http://data.cnbc.com/quotes/MSFT/tab/7
[37] http://data.cnbc.com/quotes/AAPL/tab/7
[38] http://data.cnbc.com/quotes/GOOG/tab/7
[39] http://data.cnbc.com/quotes/YHOO/tab/7

The atmosphere is similar in other countries such as England that increased cash as the global recession hit, and at a time when spending would have helped the employment picture.

> **Remark 3.23:** "Firms Hoarding Cash to Weather Storm, Says Bank, By Richard Tyler, Enterprise Editor, July of 2008—Businesses are hoarding cash as they prepare to weather what they believe will be the worst trading conditions in 16 years. High street bank Lloyds TSB has said that smaller firms, those with sales of less than £15m, are depositing "record" sums of money into their business accounts as its six-monthly survey of business conditions shows collapsing sales, profits and confidence.... "We are taking record levels of deposits from businesses. What it says is that businesses are looking to conserve cash." [40]

What can be done about companies that hoard cash during a recession? The answer is: it is recommended that anti-hoarding legislation for wealthy companies be implemented during a recessionary period. We have provided two such proposals on our website, www.SolutionsWithoutUSDebt.com.

First of all, this author proposes a hoarding quota amount something in the neighborhood of:

**$300,000 per employee**

The amount of $300,000 is a guideline. The actual amount would have to be set by the FOMC (Federal Open Market Committee). This kind of quota could also help save jobs, as companies would be allowed to keep more cash if they had more employees. After this amount, all other monies should be invested either in company growth or in corporate America. More guidelines are provided in our anti-hoarding legislation at our website.

### 3.2.3: The Financial Crisis—Money Market and Demand Deposit Hoarding Issues

Look closely at the Table 3.2 three year snapshot; most of the wealthy individuals have not lost much of their assets (with the exception of Warren Buffett). Sophisticated and average investors will, in a recessionary period, flee to take their money out of the stock market and put it into more safe investment areas such as money markets and demand deposits (e.g. checking and saving accounts

---

[40] www.telegraph.co.uk/finance/yourbusiness/2793649/Firms-hoarding-cash-to-weather-storm-says-bank.html

for which money can be withdrawn upon demand). Figure 3.4 shows a snapshot of the demand deposits over time which rose dramatically in 2008–2009.

This also reflects investors pulling money out of risky assets (basically, everything except U.S. treasury bonds) and adding assets to FDIC-insured accounts. The Feds really have no control over the velocity of money.

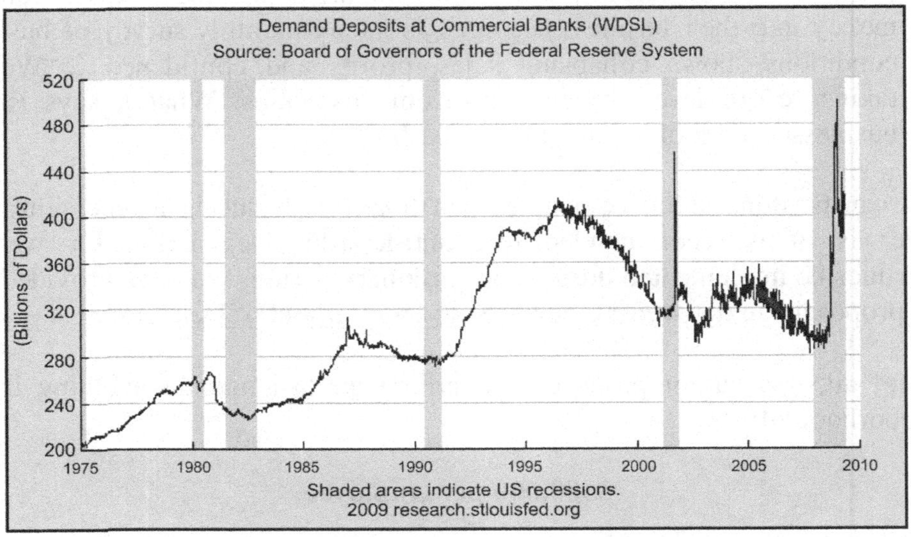


**Figure 3.4** Rise in demand deposits with clear spike in 2009 (from Federal Reserve System).

In the start of a recession, the well-known cycle occurs where the average person worries about possible job loss and starts saving. As people lose their jobs, money gets tighter, resulting in decreased consumer spending and creating more job losses. The increase in savings with reduced spending is not the best scenario for job preservation and creation. Even though much of the money may reside in banks, lending becomes tight, as we just previously discussed. Banks can be at risk of failure as well. Besides banks, the well-to-do flee from the stock market typically to money market holding accounts.

**Remark 3.24:** "Money markets are booming ($3.5 trillion as of June 2008)" [41]

The well-known drop in the stock market that started in September of 2008 resulted in early layoffs. Falling stocks prompt layoffs—although it is not a direct relationship, stock problems are a key troubling indicator to companies.

This swelling of money markets, a possible concern of unreliability, had actually started as early as the 2nd quarter of 2005. Figure 3.5 confirms the trend. Such trends are another reason why reliability economics is needed in the government's economic team's plan in order to help in their financial design policies. One has to ask, "Why did money markets swell over this long time period? It is safe to have such high liquid assets in one area of our economy? Is this a concern?" Eventually, as it turned out, it became more of a crisis at the end of 2008 than many people realized.

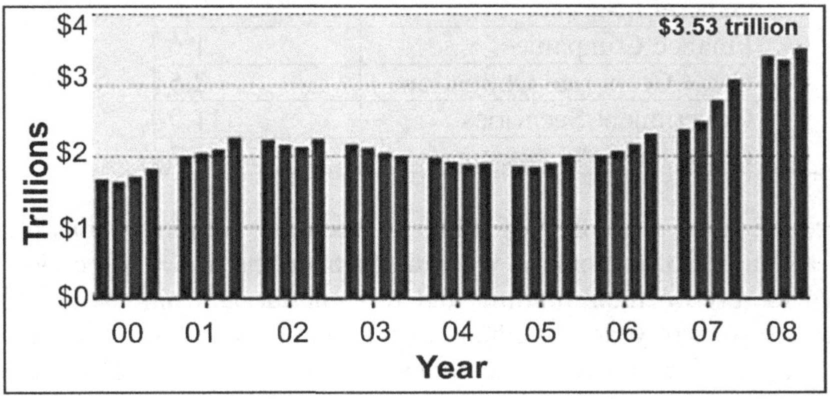


**Figure 3.5** Money market investments from 2000 to 2008 [42].

Money markets are very important to our economy. Over the years they have grown to be an incredibly important investment entity to our financial institutions.

**Remark 3.25:** "Money markets are integral to the financial infrastructure of industrial countries…central to the allocation of capital, the efficient distribution of liquidity among financial institutions, and the hedging of short-term risks..." [43]

---

[41] www.economist.com/finance/displaystory.cfm?story_id=11554685, also see http://afp.google.com/article/ALeqM5jw7OL2Rak5smvpfRB4CQhs441okA

[42] *Los Angeles Times*, Money Fund Report, August 2008. (see also http://latimesblogs.latimes.com/money_co/2008/09/the-credit-cris.html)

[43] www.newyorkfed.org/research/conference/2008/role_money_mkts.html

Because of their importance, such investments constantly need to be monitored. On the one side, we have individual investors that have put their dollars into money markets expecting stability and quick access to their funds (i.e. liquidity). On the other hand, the money market managers have the responsibility of short-term safe investments for which they put most of their money in banks.

**Remark 3.26:** A typical money market fund such as Fidelity, shown in Table 3.3, indicated that about 2% of the money goes into corporate funds while about 72% into banks and trusts. [44]

**Table 3.3** Fidelity Money Market Fund (SPRXX) as of January 2009

| | |
|---|---|
| Asset-Backed | 4.3 |
| Finance (Auto) | 0.6 |
| Banks and Trusts | 71.9 |
| General Insurance | 2.6 |
| Finance Companies | 1.6 |
| Other Corporate Obligations | 2.5 |
| Government Securities | 11.9 |
| Repurchase Agreements | 4.7 |

Here we have a number of things happening. As money markets grow, they drive a number of sectors, as we can see from the above allocation. Banks have grown to rely on their funding and this encouraged high volume of loan activity in the last eight years. The bank business does help also with job creation and retention, housing industry, car industry, and businesses. However, direct corporate investing is believed to be more important for job-friendly investing. As we know, the main business of banking is the mortgage and business lending. The problem is that there exists a lack of bank safety in a time of a recession. The key factor here is that banks have become accustomed to receiving money market funds to lend. In normal times, access to money markets allows many banks to lend many more funds than those taken from their average depositors. Thus, there was a huge build up of over $3 trillion at the end of 2007, and growth in investments as indicated in Figure 3.5.

**Remark 3.27:** September 22, 2008—"Money funds overall have taken in $400 billion in fresh cash this year alone as nervous investors have sold stocks, bonds and other assets and sought a haven where they believed their principal was protected".[45]

---

[44] http://personal.fidelity.com/products/fixedincome/fimoneymarket.shtml.cvsr

[45] http://latimesblogs.latimes.com/money_co/2008/09/the-credit-cris.html

Money markets were effectively a banking pipeline!

> **Remark 3.28**: An article briefing called "Blocked Pipes," posted on the economist.com, explains that money markets are the plumbing of the financial system. They are hardly noticed as they help investment institutions, companies, and banks to lend and borrow trillions of dollars. However, the article notes that they become very noticeable when things go wrong.[46]

However, the commentary explains the pipeline broke and money came pouring out of banks as money market managers had warranted concerns for bank investments, in particular mortgage issues.

> **Remark 3.29:** "The money markets' difficulties began in July 2007, when two Bear Stearns hedge funds revealed the damage done to their portfolios by subprime mortgages." [47]

Many investors, including managers of money market funds, became worried about bank exposure to risky financial paper - allowed due to a 1999 repeal of a Glass-Steagall act (described below –see top down view). The run on banks had started, and could have resulted in a full collapse if the FCIC had not stepped in.

> **Remark 3.30:** September 22, 2008—"From Lehman, the worries spread to Wachovia, Washington Mutual, and beyond...The runs meant that all the money market funds were in the same boat: everyone wanted to sell and hoard cash in case of a run....Ultimately, despite last week's bailouts, no one wanted to hold financial company paper. If the FDIC hadn't stepped in to backstop the runs on the money market funds…"[48]

The incredible systematic risk that occurred in a very liquid pipeline, was built without enough reliability designed into the economics for such situations. It was costly to our system, our national debt, and became another fire that had to be put out. There was no proactive reliability effort, nor oversight of what was going on in the money market pipeline. In fact, there are those in the financial sector who believe money markets were the root cause problem to the collapse of the financial sector.

---

[46] www.economist.com/displayStory.cfm?story_id=12342237
[47] www.economist.com/displayStory.cfm?story_id=12342237
[48] http://meganmcardle.theatlantic.com/archives/2008/09/how_close_was_the_financial_sy.php, the *Atlantic Magazine*, by Paul Krugman

**Remark 3.31:** "The $4 trillion money-market fund industry is the 'greatest systemic risk' to the financial system, James Staley, head of JPMorgan Chase & Co.'s investment unit, said today at the World Economic Forum in Davos, Switzerland. Money-market funds, not banks, were responsible for the collapse of Lehman and the near bankruptcy of Bear Stearns Company last year, he said. The funds, which typically hold highly rated, short-term debt instruments, were forced to pull their money from the firms when they saw signs of trouble, he said. "The people who brought down Lehman and almost Bear Stearns weren't the banks, they were the money funds," Staley said at a lunch discussion hosted by Credit Suisse. "You have this huge industry with $4 trillion of capital, immediate intraday liquidity to the client who wants it with no capital behind that statement and no insurance behind that statement." [49]

### 3.3: Financial Crisis—Housing Bubble & Bank Failures – A Reliability Economic Top-Down versus a Bottom-Up Approach

There will always be much discussion on root cause issues that need to be identified to prevent fires from occurring. We need to act on all the facts. The view presented here is that reliability economics needs to be analyzed by using both a bottom-up and a top-down approach.

#### 3.3.1: Bottom-Up View:

From a bottom-up view, much press has been given to financial/housing market industry that was been turned into a "House of Cards." Failure started with increases in adjustable-rate mortgages and job losses where homeowners had an inability to pay their mortgages as house prices spun out of control. The root cause issue goes up the line from here, directed at the loans made by an unregulated banking industry that has been blamed for making bad loans to too many unqualified homeowners. In many cases, the lender (driven more by greed) did not check out the qualifications (assets and income) of the home borrower. Furthermore, we had an industry that encouraged this selling behavior, offering packages of loans (good and bad) in bundles called mortgage-backed securities; individuals who sold and bought them as a bond had no idea of their actual intrinsic value other than they had an apparently improper triple A rating.

However, we now know that many good loans are, and have been, failing along with these bad loans (see Chapter 2, Remark 2.2). Homeowners may have been misled or misunderstood the issues with, for example, an adjustable-rate

---

[49] www.bloomberg.com/apps/news?pid=newsarchive&sid=aygKgy3VDgS8
Also see: http://money.cnn.com/news/specials/storysupplement/bankbailout and http://money.cnn.com/news/storysupplement/economy/bank_failures/list

mortgage; they may have had a good job and lost it. There are many reasons why people buy homes they feel they can afford. We cannot ignore the fact that we have a very high unemployment rate that affects a homeowner's ability to pay bills. Once many loans started to fail in large numbers, financial institutions which had huge investments in mortgage-backed securities found themselves owning these bonds with falling values, and this started the financial crisis leading to the money market withdrawals, etc. It also dragged other securities down that were unrelated to the mortgage industry.

In the bottom-up approach, the solution revolves around:
**1) Governmental oversight with tighter mortgage restrictions and**
**2) Financial bailouts of lenders.**

### 3.3.2: Top-Down View

In this section on corporate hoarding, we actually have taken a top-down view rather than reiterate the bottom-up view that has been discussed frequently in the news. This has led to some other conclusions compared to the bottom-up mainstream approach. We have found that bank hoarding is costly to businesses, home owners, and jobs. Large-business hoarding also costs jobs, and this factor cannot be ignored. Money markets' liquidity played a key role in the financial crisis; banks had far too much money to lend and many in the industry acted with greed in bundling available funds into mortgage-backed securities. Now you had simple mortgages loans becoming exposed like equities to economic sentiment, and the security value fluctuating like a stock, which put over-exposed security holders like Lehman Brothers at risk to market pressures. The failure of these securities occurred much faster than home-owner mortgage delinquencies indicating economic sentiment and marketplace rumors were key root causes. Some companies (Goldman Sachs for example) profited by the failure of the mortgage securities through hedging with firms like AIG. We tax payers paid the price. AIG received $180 billion in bail out (more details are provided in Sec. 5.6). Thus it would be wrong to blame the crisis entirely on bad loans; the mortgage-backed securities were themselves part of the problem, compounded with an unregulated banking industry that became too big to fail.

Much of this issue has an underline root cause that many blame on the repeal of a Glass-Steagall act in 1999. This repeal allowed commercial banks to make risky investments. This one time successful act of 1933 had protected the banking industry for decades, now with its repeal we found that in just a short period of 10 year has partially led to enormous failures. From about October 2008 to December of 2009 there were 733 bailed out banks and financial institutions costing taxpayers $205 billion[48]. And from January 2008 to December 2009 there were 229 failed banks with a total FDIC cost of $45.4 billion[48]!

This is clearly a reliability economic issue of failed policy and most likely would never have occurred if reliability economist were available to provide proper FMEA assessments to balance the strong influences of lobbyists who fought hard for this repeal (see Chapter 6).

However, it would also be wrong to blame bank failures entirely on this repeal and a corporate hoarding crisis (money markets pulling their assets). We cannot ignore all the complex issues and root causes. We have a large system with many complex parts. All areas must be considered in trying to obtain a smooth-running economic engine.

In the top-down approach, the solution revolves around FMEA analysis for:

1) reduction of corporate hoarding,
2) reduction and/or review of allowed bank lending practices of money market funds that must require liquidity,
3) mortgage-backed securities—their issues and potential failure modes
4) review of the 10% rule during a recessionary time.
5) Reduction in large business hoarding allowing for more jobs
6) restoring a new version of the "Glass-Steagall Act". As we have briefly discussed, this repeal in 1999 permitted banks to merge with insurance companies and investment houses. With its repeal we now have financial institutions that are "too big to fail". Such large institutions (created from merged commercial and investment banks) were then able to underwrite and trade instruments such as mortgage-backed securities, collateralized debt obligation and establish these "structure investment vehicles" and thus had less oversight (i.e. deregulation) and were a main reason for our financial crisis that needed large bailout packages. Besides banks, these risky investments cause a Merrill Lynch debacle, a full collapse of Lehman Brothers, and forced a merger of Merrill Lynch with Bank of America. Risky investments prior to 1999 were not part of a normal commercial banks portfolio. We further believe this bipartisan repeal in 1999 of the Glass-Steagall Act (spearheaded by lobbyists – see Chapter 6) would not have occurred if reliability economists were involved in the decision making process and a proper FMEA was performed prior to the repeal.

## 3.4: Summary

In this chapter we discussed both individual and corporate hoarding using the concept of a fishbone analysis tool. We initially addressed the issue of why individual wealth and hoarding has more of an impact today than in prior years. For example, in 2005 it was reported that U.S. wealth is highly concentrated and unequally distributed: the richest 1% make about 40% of the total income dollars and hold about one third of the total wealth in the economy. This division of wealth has grown dramatically since 2005. Salaries of CEOs, celebrities, movie stars, and athletes have skyrocketed. Many individuals exist who own billions of dollars of U.S. assets. More money for the wealthy implies a decrease in the quantity of money supply in circulation when hoarded. This result is an economic drought that correlates to failures in the stock market, job loss, inability to make mortgage payments, bank failures, increasing stockpiles of real goods available to be sold, loss of industry, and less money for the average spender in our economy. As the speed of money circulating decreases, money tightens and eventually equates to loss of value on homes due to deflation and on the goods one might be selling. This slowing was indicated by demand deposits (e.g. checking and saving accounts) that rose over time dramatically in 2008–2009. Here we asserted that great wealth creates problems in terms of velocity of money back into our economy. Currently the Feds really have no control of the velocity of money.

In terms of corporate hoarding, we point out in an economic downturn "Cash is King". If a company shows a good balance sheet, they are viewed as a valuable business partner rather than a risk as well as the fact they can acquire weaker companies and grow with acquisitions. Here the leading corporate hoarding fishbone issues are noted by large businesses parking (uninvested) money, banks' inability to lend, money markets pulling out of the financial sector, and economic sentiment where investors hoard cash, causing stocks to fall. All of these factors affect the bottom line of high job loss, mortgage failure rates, housing deflation creating increased mortgage failure rates, business to business reduction, loss of business orders creating layoffs, big business bailouts leading to an increase in the national debt, and job outsourcing. We provide examples of a number of companies that have, for the most part, maintained a significant level of cash.

Money markets were separately discussed. The swelling of money markets actually started in 2005 and peaked in 2008 and 2009. Money markets are discussed as an incredibly important investment entity. However, when mortgages started to fail, money managers sought to protect their assets by pulling their investments. One remark (3.31) by James Staley, head of JPMorgan Chase & Co.'s investment unit, was enlightening, as he blamed money market funds, not banks, for the collapse of Lehman and the near-bankruptcy of Bear Stearns.

We discussed the financial downturn of the housing market from both a top-down and bottom-up reliability economics approach in order to identify the root causes and corrective actions. The identified root causes from a bottom-up view were not just the selling of mortgages to high-risk borrowers, but also the sales of many good loans that are failing due to the recession's high unemployment rate. In the bottom-up approach, the solution revolves around 1) governmental oversight with tighter mortgage restrictions and 2) financial bailouts of borrowers. From a top-down view, we described everything from corporate hoarding to the greed in selling mortgage-backed risky securities. In the top-down approach, the solution revolves around a reduction of corporate hoarding, a reduction and/or review of allowed bank lending practices of money market funds that must require liquidity, a review of the 10% rule during a recessionary time, and restoring the Glass-Steagall Act, where its repeal has led to financial institutions that are now too big to fail.

# ■ 4.0 ■
# RELIABILITY ISSUES OF THE U.S. TAX STRUCTURE

## 4.1: FMEA Update for the Tax Structure Issue

In this chapter, tax structure, the next key issue in our FMEA Table 2.1 is

**Table 4.1** Failure Modes and Effects Analysis on Tax Structure

| Key Issue | Potential Failure Mode | Potential Effect of Failure | Root Cause(s) (RC) | Root Cause Rating | Design Control | Possible Corrective Action |
|---|---|---|---|---|---|---|
| Tax Struc-ture (Federal Income) | 1) Loss of needed govern-ment revenue 2) Separa-tion of wealth increase 3) Wealthy may have no income to tax | 1a) Poor monetary circulation 1b) Governmental national debt increases 2) Reduce money for average worker 3) No income tax revenue from wealthy retirees | 1a) Tax bracket stops at 35% 1a) Excess tax write-offs 1, 2) Government administrative issues 3) No tax on wealthy retiree assets 4) Nonresident alien tax issues | 1) 9 2) 9 3) 7 4) 3 | 1a) Assess extending bracket 1b) Review and close loop holes 1, 2) Investigate administrative issues with fair tax implementation Review possible salary cap 3) Asset tax review 4) Increase on export serviceable tax | 1a) Extend brackets fairly 1b) Close loop holes 2) Do FMEA on govt. admin issue 3) Asset tax 4) Service export tax increase—Ex. Foreign athletes |
| Tax Struc-ture (Estate and Asset Tax) | 1) Loss of needed govern-ment revenue 2) Inherited separation of wealth increase | 1) Sudden and continual changes in velocity of money 2) Governmental national debt increases 3) Reduce money for average worker | 1a) Under taxed estates 1b) Excess wealth 1c) Admin. Issues 2) Excessive generational opportunities 3) Excessive financial control | 1) 9 2) 7 3) 8 | 1) Assess feasibility of salary & lifetime caps 2) Analyze higher estate tax 3) Analyze taxing assets 4) Review & assess charities | 1) Impose lifetime cap 2) Increase estate tax 3) Tax assets as well as income |
| Govern-ment Admin Tax Issues | Failure to implement fair tax structure | 1) Recession issues, increase in national debt 2) High interest rate payments 3) Loss of fiscal stability in U.S. 4) Default on foreign loans | 1a) Irresponsible risk tolerance 2) Under taxation 3) Conflict of interest | 1) 9 2) 10 3) 10 | 1) Review and propose improvement 2) Assess government influences 3) Implement a reliability economics team | 1) Restrictions on lobbyists 2) Set aside tax for campaign funds to avoid lobbyist influences 3) Add a reliability economics team |

analyzed. This is a crucial concern as it is the main source of government revenue and the key instrument for redistribution of wealth for a lopsided economy. From the results of Chapters 2 and 3 along with historical information found in our research, we have put together the FMEA table centering on tax structure. From here, we launch our next investigation to support our assessment based on facts.

Identified are now three key tax issues: 1) income tax, 2) estate tax, and 3) tax administrative issues. The last issue of administrative problem was found when assessing root causes. This will shortly be explained.

Note that based on the high salaries and the excess out of control wealth accumulation identified in Chapter 3, the key issue "estate tax" needs review. All of these are suspected to have an effect on velocity of money, national debt, and pose a problem for macroeconomic unreliability.

**4.2: Root Cause—Tax Bracket Stops at 35%**

The initial fact to look at is the upper 2009 tax bracket, since it is our first potential root cause.

> **Remark 4.1:** Currently the 2009 tax bracket stops at 35% for an annual income of $372,950. The progressive tax bracket increases up to that point and then stops. Why?

This immediately draws our attention. Presented in the last chapter was a rather large amount of information that showed individuals in recent years were making extraordinarily increasing yearly incomes, many times greater than $372,950 and in one case up to $3.7 billion (Remarks 3.1 to 3.3) and this individual actually paid substantially less that 35% tax (a reported 15% - the same tax as someone making approximately $34,000, see remark 4.2-A). Note that dividing $3.7 billion by $372,950 results in a factor of 9,920 times larger than the upper tax income bracket! This is a disturbing reality prompting further analysis.

It appears the upper tax bracket is not adequate to deal with today's rising income for highly compensated individuals and poses a long term reliability economic threat. This not only prompts concern regarding the tax structure, but one has to question why the government has ignored it. This is one reason for adding the 3rd suspect key administration tax issue that turns out to be complex enough that we later have devoted Chapter to it entitled "A Lobby Full of Conflicts of Interest."

To start, consider the upper tax bracket by looking first at the 2009 tax structure for a single individual in Table 4.2.

**Table 4.2** 2009 Income Tax Bracket[50]

| Salary Made From | Salary Made To | 2009 Tax Bracket | Progressive Tax |
|---|---|---|---|
| $0 | $8350 | 10% | ✓ |
| $8350 | $33,950 | 15% | ✓ |
| $33,950 | $83,250 | 25% | ✓ |
| $83,250 | $171,550 | 28% | ✓ |
| $171,550 | $372,950 | 33% | ✓ |
| $372,950 | "above" | 35% | ✓ |

In this instance, a graph seems appropriate to look at the U.S. tax model. Here we plot the upper income salary (column two) versus the tax bracket and substitute the maximum known yearly income of $3.7 billion as the last number for the word "above" in the table to arrive at the plot in Figure 4.1.

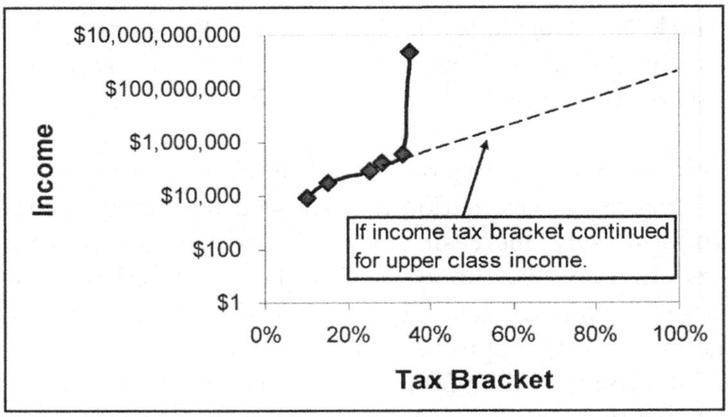


**Figure 4.1** 2009 tax bracket versus upper income level with dashed line showing the logical continuation of the bracket for upper class income.

Looking at the plot, the irregular line more clearly illustrates the issue in the tax bracket structure. The logical increase has been added using a dotted line. The figure shows our tax structure clearly is uneven and favors the **upper income individuals** since it is not extended. That is, prior to 35% the more money a person makes the higher his tax bracket, except after $372,950. **The question is, why does it stop there?** It should continue to be consistent and fair. This indicates that a disproportionate tax is removed at the lower end compared to the upper income tax bracket (i.e. it is unequal at the upper and lower ends). The upper level should be equally weighted as shown by the dotted line.

50 www.moneychimp.com/features/tax_brackets.htm

There is a strong precedent for a higher income tax rate. In fact the income tax during World War II reached 94%.

> **Remark 4.2:** "The rate had reached 94% during World War II, on income over $200,000 (approx. $2.5 million in today's dollars). It dropped down to 91 percent in 1946 and remained there until the Kennedy tax cuts in 1962-64. Brackets weren't inflation adjusted back then, so it still applied on income over $200,000, which by then had reached $1.4 million in today's dollars."[51]

**4.3: Root Cause—Excess Tax Write-Offs**

The next root cause to be addressed is "excess write-offs". In the last chapter statistics from 1980 to 2006 (Table 3.1) were provided. Let's take a closer look at 2006 since the data is readily available. Here we'll look at what the top 1% to 5% in 2006 actually paid in taxes compared to the 35% bracket. First note that the tax structure in 2006 was almost the same as in 2009 as illustrated in Table 4.3.

**Table 4.3** 2006 Tax bracket (similar to the 2009 structure)[52]

| Joint return | Single taxpayer | Rate |
|---|---|---|
| $0—$15,100 | $0–$7,500 | 10.00% |
| $15,100—$61,300 | $7,500—$30,650 | 15% |
| $61,300—$123,700 | $30,650 –$74,200 | 25% |
| $123,700—$188,450 | $74,200 –$154,800 | 28% |
| $188,450—$336,550 | $154,800 –$336,500 | 33% |
| $336,550 and up | $336,500 and up | 35% |

The information furnished by the tax foundation for 2006 is listed in Table 4.4 on what the top individuals actually paid in percent compared with the 35% bracket. This indicates that even though individuals were either in the 33% or 35% bracket, they paid a much smaller percentage, between 17.5% and 22.8%. We might deduce that this is because we have a "progressive" tax structure rather than say a flat tax. Therefore, individuals typically pay less than their bracket and this may be the reason. However, an analysis for single individuals shows that the progressive tax structure is really not that forgiving for high salaries. In fact, for larger incomes, it starts to be close to a flat tax!

---

[51] www.taxfoundation.org/blog/show/23697.html
[52] www.infoplease.com/ipa/A0106989.html

**Table 4.4** Average Tax Rate Actually Paid in 2006 in the 33 or 35% Bracket [53]

| Wealthy Top Percent | **Number of Returns with Positive AGI** | **Group's Share of Income Taxes** | **Income Split Point** | **Bracket** | **Average Tax Rate** |
|---|---|---|---|---|---|
| Top 1% | 1,357,192 | 39.89% | > $388,806 | 35% | 22.79% |
| Top 2–5% | 5,428,766 | 20.25% | > $153,542 | 33% or 35% | 17.48% |

Table 4.5 illustrates this for incomes above $150,000. Table 4.5 illustrates what high-salaried individuals should have been paying in a progressive tax system without any "write-offs" in 2006.

**Table 4.5** Actual Tax Rate/Percent That Should Be Paid Without Write-Offs in 2006

| Income 2006 | Bracket | Actual Tax | Actual Rate |
|---|---|---|---|
| $150,000 | 28 | $36,332 | 24.2 |
| $330,000 | 33 | $94,492 | 28.6 |
| $1 million | 35 | $329,861 | 33% |
| $10 million | 35 | $3,479,660 | 34.8% |
| $100 million | 35 | $34,979,861 | 34.98% |

From the above table, for an individual in the 35% bracket, the most the progressive tax bracket rate reduction allows is about 3%, i.e. 32 to 35% (last column) required tax for the 35% bracket. Yet wealthy individuals, according to Table 4.4, have averaged paying only a 17% to 23% tax rate!

As an example of a giant tax loophole, many people are angry that hedge fund managers, the highest paid individuals in the country are subject to only 15% on many of their investments. This is a sad statement from our congress showing little attempt to provide redistribution of wealth for our lopsided economy (see Fig. 1.1).

**Remark 4.2-A** "...Yet the $3.7 billion all went to one man (Hedge fund manager John Paulson). He did nothing to contribute to America's productivity or to society, he used other people's money, he took advantage of investment tools that have been set

[53] www.taxfoundation.org/news/show/250.html

up to benefit people like him. He paid a 15% capital gains tax, compared to a 40% total tax paid by many working people…" [54]

Yet when this tax loophole came before congress, it was apparently dropped??

**4.2-B** "…Last year, the Democratic Congress quietly dropped a proposal to end a tax windfall for hedge fund managers, whose income is taxed at the 15 percent capital gains rate, rather than higher income tax rates…"[55]

In summary we have found:

1) The upper tax bracket stopping at 35% is not equally weighted, having an unfair distribution for modern salaries well above the upper tax limit.
2) The actual tax paid by the wealthy (in 2006) was well below their actual bracket, even for a progressive tax averaging about 23% for the 35% bracket.
3) Our congress has serious administrative issues regarding their inability to tax the wealthy and close tax loopholes (see Chapter 6 on Conflict of Interest). In light of our national debt and high unemployment rate, it is fiscally irresponsible.

We see that the statement, "the rich find tax loopholes" has credibility and requires further investigation. We suggest in the FMEA table a design control to find and fix tax loopholes. We have illustrated on tax loophole, other data are not readily available and is outside the scope of our work. However, it is a fiscally irresponsible severe issue of unreliability in our economy and requires a multi-discipline full FMEA special committee approach to resolve the loopholes.

### 4.4: Root Cause of Ultra Wealthy Retirees – A Proposed Asset Tax Corrective Action

Lastly, in the FMEA table we would like to mention the problem of root cause number "3" (first row) regarding wealthy retirees. Individuals who are in the lower income bracket and only pay 15% of their income may actually be paying more taxes than a truly retired wealthy person who is living off his or her assets. That is, **no income, no income taxes**. Logically, a retiree who has over

[54] www.stateofnature.org/whereHaveYouGone.html, "Wher Have You Gone, Gordon Gekko? Oh Right, You'r Still Here, article by Paul Buchheit (summer 2008)

[55] www.wsws.org/articles/2008/apr2008/hedg-a17.shtml, In midst of recession, multi-billion-dollar paydays for US hedge fund managers, by Barry Grey, April 17, 2008.

$10 million or a billion dollars in their mattress account does not need to bother investing for income? This can be viewed as a tax loophole. Some might actually view it as the Grand Canyon of untaxed assets. From the arguments above, these monies would appear to have been under-taxed in the first place, and now the assets are free from taxation. It allows individuals to do as they see fit with their finances. They may hoard it, keeping it out of the economy, or invest it in some manner that may or may not be productive economically.

Remember, our goal is a reliable economy. This requires keeping money in circulation. The main corrective action on this type of issue would of course be an asset tax. Currently, however, individuals do not list assets, and there is a measure of undetectability to this issue. It would therefore help to correct the problem if assets were required to be declared over a certain amount and subjected to audit.

There is a Precedent for an asset tax. Florida had an annual intangible personal property tax on stocks, bonds, mutual funds, money market funds, shares of business trusts, and unsecured notes, enacted in 1931. This tax was discontinued in 2007. For example, this small tax (of 0.05% on assets exceeding $250,000) raised an estimated $1.074 billion in Florida in 2000. Here we view this tax as a way for us to help pay-off the deficit and provide badly needed revenue.

**4.5: Opposing Views on Increasing Upper Tax Bracket & the Laffer Curve**

Unfortunately, there are many articles declaring that the wealthy already pay too much tax. That is, the articles typically look at the face value fact that the top 1% pay 40% of all federal taxes and draw their conclusions. Looking at that statistic can be misleading and cause an opposing interpretation. This kind of analysis can create overly opinionated articles by non-analysts and therefore present an inaccurate picture. This fact will make change difficult. In the reader's interest, excerpts are provided from a number of opposing viewpoints.

> **"Guess Who Really Pays the Taxes**—Yes, income in America is skewed toward the rich. But taxes are skewed far, far more....The top 5 percent pay well over half the income taxes..."[56]

> **"Who Pays the Most Taxes?...**cites a Tax Foundation study that finds "the top 1% of tax returns paid about the same amount of federal individual income taxes as the bottom 95% of tax returns...but it's hard to argue that those who earn 21.2% of the nation's income should pay 39.4% of all federal income taxes when taken in isolation..."[57]

---

[56] www.american.com/archive/2007/november-december-magazine-contents/guess-who-really-pays-the-taxes

[57] www.outsidethebeltway.com/archives/who_pays_the_most_taxes/

> **"Those Rich People Don't Pay Taxes**—December 10, 2008 Just a question: If the evil rich aren't paying their taxes, then just how is it that the Imperial Federal Government is collecting about 40% of all income taxes paid from the top 1% of income earners? Somebody 'splain that to me please." [58]
> **"The Rich and Their Taxes**—April 15, 2008 One of the most persistent themes in this presidential campaign is that the rich are not only getting richer, but that they are also not paying their fair share of taxes, mostly because of tax cuts that favor the wealthy.....As Internal Revenue Service data demonstrate, the rich are getting wealthier, but they are also paying a steadily increasing share of the federal tax burden. Over 25 years, in fact, the percentage of the federal income tax bill paid by the wealthiest Americans has doubled, even as it has shrunk for all others...."[59]
> **"New IRS Tax Numbers: "Rich" Pay Highest Share in 40 Years July 21, 2008...**the Democrats and Obama continue to say that these tax cuts have been a giveaway to the rich and it's a figment of their imagination. Taxes paid by millionaire households more than doubled to $274 billion in 2006, from $136 billion in 2003." ...."[60]

Another reason often cited for not raising taxes are arguments behind a **Laffer curve**[61]. We will not show this over simplified curve but mention the concept argues that higher taxes inhibits economic activity and can be counterproductive for tax revenue. The arguments are irrelevant for the following reasons, the theory is based on a flat tax, not a progressive tax, it doesn't relate to the large separation of wealth that plagues the U.S. hoarding culture, it is not relevant to war time where we argue in Chapter 7 that we need to declare war on the national debt, finally, the curve while famous is unsubstantiated with data. We base our decision in reliability economics on data not ideology. For example, data suggests the 2004 Bush job creation bill that cut corporate tax breaks failed to have an impact on the job market. The reader should research this curve and realize that it is not only irrelevant but is hurting the U.S. due to its significant ideological following.

### 4.6: Obama Tax Structure Corrective Action

There is a current proposed 2011 Obama Tax Increase, but it is only a minor increase compared to what we showed for the proposed dotted-line increase in Figure 4.1. This Obama tax increase does not appear to go far enough to reduce

[58] http://boortz.com/nealz_nuze/2008/12/those-rich-people-dont-pay-tax.html
[59] www.realclearmarkets.com/articles/2008/04/the_rich_and_their_taxes.html
[60] www.rushlimbaugh.com/home/daily/site_072108/content/01125110.guest.html
[61] http://en.wikipedia.org/wiki/Laffer_curve

the separation of wealth, significantly pay off the national debt, and run an effective government while currently facing our health care issues and the other problems in our economy.

> **Remark 4.3:** "The president has proposed raising the top two tax brackets. The 35% top rate on ordinary income would increase to 39.6%, and the 33% rate would rise to 36%. The president also has proposed new limits on itemized deductions, and the top rate on long-term capital gains and most dividends would rise to 20% from 15%. The president says these plans would affect upper-income Americans, described as families making more than $250,000." [62]

**4.7: The One Hundred Percent Equitable Progressive Income Tax Structure with Salary Cap as a Potential Corrective Action**

A realistic and logical extension of the tax structure is shown by the dotted line in Figure 4.1 that indicates how the tax bracket could be fairly increased. Table 4.6 has been generated by following the dotted line in the figure. It provides one possible scenario for a realistic corrective action. We call this the one hundred percent equitable progressive income tax structure with salary cap. (Note that this table is a continuation of the 2009 tax structure. Our new suggested brackets occur after the 35% point. However, we would actually recommend lower taxes for individuals making under $8,350.)

The table provides results based on the logical continuation (fitted data of last 2 points for 33% and 35% bracket points) of the upper 2009 tax brackets (dotted line in the graph). Here we still have a progressive tax, meaning that 100% tax (unlike a flat tax) still provides quite a bit of income to the individual. One needs to use the progressive tax equations to see how this occurs (see for example Ref. 63). Table 4.6 shows the amount a single individual would pay (and keep) if he or she made the maximum amount in each bracket. We also suggest a salary cap below so that the most income a single individual could "keep" is $100 million. A person will pay income in excess of $100 million to taxes. This is just one possible scenario to extend the tax bracket equally and have some measure of limitation on wealth. Our preference here is also to include a salary cap. Later, we argue that a salary cap is reasonable. In any case, we see that the logical extension of the dotted line has led to much higher income tax revenue.

---

[62] online.wsj.com/article/SB123707638051931241.html

[63] www.moneychimp.com/features/tax_brackets.htm

**Table 4.6** Logical Continuation of 2009 Income Tax Bracket (Single Person)

| From | To | Bracket | Tax to Pay | Amount to Keep |
|---|---|---|---|---|
| 0 | $8,350 | 10% | $835 | $7,515 |
| $8,350 | $33,950 | 15% | $4,967 | $28,983 |
| $33,950 | $83,250 | 25% | $19,571 | $63,679 |
| $83,250 | $171,550 | 28% | $42,554 | $128,996 |
| $171,550 | $372,950 | 33% | $109,031 | $263,919 |
| *$372,950* | *$489,983* | *35%* | $133,333 | $356,650 |
| Below is how a fair continuation of 2009 Income Tax Bracket would appear for upper income class based on dotted line logical extension (dotted line in the graph) | | | | |
| *$489,983* | *$921,031* | *40%* | $315,079 | $605,952 |
| *$921,031* | *$1,607,095* | *45%* | $581,407 | $1,025,688 |
| *$1,607,095* | *$2,644,295* | *50%* | $1,031,444 | $1,612,851 |
| *$2,644,295* | *$4,149,046* | *55%* | $1,714,681 | $2,434,365 |
| *$4,149,046* | *$6,259,680* | *60%* | $2,726,999 | $3,532,681 |
| *$6,259,680* | *$9,138,012* | *65%* | $4,167,158 | $4,970,854 |
| *$9,138,012* | *$12,970,879* | *70%* | $6,162,605 | $6,808,274 |
| *$12,970,879* | *$17,971,635* | *75%* | $8,856,773 | $9,114,862 |
| *$17,971,635* | *$24,381,620* | *80%* | $12,419,878 | $11,961,742 |
| *$24,381,620* | *$32,471,597* | *85%* | $17,043,961 | $15,427,636 |
| *$32,471,597* | *$42,543,169* | *90%* | $22,949,287 | $19,593,882 |
| *$42,543,169* | *$54,930,163* | *95%* | $30,381,832 | $24,548,331 |
| *$54,930,163* | *$70,000,000* | ***100%*** | $39,618,168 | $30,381,832 |
| *$70,000,000* | $109,833,906 | ***100%*** | $70,215,738 | $39,618,168 |
| $109,833,906 | $165,706,781 | ***100%*** | $95,491,043 | $70,215,738 |
| $165,706,781 | $241,902,246 | ***100%*** | $146,411,203 | $95,491,043 |
| $241,902,246 | "Above" | ***100%*** | Pay All but $100 Million | $100,000,000 |

We anticipate that if this tax extension was implemented for income exceeding $372,950, the following economic results would be possible:

- National debt eliminated in less than 8 years (see Chapter 7)
- Any need for a tax bailout to aid corporations would be totally funded by our tax structure rather than a U.S. debt increase
- Millions of jobs would be saved and opportunities created
- Business owners will be encouraged to grow their companies rather than pay higher individual income taxes

- Quicker end to the Modern Recession
- Provides badly needed redistribution of wealth (see Fig. 1.1)

The analysis here leads to the conclusion that our federal representatives are either not looking at the tax structure correctly or are highly swayed by perhaps their wealthy sponsors and their own personal tax views. It is difficult to understand how the latter would be occurring since we are in problematic times. However, we cannot discount this failure mode, and will have to address this in a later chapter. The reader will be directed to our Chapter 6 titled, "A Lobby Full of Conflicts of Interest."

*"Change doesn't come from Washington. Change comes to Washington."*

—BARACK OBAMA, DNC speech, August 28, 2008

**4.8: Playing Chess with Increasing Taxes on the Rich**

At this point, we would also need to do an FMEA on the potential failure modes of this proposed corrective action to understand the consequences of a major 100% tax bracket increase. While instructive, it would be presumptuous to assume this proposal would be acceptable. Therefore, rather than proceed with this FMEA, we will at least point out some of the current historical pitfalls regarding known minor tax increases.

Taxing the rich can be somewhat of a game of chess, especially on the state level. For every move by the government, there may be a counter-move by highly compensated individuals being taxed. For example, consequences have been found by increasing state income taxes; many states have found that it made matters worse, since individuals and businesses are mobile and often moved to another part of the U.S. with a lower tax rate.

> **Remark 4.4:** In an article by Stephen Moore entitled, "Soak the Rich, Lose the Rich" he notes that "... in Connecticut, which raised its tax rate in 2003 to 5% from 4.5%; in New Jersey, which raised its rate in 2004 to 8.97% from 6.35%; and in New York, which raised its tax rate in 2003 to 7.7% from 6.85%. Over the period 2002-2005..." He also noted in this article that in each of these states there was a significant reduction in the number of well-to-do taxpayers compared to the expected national average.... His conclusion was there were consequences from states raising tax rates on the rich. He felt that some rich residents sell their homes and leave the state; as well, many seem to pay less taxable income

on their tax returns; and finally there was a reluctance for some rich people to locate in high-tax states.[64]

Taxes on the federal level are, of course, a different story. Similar consequences could occur if Washington decides to increase the federal income tax on the wealthy, especially to any significant level as proposed here. It is important to realize that corporate versus individual tax usually has a dotted line connection. Business owners who feel they are overtaxed may decide to move to another country to avoid a large federal income tax hike and take their company with them, or they may look for tax loopholes that create fewer jobs.

**Remark 4.5:** In an article by Nonoy Oplas on "The Retreat of High Income Tax Rate Philosophy in the World" he notes that globalization in the 1980s made many politicians realize that they needed to reduce their level of income, as now income tax competition among countries was emerging. The concern the author points out is that a number of people and businesses were moving to other countries where the income taxes were lower. This actually forced government in the mid-90s to further slash their income tax rates. [65]

The government cannot blindly go about increasing individual taxes without understanding the risks and consequences. One logical step would be a pact with our key trading countries to align their income tax structures with ours. The U.S. might be able to dictate such a policy since we are, after all, a leader in imports that could be used as a bargaining chip.

Finally, let's be perfectly clear, we cannot avoid the fact that we have an unfair federal income tax policy, illustrated in Figure 4.1, and as a huge national debt that must be addressed ASAP. The government should do the right thing and provide an equitable tax structure to help pay off this debt by providing a fair tax bracket for each income level. Otherwise, anything less is fiscally irresponsible.

### 4.9: Further Corrective Action with Salary Caps or Luxury Tax

One of the design controls in our FMEA table is to review the possibility of a salary cap. President Obama has asked CEOs and federal employees in February 2008 to take lower salaries; a voluntary suggestion that, while logical, is apparently not possible.

---

[64] online.wsj.com/article/SB124260067214828295.html, Soak the Rich, Lose the Rich, By and Stephen Moore

[65] www.grassrootinstitute.org/system/old/PRPersp/retreat0907.shtml, Grassroot Institute of Hawaii, by Nonoy Oplas, Sept. 2007.

The number one hazard for reliability economics is GREED.

The greed factor is a main reason why this book opposes "Laissez-faire" economic policy (i.e. allowing industry to be free of government restrictions). As you can see from the facts in this chapter, people can never have enough money! One possible suggestion to force the issue is mandatory salary caps. According to our assessment, a salary cap of $70 to $100 million was roughly indicated as a logical extension to the 2009 tax bracket. Therefore, a salary cap is nothing more than a reasonable part of a fair tax structure (see Table 4.6).

There is precedence for a salary cap; although, we have to look at sports to find it. Salary caps are used by the following major sports leagues around the world:

- North America: The National Hockey League, National Football League, Major League Soccer, National Lacrosse League, and the National Basketball Association and minor leagues in various sports.
- England: The top-level leagues in both rugby codes—the Guinness Premiership in rugby union and the Super League in rugby league—have salary caps. Recently, several European soccer leagues have also discussed introducing salary caps.
- Australia: The National Rugby League, The Australian Football League, and A-League all include salary cap provisions.
- "Instead of a salary cap, major league baseball implemented a 'luxury tax,' an arrangement by which teams whose aggregate payroll exceeds a certain figure, determined annually, are 'taxed' on the excess amount. The tax is paid to the league, which then puts the money into its 'industry-growth fund ."[66]

In theory, there are two main benefits derived from sports salary caps—promotion of equality between teams and control of costs.

Here we suggest a salary cap or luxury tax for highly paid individuals to promote some degree of parity amongst citizens. A salary cap will help disperse money into more consumer hands with many possible benefits depending on how it might be implemented.

For example:

- Help job growth—CEOs would take less money, leaving more money for workers
- Less cash hoarding.
- A luxury tax would increase U.S. government taxes.
- Reduce separation of wealth—more consumer spending

[66] http://en.wikipedia.org/wiki/Salary_cap#Luxury_tax_in_Major_League_Baseball

- Beneficial to the consumer as the price of goods could be lower since CEOs would take less
- Lower spectator costs (sports, movies, etc.)

One argument against salary caps is that higher salaries equal more income taxes. However, from the above list, CEO salary caps may be deferred to more jobs, less money spent on unemployment, aid programs, and so forth. Another argument is that people will lose motivation. However, many highly compensated people continue to work even though they do not need the money. We see this all the time in sports, as well as business. Nevertheless, people "whose cup runneth over" will hold out for even higher salaries most of the time. We see this most clearly in athletes whose persistence does nothing more than raise ticket prices. If the individual decides to quit because of a salary cap or luxury tax, a new job is created. Today that's a good thing!

**4.10: Estate and Asset Tax—Generations of Separation of Wealth**

According to the FMEA Table 4.1, the next key issue is under-taxed estates. It would be difficult to ascertain approximately how long it takes for the average multimillionaire to pass money back into circulation through spending, job-friendly investing, government taxes, or through a death tax. Even if the money resides in bank investments or stocks, it may not be enough to provide helpful circulation for good job growth and consumer spending. We noted from Chapter 3, Table 3.2, many billionaires can maintain a relatively stable estate through safe holding practices, and through inherited generations. Today, the build-up of wealth by the few is both a major cause and a potential cure for the Modern Recession. One assumed purpose of the estate tax is the reduction of separation of wealth in the U.S. Unfortunately, the death (i.e. estate) tax is not doing its job. Because of the 2005 total repeal bill known as H.R. 8, when a wealthy person dies in 2010, their estate will be completely untaxed!

> **Remark 4.6:** Estate tax: highest rate in 2001 was up to 60% and has gradually been reduced to 45% in 2007. This was after a certain exemption level as in Table 4.7. However, under current law there will be no estate tax in 2010 and this will not be repealed for 2010. Currently, many members of our government want this law to be made permanent.

**Table 4.7** Federal Estate Tax Exemption from 2004—2011[67]

| Exemptions and Maximum Tax Rates | | |
|---|---|---|
| **Year** | **Estate Tax Exemption** | **Highest Rate** |
| 2003 | $1 million | 49% |
| 2004 | $1.5 million | 48% |
| 2005 | $1.5 million | 47% |
| 2006 | $2 million | 46% |
| 2007 | $2 million | 45% |
| 2008 | $2 million | 45% |
| 2009 | $3.5 million | 45% |
| 2010 | (taxes eliminated) | 0% |

It is uncertain what the government will do with regard to the 2011 estate tax.

> **Remark 4.7:** "For this year (2009), the basic federal estate-tax exemption is $3.5 million, and the top rate is 45%. (However, transfers from one spouse to the other typically are tax-free.) Based on current law, the estate tax is scheduled to disappear in 2010—but only for that one year. The president's plan would extend this year's $3.5 million estate-tax exemption level—and the 45% top rate—into future years."[68]

We know many wealthy individuals like the Waltons of Wal-Mart have and continue to amass huge estates. What will happen to their estates when they die? What estate taxes will be collected, and what charities will their dollars go to, and who will control these assets? A lot will depend on what the current estate tax law is at the time of their death. Powerful people like the Waltons have apparently lobbied to affect our tax structure. This is another aspect of our government's administrative issues.

> **Remark 4.8:** "Wal-Mart and the Waltons have, after all, been notably reluctant to pay taxes. Not only has the company lobbied for tax breaks in communities all over the nation, the Waltons...have campaigned vigorously against the estate tax. They have donated money to its opponents, Republicans like John Thune of South Dakota and David Vitter of Louisiana, and enlisted one of Washington's top lobbying firms,

[67] http://estatetalk.nase.org/estatetalk/FedEstateTaxExempt.pdf
[68] online.wsj.com/article/SB123707638051931241.html

Patton Boggs—a leading anti-estate tax lobbyist—to represent their interests."[69]

Such administrative influences and wealth prejudices are present in our Congress. This has been explored quite a bit in the chapter on conflicts of interest (Chapter 6). It is hard to imagine the Waltons and other billionaires' estates such as Bill Gates' going untaxed by the estate tax, and their money being passed on to their heirs to potentially hoard. However, it is quite possible that these estates may find tax shelters due to our politicians' conflicts of interest (see Lobby Full of Conflicts of Interest, Chapter 6). That is, the U.S. dollars may end up staying in their estate or in a charitable foundation with little or no estate tax collected. This is one current major taxation failure for reliability economics. These untaxed estates equates to loss of government revenue that is passed onto the average American via the national debt.

### 4.10.1: Corrective Action for the Estate Tax

The U.S. needs to maintain some logical level on inheritance similar to the 2009 estimate, but it appears a 45% rate would still be irresponsible. The percentage is very low in value for a reliable economy when you consider the extraordinarily wealthy family such as the Waltons. It would be more logical to increase the 45% level incrementally based on the size of the estate to as much as 95%. It would be presumptuous for us to provide details. The tax assessment should be provided without administrative issues. This will be difficult since there is a strong opposition in Washington to protect the wealthy. The administrative key issue is very deep. The actual vote breakdown on the 2005 bill (H.R. 8) by our Congress is given in Table 4.8.

**Table 4.8** Vote Results on Permanent Death Tax Repeal[70]

| | **For** | **Against** |
|---|---|---|
| Republican | 230 | 1 |
| Democratic | 42 | 160 |
| Independent | | 1 |
| **Totals** | **272** | **162** |

Here again there appears to be a conscious effort by Congress (primarily republicans) to maintain the separation of wealth in our country. Improper taxation is fiscally irresponsible and can stem from a conflict of interest, creating

[69] www.reclaimdemocracy.org/walmart/2005-06/charity.php, "Wal-Mart Charity Evaluated," By Liza Featherstone. First published in the Nov. 21, 2005 issue of *The Nation*
[70] http://clerk.house.gov/evs/2005/roll102.xml

an unreliable economy. The government has no control over how money is invested by individuals who inherit large sums, thus taxation is crucial to bringing money back into the economy so the consumer can have access to it.

> **Remark 4.9:** CNBC reported that the wealthy are likely to pass onto the next generation $27 trillion. To put this in perspective, as of March 2009, the national debt is just over $11 trillion.

Many opponents claim the death tax is a form of double taxation (as a person's income is already taxed during his lifetime). From the view of the inheritor(s), this is true. From the viewpoint that we are all rightful inheritors, as the money originated from U.S. profits, this is false, as there would be no other means to bring this money back to the rightful heirs: the U.S. consumers.

Prior to this bill, H.R. 8, the Charitable Organization Independent Sector, a national, nonprofit organization with over 500 member charities, foundations, and corporate philanthropy programs, urges opposition to the death tax repeal (H.R. 8) stating in a letter to our representatives:

> **Remark 4.10:** "For decades, charitable organizations have worked with donors wishing to make bequests, establish endowments or set up foundations from their estates. Increasingly, charitable gifts are coming from donors' estates. Full repeal of the estate tax would wreak havoc on planned giving decisions and would also guarantee the loss of billions of dollars to charity annually. A recent study by the Congressional Budget Office (CBO) estimated that charitable organizations would have received $13 to $25 billion *less* in 2000 alone if the estate tax had not existed. Annual losses in this range will be disruptive to charities—from universities to neighborhood health clinics, homeless shelters to symphony orchestras." [71]
>
> ***(See Appendix 4A for full details)***

We have illustrated how wealth accumulation leading to hoarding creates money tightening which, in turn, causes our economic downturns in the market and job losses. Inappropriate taxation also creates loss of opportunities for government jobs and hampers the ability for our government to help the needy and effect charities as described by the protest over this H.R. 8 bill.

---

[71] www.independentsector.org/programs/gr/estatetaxalert.html

### 4.10.2: Charities and the Estate Tax

At this point we would like to look at the design control in Table 4.1, requiring a review and assessment of charities in the estate tax key issue. In many ways charities are a cyclic problem. Separation of wealth is problematic; CEO billionaires have outsourced jobs while becoming wealthy. This creates unemployment issues and to a certain extent, charitable needs. Wealthy then hire tax specialist to create trusts and tax foundations to avoid taxes. Since the well-to-do can't spend their money in their lifetime, they typically give it to their charity which is helpful but in many ways does not serve the common good. This lost tax revenue adds to the national debt leaving more burdens on Middle America to pay it off. Less government revenue tightens the job market and creates more charity needs. It would of course be better to have a proper balance. People would rather have a job than need food stamps.

> **Remark 4.11:** Charitable bequests are exempt from the estate tax.

Charity write-offs are then an expense to every American citizen through reduced tax collection. It is a cyclic good and bad problem. As such, this is a key item that needs to be reliable and reviewed appropriately. What happens to charitable collections if we increase the estate tax?

> **Remark 4.12:** "Repealing the estate tax would cause charitable giving to decline. One prominent analysis concludes, for example, that repealing the tax would cause charitable bequests to fall by about 12 percent.[72] Other analyses suggest that charitable bequests could fall much more than that: one concludes that charitable bequests would decline almost 40 percent, and another analysis estimates a 22 percent drop.[73] The potential decrease in charitable bequests has been cited by Independent Sector in their opposition to repealing the estate tax."[74]

According to this assessment, there should not be a consequence, and it is actually beneficial to charities when the estate tax is increased. On the other hand, looking at the extreme case from a tax collection point of view, the government does not collect any tax revenues from individuals that choose to give all their lifetime assets away. In many cases this is not an issue as few individuals do so. However, much debate can occur when we have prominent billionaires such as the Waltons, Bill Gates, and Warren Buffett expected to make high donations.

---

[72] David Joulfaian, "Estate Taxes and Charitable Bequests by the Wealthy," *National Tax Journal*, vol 53, no. 3 (September 2000), pp. 743-764.

[73] www.urban.org/UploadedPDF/310810_TaxPolicy_6.pdf;

[74] www.independentsector.org/programs/gr/estatetaxalert.html

The latter two have pledged their estates to charity (collectively they could well contribute over $100 billion; see Table 3.2). Currently the Gates Foundation is the largest in the nation.

**Remark 4.13:** "Gates Foundation Asset (April 2009): $27.5 billion" [75]

**Remark 4.14:** Reported in February 2007—"Buffett's donation, $36.1 billion of which goes to the Bill & Melinda Gates Foundation, which was already the nation's largest private charity, has some calling this a 'golden age' of philanthropy ....Buffett, 76, chairman of Berkshire Hathaway, an insurance and investment company in Omaha, Neb., paid $1.6 billion (2006) of his record $36.1 billion pledge to the Bill & Melinda Gates Foundation. He said he would continue to pay the foundation 5 percent of the remaining balance of the earmarked shares every year until his death." [76]

**Remark 4.15:** "Wal-Mart makes the majority of our charitable donations at the local level where we can have the most impact on improving people's lives. In 2007, Wal-Mart stores, Sam's Clubs and the Wal-Mart Foundation gave more than $296 million to 4,000-plus communities in the U.S." [77]

**Remark 4.16:** "The Oprah Winfrey Foundation is run exclusively by Oprah Winfrey and provides grants for not-for-profit organizations....The foundation has more than a whopping $190 million in assets and funds." [78]

At that point, when an entire estate is donated to charity, since no money is collected; such trends for billionaires, while good for charities, is a special concern for tax revenue. America needs jobs not hand-outs.

**Remark 4.17**: In an article by Liza Featherstone on Wal-Mart charity, the author notes that on the one hand we are "supposed to applaud philanthropy—because it aligns itself with altruism and 'giving back.'" However, she points out that philanthropy provides an alternative to taxation due to the tax write-off. She then questions whether this type of philanthropy serves the common good, since the tax payers have to end up making up the public (tax write-off) revenue. [79]

---

[75] www.gatesfoundation.org/about/Pages/foundation-fact-sheet.aspx
[76] www.slate.com/id/2159774/fr/rss/
[77]http://walmartstores.com/FactsNews/,
http://walmartstores.com/FactsNews/NewsRoom/7991.aspx
[78] http://charity.lovetoknow.com/Charities_of_Oprah_Winfrey
[79], www.reclaimdemocracy.org/walmart/2005-06/charity.php, Wal-Mart Charity Evaluated, By Liza Featherstone , First published in the Nov. 21, 2005 issue of The Nation

The question of charity funds being exported overseas can also be debated. This is an excellent use of dollars but does not create U.S. jobs and, in many cases, actually does not help needy Americans get a job and make a living. As the old saying goes,

*"Give a person a fish and he will eat for one day, give a person a fishing pole and he will be able to eat for a lifetime."*

It is a serious issue, we certainly need charitable donation. However, if all our billionaires give most of their money to charity, it burdens the rest of us to pay off the national debt. That is, if these monies are not collected in taxes, the average American has to make up for the lost revenue. The debt is forwarded to each generation; we all end up paying for the charity. Many feel it is really the job of the U.S. government to decide what countries and charities to support and how a charity should be represented. For example, charities often are presented in the philanthropist's name, such as the Bill & Melinda Gates Foundation. It is important to address this issue. The U.S. seems to be making huge sacrifices, outsourcing jobs, which also supports many outside poor countries through the free trade imbalance, U.S. foreign charities, fighting wars to help spread democracy, and helping fight nuclear proliferation and so forth. Since the reality is that out-of-the country charitable tax deductions are actually an expense to every U.S. citizen, then it makes sense that large charitable donations should be provided under the U.S. name and control of our elected officials.

### 4.11: Other Corrective Actions—A Lifetime Wealth Cap or Luxury Tax

How much wealth is excessive? Currently this question is really left up to the individual. Seemingly, the saying goes, "Money is Power." Some individuals can never have enough as greed persists. It is time to ask the question:

**How much is too much?**

Does excessive wealth cause an unreliable economy? This is currently a root cause in the FMEA table. According to Figure 1.1, our findings in Chapter 2 and 3, and the most thorough study we could find summarized in Remark 3.9 (in 2005), a very small number of wealthy individuals control most of the assets in the U.S. The wealthier an individual is, the more likely it will be that he invests conservatively. This can be bad for job growth. In Chapter 8, on job-friendly investing, we find that as a general rule, the safer the investment, the less friendly it is for job creation. If this is correct, it is a serious root cause to the Modern Recession.

It is logical to deduce that the upper-echelon investors mainly use brokers and hedge-fund managers. And, in light of the computer models and the media today, it is no wonder that the markets and velocity of money (Figure 2.1) can suddenly be affected by economic sentiment. We anticipate that many IRA accounts will have difficulty keeping up with the sudden changes in the stock market. This is one argument that indicates large individual wealth in the hands of a small fraction of society can make for an unpredictable and unreliable economy.

A wealth cap or luxury tax appears appropriate in order to limit one's estate. There are many advantages that apply, similar to salary cap or luxury tax on a salary. We anticipate:

- Less hoarding and more opportunities for job growth
- A luxury tax increases U.S. government tax revenues
- Reduced separation of wealth increase consumer spending

A Pew Research Study found in 2007 that many more individuals today feel we have become a nation of "haves" and "have-nots."

> **Remark 4.18:** September 13, 2007, Pew Research Center—"A Nation of 'Haves' and 'Have-Nots'? Over the past two decades, a growing share of the public has come to the view that American society is divided into two groups, the 'haves' and the 'have-nots.'.... Of equal importance, the number of Americans who see themselves among the 'have-nots' of society has doubled over the past two decades, from 17% in 1988 to 34% today." [80]

The opinionated study is supported in our previous chapters by facts. Now in 2009, we know that things have gotten worse in this regard. In terms of a lifetime wealth cap, if a person cannot clearly demonstrate that their capital is serving the greater good through job creation and benefits to our society, than their ability to amass a huge estate should be limited. This kind of question really requires serious attention by economists and cannot be solved by one author. One specific amount may not be correct. The logical method is to use a full team to review the problem and look at the issues and consequences of this corrective action. There really is no strong mechanism for redistribution of wealth but taxes.

### 4.12: Non-Residential Alien Under-Taxation Issues

Many situations most likely exist of under-taxation on non-residential foreigners. However, with globalization, it is a growing debacle in a number of areas for U.S. taxation. For example, in the area of athletes and entertainers, the IRS has their hands full.

---

[80] http://pewresearch.org/pubs/593/haves-have-nots

**Remark 4.19:** "Why the spotlight on foreign athletes and entertainers? It is probably because athletes and entertainers are some of the most globally mobile individuals who can earn substantial amounts of money in many countries without establishing a fixed base in any country. Given their ability to move quickly through countries while earning high income, it is not surprising that the IRS is concerned over their compliance efforts."[81]

**Remark 4.20:** At the start of October, Helio Castroneves, a two-time Indianapolis 500 winner and *Dancing With the Stars* champion, was indicted on six counts of tax evasion for allegedly failing to report about $5.5 million of endorsement income between 1999 and 2004.[82]

A new type of trade deficit is also now apparent. We cannot address the multitude of issues but will briefly look at athletes as one example. This group is a good case since they appear to offer little in the way of irreplaceable services to the U.S. economy. In addition, they have no real positive impact on the ordinary U.S. citizen (with the exception of an occasional "expensive" role model). Here we address the root cause of under-taxation of non-resident alien athletes. The issues created have drawn some topics for discussion but have not really been put under the microscope economically.

**Remark 4.21:** "America's New Trade Deficit: Elite Athletes?—Then it got even better—and became a terrific favorable rate of exchange when the best foreign athletes started coming over here…."[83]

**Remark 4.22:** "Foreign Invasion: International Athletes Taking Over American Games," by Kevin Quinn—Foreign athletes continue to enter the American market and increase the globalization of sports….Games, once dominated by Americans, are now being conquered by the likes of such basketball stars as China's Yao Ming and Germany's Dirk Nowitzki. In baseball, players like Pedro Martinez from the Dominican Republic and Japan's Ichiro Suzuki are dominant forces…."[84]

Clearly, foreign athletes are good for the sport but create a negative economic reliability impact for the U.S. and average American. Their median tax on prize money is about 30%, well under the current 2009 tax bracket exceeding

---

[81] www.thefreelibrary.com/The+IRS+spotlight+on+foreign+athletes+and+entertainers.-a0188604712

[82] www.webcpa.com/ato_issues/2009_6/-31193-1.html (APRIL 20, 2009)

[83] www.npr.org/templates/story/story.php?storyId=96861875

[84] www.academic.marist.edu/mwwatch/spring03/articles/Sports/sports4.html

$380,000. Foreign athletes take away opportunities for American athletes, create an athletic financial trade deficit, and typically do not spend their winnings inside the U.S. This directly reduces the U.S. housing market and many related job opportunities. As discussed in the chapter on trade deficit, the dollars must come back in foreign exchange, but the direct impact on the velocity of money will be akin to great accumulation of wealth with hoarding and serve to reduce job growth in the U.S. with loss of opportunity to U.S. athletes and their related financial activities.

The rate at which money is exported to foreign athletes on the PGA tour, baseball, football, soccer, basketball, etc., is exceedingly high and is somewhat of a crisis. One does not have to look hard to find simple examples on the PGA tour and baseball.

> **Remark 4.23:** "In January 1997, Norman an (Australian professional golfer) won his largest winner's check to date, $1 million (for a Skins game in one day), when he won the Andersen Consulting World Championship of Golf at Grayhawk (Golf Club in Scottsdale, Arizona, USA)"[85]

> **Remark 4.24:** "I've never had to make a par for $800,000 in my life," Norman said. "It was hard trying to figure it out."[86]

**The average American has a hard time understanding these prizes.** And America attracts athletes from all over the world. Why not? The U.S. is just giving money away!

> **Remark 4.25:** Angel Cabrera is a golfer from from Argentine who won the 2009 Masters Golf Tournament for $ 1.35 million and the U.S. open in 2007 for $1.26 million. Both were 4-day tournaments.

> **Remark 4.26:** Daisuke Matsuzaka, Japanese baseball player for the Boston Red Sox, held contracts for $6.3 million in 2007 and $8.3 million in 2008 and 2009, each year for a season of baseball.

Foreign prize money in tournaments is considered exported serviceable earnings. It provides few jobs in the U.S., which we have determined is a bottom line in the Modern Recession. In a recessionary period where money is tight, increased prize money on the PGA tour per tournament in 2008 and 2009, and our ever-increasing nation's trade deficit now to foreign athletes, illustrates the

---

[85] http://en.wikipedia.org/wiki/Greg_Norman
[86] www.shark.com/sharkwatch/sharkive/sharkive53.php

continued isolation and lack of ability to change such issues for the average American who faces a future in a country of "haves" and "have-nots".

One proposed corrective action from this author's perspective would be to raise the foreigner's non-residential taxation rate for athletes on prize money from the current base rate of about 30%, to 95%, and also on other types of longer-term seasonal income in order to discourage this continual activity and behavior. This would promote reliability for a struggling U.S. economy. In actuality, a full FMEA needs to be performed on raising such tax rates for different non-residential alien groups such as athletes, entertainers, etc. This is an unusual issue to the trade deficit problem. Typically, one thinks of a trade deficit as being related to imports that provide some benefits to consumers through cheaper goods found in stores like Wal-Mart. In this case, the financial benefits are most likely found to favor only a small population of businessmen and of course, foreigners and their countries.

**4.13: Summary**

In this chapter we identified three key issues on the tax structure: income tax, estate tax, and tax administrative problems. We found the upper 35% tax bracket is not adequate to deal with today's rising income for highly compensated individuals, and poses a long-term reliability economic threat. Prior to the 35% bracket, the more money a person makes the higher his tax bracket, except after $372,950. The upper tax bracket stopping at 35% was identified as not equally weighted, having an unfair distribution for modern salaries well above the upper tax limit. The correct continuation was shown by a dotted line in Figure 4.1. As a corrective action we provided a progressive tax structure in Table 4.6 where brackets continued to 100%. We also suggested a salary cap so that the most yearly income a single individual could "keep" is $100 million.

Next root cause to be addressed was excess write-offs. This indicates that even though individuals were either in the 33% or 35% bracket, they paid a much smaller percentage, between 17.5% and 22.8%, with available data provided on tax year 2006. A design control study was suggested to find and fix loopholes.

Well-to-do retirees whose assets may be between $10 million or $1 billion (or more) were identified as another loophole. This is a problem because they may hardly pay any income tax where they can live off their assets. It would therefore help to correct the problem if assets over a certain amount were required to be declared and could be taxed.

The U.S. estate tax was reviewed. It appeared a 45% tax rate was identified as very low in value for a reliable economy. There are too many extraordinarily wealthy estates in the U.S. as pointed out in Chapter 3. It appeared to be logical to increase the 45% level incrementally based on the size of the estate. We have note in prior chapters that large estates can lead to hoarding and contribute to poor velocity of money.

Many situations of under-taxation most likely exist for non-residential foreigners. An example of foreign athletes was noted that leads to a negative economic reliability impact for the U.S. and for the average American. Their median tax on prize money is about 30%, well under the current 2009 tax bracket of 35% for prize monies over that bracket value. Foreign athletes also take away opportunities for American athletes, create an athletic financial trade deficit, typically do not spend their winnings inside the U.S. (such as in our housing market), and appear to be flooding our athletic structure.

## Appendix 4A: Independent Sector's Letter to Congress on Estate Tax Repeal[87] April 12, 2005

Dear Representative:

Independent Sector, a national, nonprofit organization with over 500 member charities, foundations, and corporate philanthropy programs, urges you to oppose H.R. 8, which would permanently repeal the estate tax. Only a very small number of estates would benefit from this bill, while tens of thousands of charitable organizations serving millions of individuals, families and communities would be greatly disadvantaged.

For decades, charitable organizations have worked with donors wishing to make bequests, establish endowments or set up foundations from their estates. Increasingly, charitable gifts are coming from donors' estates. Full repeal of the estate tax would wreak havoc on planned giving decisions and would also guarantee the loss of billions of dollars to charity annually. A recent study by the Congressional Budget Office (CBO) estimated that charitable organizations would have received $13 to $25 billion *less* in 2000 alone if the estate tax had not existed. Annual losses in this range will be disruptive to charities—from universities to neighborhood health clinics, homeless shelters to symphony orchestras.

Independent Sector's member organizations often partner with governments at all levels to provide services throughout this country and around the world. The loss of revenues to federal and state treasuries caused by repeal of the estate tax would require further cuts to critical programs and services already strapped for funds. This vital source of public revenues benefits all taxpayers and should not be traded for a tax cut benefiting less than one-half of one percent (0.005) of taxpayers (the estimated number that will be subject to estate taxes in 2009).

We understand the need to reform the estate tax laws and support efforts to give relief to family farmers and small businesses. These are important assets to families and communities, and heirs should be able to maintain them without the burden of estate taxes. But the very wealthiest estates should contribute to meeting the needs of the nation. A reformed tax will not negatively impact their heirs who will still be extremely rich.

IS (independent Sector) urges you to support reasonable reform options instead of full repeal of the estate tax—and to oppose H.R. 8. Too much is at stake to do otherwise.

Sincerely, Diana Aviv President and CEO

---

[87] www.independentsector.org/programs/gr/estatetaxalert.html

# ■ 5.0 ■
# HOARDING ISSUES

## 5.1: FMEA on Velocity of Money

Our findings in Chapter 3 indicated that the dramatic slowing of the velocity of money was a key economic indicator for the Modern Recession. We are now in a very good position to perform an FMEA on this key issue.

Table 5.1 indicates that there are two main potential failure modes in which velocity of money either slows suddenly or gradually. There are many effects resulting from these failure modes, and we will focus on the ones listed. Some of the key root causes that we'll discuss are economic sentiment, wealth accumulation, job outsourcing, and hoarding. We have already discussed a number of corrective actions in the area of taxes in Chapter 4. Here we look for more supporting facts for our FMEA analysis.

**Table 5.1** Failure Modes and Effects Analysis on Velocity of Money

| Key Issue | Potential Failure Mode | Potential Effect of Failure | Root Cause(s) | Root Cause Rating | Design Control | Possible Corrective action |
|---|---|---|---|---|---|---|
| Velocity of Money | 1) Velocity of money slows suddenly<br><br>2) Velocity of money slows gradually | 1a) Companies lose orders<br>1b)Abrupt job losses<br>1c) Abrupt mortgage defaults<br>1d) Deflation<br>2a) Companies order slow down<br>2b) Hiring freeze<br>2c) Mortgages start to default<br>2d) Deflation | 1a,b,c) – Economic sentiment leading to:<br>- Small Sector of wealthy controlling U.S. investment dollars.<br>- Job outsourcing. Company hoarding.<br>- Rapid decline in stock prices,<br>- Decline in GDP<br>1c) Lack of government oversight. Greed.<br><br>2) Job outsourcing, - Separation of wealth,<br>- Wealth accumulation,<br>- Decline of GDP | 1) 9<br><br>2) 6 | 1a,b,c) Investigate proper income and estate taxation,<br>2) Assess govt. administra-tion failures<br>3) Assess free trade issues<br>4) Assess wealth separation<br>5) Review historical parallels | Add income and estate tax overhaul (see Chapter 4)<br><br>Review possible anti-hoarding legislation<br><br>Free trade protec-tionism (Ch. 9); U.S. job quotas (Ch. 9) |

**5.2: Looking at the Potential Effect of Failure "Deflation"**

From the table, we see one clear effect is deflation. It is instructive to start with this indicator, since it is commonly discussed in the news. And deflation will continue, as long as velocity of money remains slow. Deflation illustrates that money is not, in the strictest sense finite, i.e. it is not conserved. This means it can change value by inflating or deflating. Currently as of August 2009 the deflation rate (according to the Consumer Price Index) is about 2.1% [88]. That means a basket of goods costing $100 in a non deflation time will now only cost on average $97.90. This is extremely helpful when money is hoarded. As money slows, eventually prices will fluctuate on goods; and things typically get cheaper as we are all watching dollars. Another aspect that helps with a hoarding event is that such dollars are a potential money source, stored for later use. In light of these two aspects, one might feel that hoarding is not a key issue. In the next section we clarify this concept a bit.

**5.3: Failure Mode—Slow versus Abrupt Change in Velocity of Money**

As we have discussed previously, there is a serious time factor regarding the velocity effect. The effect of deflation takes time, and stored assets may take even longer to go back into circulation. Looking at Figure 2.1 we have had a very gradual slowing of the velocity of money (1989 to 2001), then a small recovery. In that period, there was time to adjust somewhat. Housing prices even inflated during that time. This root cause for the second failure mode, number 2, rated as a 6, is not as severe as failure mode number 1, rated as a 9.

Failure mode number 1, with the high rating, creates bigger problems. For example, when the mass-hoarding rate increased quickly as in 2008 (see Analysis 2.1), then the velocity of money decreased rapidly, possibly at the same rate or faster depending on the GDP (see Equation 2.1). The effects reflected in the table prompts concern: companies lose orders, job losses occur, and mortgage defaults increase, all in a short time frame. These contribute to a decrease in the velocity of money. It should be stressed that the slowing of the velocity of money is not a root cause; it is a key issue. The root causes are found in the reliability FMEA analysis by viewing the issue from both a bottom-up and a top-down assessment. In the top-down view, we have corporations losing orders as one root cause. We will discuss other ones shortly.

Job loss and deflation of housing prices are key reasons from a bottom-up root cause perspective. Table 5.1 illustrates why we currently continue to have a slowing in the velocity of money, which has contributed to problems like the mortgage failure rate. As of June 2009 the foreclosure rates in the U.S. are

---

[88] http://www.bls.gov/news.release/cpi.nr0.htm

spiking. The average U.S. statistic is not well-known but it is probably around 1 out of every 400 homes (CNN reported in June 2009).

> **Remark 5.1:** More than 1.3 million homes have now been lost to foreclosure since the market meltdown began in August 2007…(as of May 2009) "We had been predicting 3.4 million foreclosure filings for the year," he said, "but we'll blow those numbers out of the water." [89]

> **Remark 5.2:** In California, 1 out of every 173 homes in the state has received a foreclosure filing. Yet this is nothing compared to Nevada where 1 out of every 76 homes received a foreclosure notice! [90]

Often, in 2009's Modern Recession, people worry about inflation. They fail to understand the importance of the velocity of money remaining slow. So that in actuality we are still in a deflationary period. One article reports in June 2009,

> **Remark 5.3:** "In case you're wondering why interest rates are climbing along with the price of filling up your gas tank, the answer is simple: fear of inflation. The U.S. has pumped so much money into the economy—including $12.8 trillion to bail out banks and others along with cutting the Fed Funds rate to almost zero—that people around the world are beginning to question the strength of the dollar."[91]

However, we anticipate this fear is unfounded, as the velocity of money is still too low to cause any inflation and, with foreclosures still climbing, home sales faltering, and unemployment still increasing, there is no real indication of inflation as of June 2009.

> **Remark 5.4:** February 2009, blog excerpt by Espen Haug entitled "The Velocity of Money and Time Stamped Money."—In this blog Haug notes that injecting a lot of money into the economy by the government should spur inflation. However, this most likely will not happen due to the velocity of money. Espen Haug notes that some macro-economists think the velocity of money is not very important while others feel it is very significant. The author agrees with the view (similar to this book) that it is important. The author notes that if the money supply continues to grow

---

[89] www.money.cnn.com/2009/05/13/real_estate/April_foreclosure_stats/?postversion=2009051310

[90] www.mrswing.com/articles/Monthly_Foreclosures_and_the_Dreaded_Road_Ahead_On.html

[91] www.dailyfinance.com/2009/06/12/will-inflation-fears-send-oil-to-250/

that we can still get deflation of common goods, and this can cause many respectable businesses to close due to less demand. Haug forewarns that businesses could go bankrupt with falling production, and that unemployment problems will increase the cycle.[92]

**5.4: Historical Review of Hoarding**

From the FMEA table, we see that hoarding among the wealthy and mass hoarding are both indicated as root causes to the velocity of money. It is important to look at history, since this helps with verification and reliability lessons learned. Historically, hoarding has been shown to be a key reason for the fall of the Roman Empire.

> **Remark 5.5:** Multiple scholars have contended "One of the primary catalysts to the deterioration of the Roman economy was the lack of circulating currency in the Western Empire. Two reasons for the lack of funds are **wholesale hoarding** of bullion by Roman citizens, and the widespread **looting of the Roman treasury** by the 'barbarians'. These two factors, coupled with the **massive trade deficit** with Eastern Regions of the Empire served to stifle the growth of wealth in the west."[93]

There are strong U.S. parallels in our economy that, while not totally equivalent, are concerning:

- The monetary saving is surging (as shown in Figure 3.4 and Remark 2.3). This is one key parallel effect to bullion hoarding. (Note: though money is no longer on the gold standard, gold bullion, a more finite conservative quantity as we mentioned above, is less like the dollar). There are also fewer tendencies as well to stuff money in a mattress, yet strong job-friendly investing is also not occurring:

> **Remark 5.6:** As of June 11, 2009—The *Los Angeles Times* reports that there is still an enormous mountain of cash in savings accounts ($4.5 trillion), money market funds ($3.7 trillion), and short-term CDs ($1.3 trillion). Right now, there is a $9.5 trillion cash hoard.[94]

---

[92] www.wilmott.com/blogs/collector/index.cfm/2009/2/15/The-Velocity-of-Money-and-Time-Stamped-Money, by Espen Haug

[93] ancienthistory.about.com/gi/dynamic/offsite.htm?zi=1/XJ&sdn=ancienthistory&cdn=education&tm=106&gps=264_1163_921_556&f=00&su=p897.4.336.ip_&tt=2&bt=1&bts=1&st=34&zu=http%3A//web.archive.org/web/20040412123321/http%3A//www.acs.ohio-state.edu/history/isthmia/teg/Hist111H/issues/rome2.html

[94] www.fundmasteryblog.com/2009/06/11/95-trillion-cash-hoard/ , Sources MoneyNet Inc., Federal Reserve.

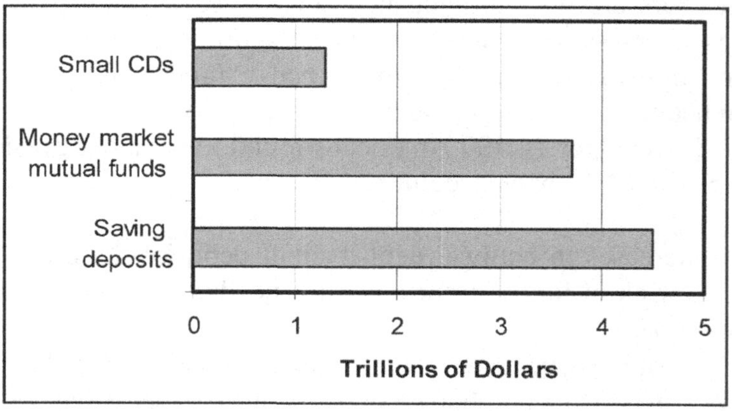


**Figure 5.1** Company hoarding is increasing in 2009 for the most part. See Remarks 3.16 to 3.22

- In parallel to the Roman Empire looting, we have problems on Wall Street. Three good examples are:

**Remark 5.7:** The $50 billion Ponzi scheme by convicted former Nasdaq chairman (hedge-fund manager) Bernard Madoff. [95]

**Remark 5.8:** "Robert Allen Stanford and James M. Davis, accused of carrying out a 'massive Ponzi scheme' over the last decade….more than $1.6 billion in 'bogus' loans."[96]

**Remark 5.8-A:** Companies can be legally bought, drained and sold, then sent to bankruptcy after executives and bankers take extreme profits leaving bond holders and company workers to bear the burden, says NY times of Simmons Mattress by a Boston firm THL.[97] (such buyouts are not uncommon![98]

**Remark 5.9:** December 8, 2008— "…Over the last five years, the SEC has brought more than 125 enforcement actions involving hedge funds,

---

[95] www.time.com/time/business/article/0,8599,1866680,00.html

[96] http://dealbook.blogs.nytimes.com/2009/02/27/us-accuses-stanford-of-running-huge-ponzi-scheme/

[97] www.nytimes.com/2009/10/05/business/economy/05simmons.html?pagewanted=1&_r=1&sq=simmons%20company&st=cse&scp=1 , October 4, 2009

[98] The Buyout of America: How Private Equity Will Cause the Next Great Credit Crisis by Josh Kosman

and regulators are now probing new areas such as trading in derivative securities, controls over valuation, naked short-selling, use of high value investors, information sharing among hedge funds, and the relationship between hedge fund managers and their prime brokers....”[99]

**Remark 5.9A:** Over 14,700 Americans found to have tax evasion foreign (mostly Swiss UBS) bank accounts.[100]

- With increases in national debt, bailout debt, job loss, and recession, we face lack of funds in our government (due to improper taxation see Chapter 4).
- We have a massive trade deficit, primarily with China, Japan, Canada as well as with a number of other countries (see Chapter 9 on Free Trade Failures).

The reader should not take these historical parallel to the fall of the Roman Empire lightly. The U.S. as of September 2009 has done little in the area of structural economic changes that plague our recession to remedy such problems (see Chapter 11 on What the Reader Can Do).

**5.5: Wealth Accumulation Issue to Hoarding**

The wealth accumulation factor in Table 5.1 is certainly a strong confounding problem with hoarding. Here individuals who are able to amass millions or billions of U.S. dollars provide mathematical challenges since it is typically more money than can be spent in a lifetime.

> **Remark 5.10:** If a person lives for 100 years and tries to spend a billion dollars, this would equate to $10 million a year or about $27,400 per day over his lifetime. If his lifetime were limited to 50 years, this would equate to spending $20 million per year or $54,800 per day.

Of course, such spending is not likely to occur. Most likely a small percentage will be spent and the rest will be used in a number of different ways. The best scenario is investing in a company that can create jobs. This is the capitalistic way of thinking. However, we now have to question the motivation of an extremely wealthy person to risk investing or in working hard to create or expand his own company. Furthermore, many multi-millionaires do not own companies. Movie stars, athletes, hedge-fund managers, for example, do little to employ the masses and create jobs. And when wealthy individuals are in control of a manufacturing corporation, worse yet, they are pressured to find ways to

---

[99] www.pli.edu/product/clenow_detail.asp?id=38831

[100] New York Times, Business Day, Nov. 18, 2009.

streamline their bottom line, outsourcing jobs overseas and reducing their company's U.S. work force. See for example:

> **Remark 5.11:** "Exporting America: Why Corporate Greed Is Shipping American Jobs Overseas"[101]

> **Remark 5.12:** "Despite Criticism, U.S. Firms Look to Outsource More Information Technology Jobs Overseas, Says CEO of Outsourcing Advisors, Alsbridge, Inc."[102]

As we continually stress, there is just too much money in the hands of the few who are not interested in providing nor required to provide job-friendly investing. Nor are they able to spend their wealth in a timely manner. We know that it is the lower- and middle-class (~70%) Americans who are the main consumers. And they are now having problems keeping jobs, paying bills, and in general, find money very tight, leading to the fact that they are not spending. Still persistent during the Modern Recession, we have articles such as this one in a Colorado business paper that reports CEO salaries are still on the rise as of June 2009.

> **Remark 5.13:** "In a year that saw a national recession eroding corporate profits and creating double-digit unemployment rates, the top officers at Colorado's 50 largest public companies saw their compensation increase by more than 5 percent. Stocks of only three of those firms rose in value....The article continues to name M. T. Fries, CEO Liberty Global Inc, 19.1 million, J. H. Schwartz, former CEO ProLogis, $15.1 million, G. B. Maffei, CEO Liberty Media Corp, $12.2 million, E. A. Mueller, CEO Quest Communications, $10.4 million and others...total compensation increased to $524.7 million in 2008 from $498.99 million the year before a 5.2% increase..."[103]

> **Remark 5.14:** Blackstone's chief executive officer, Stephen Schwarzman, tops the list of the top 10 highest-paid executives in the U.S. last year (2008), with a staggering package of $702 million, according to reports from the corporate library. The stock went from a little over $20 in

---

[101] www.cceia.org/resources/transcripts/5054.html
[102] www.prnewswire.com/cgi-bin/stories.pl?ACCT=104&STORY=/www/story/10-22-2008/0004909753&EDATE=
[103] *The Denver Post*, June 14, 2009, Business Section.

January 2008 to about $5 in January 2009 (as of August 2009 it has rebounded to about $13). [104]

With salaries (Remarks 3.1 to 3.8 and Figure 1.1) and estate values still on the rise (Table 3.2) in the wealthy communities even in our recession, U.S. dollars, while not finite are also not infinite. There will just be less money in circulation, continually slowing the velocity of money and creating tight money issues. The primary way to get this "stored" money back into circulation is through the corrective action of proper taxation as suggested in Chapter 4.

**5.6: Top-Down FMEA Special Issues to the Financial Housing Crisis**

From a top-down FMEA view to the housing crisis, government oversight, greed, and economic sentiment play key roles in the financial system's root causes as indicated in Table 5.1. We start briefly with a top-down view on greed and government oversight in an enlightening interview with Alan Greenspan by CNBC, during a special program entitled, "House of Cards" on free market bank failures, aired on July 3, 2009.

> **Remark 5.15: Interviewer:** "If anyone along the way would have raised their hand and said, guys at the banks, you are doing the wrong thing at the lenders; you're doing the wrong thing. Maybe we could have averted this crisis, nobody was willing to step back and say, you know what, this is going to end badly."
> **Greenspan:** "Ya that's true, and there is a very good reason for that. It's not that they weren't aware that the risks were there, and I spoke to them. It wasn't that these people were dumb, they knew precisely what was going on, the vast majority of them thought that they knew when to get out. It was a failure of our best and our brightest."
> **Interviewer:** "You seem to have been maligned on the good judgments of managements to say we're going to step out now, but nobody or very few actually did that. These were not poor decisions—these were the worst decisions financial executives have ever made! Greed runs through this."
> **Greenspan:** "Absolutely—and you are going to pass legislation which is going to outlaw all that—try it."
> **Interviewer:** "You still firmly believe in the power of the free market?"
> **Greenspan:** "I firmly believe that because I know of nothing in the evidence of the alternatives."
> **Interviewer:** "Fully acknowledging the bad things that go along."

---

[104] www.ibtimes.com/articles/20090814/blackstonestephen-schwarzman-tops-list-highest-paid-ceo-s.htm

> **Greenspan:** "This is one of the most extraordinary things about this whole episode. Looking at the way we all behaved. How is it possible that this species built up such an extraordinary world standard of living which has drawn hundreds of millions of people out of poverty? The thing that we should be most extraordinarily appreciative of is how far this system has carried us. Because there is no doubt that somewhere in the future we are going to have this conversation again—it will not be for quite a period of time, but it will occur. Because the flaws of human nature are such that we cannot change that—it doesn't work."

From this interview, we see two things that stick-out regarding the housing crisis. First, Mr. Greenspan's agreement that greed runs through this crisis. Next is his contradictory statement that in spite of acknowledging this issue, he still believes in the power of an open market for the banking industry. As well, he apparently feels government oversight in the banking industry, will not work by his comment "try it"! Perhaps this is another statement for reliability economics. We are befuddled with the lack of today's economists to really only understand the greed factor after a failure has occurred and not build-in protection against it in our economic policies. Such "Laissez-faire economics" is a root cause issue. This could be recognized more quickly if potential economic policies were first subjected to a financial FMEA analysis team requiring such design controls. However, without a reliability economics team in place, we believe that Mr. Greenspan is correct stating this conversations will again occur in the future. Currently, it is really left to the government to provide appropriately corrective actions when necessary. We have to also question, the reasons for the free market failure still since mortgage loans illogically became subjected to another main root cause issue economic sentiment via mortgage backed securities!

When businesses fail due to a sudden drop in product demand, whether it is financial or manufacturing orders, economic sentiment is often a key. Now we had mentioned in Chapter 3 that simple mortgages got bundled into mortgage-backed securities. This meant that they were exposed to economic sentiment and market pressures. A number of firms held these securities such as Lehman Brothers. Many see the fairly sudden collapse of Lehman Brothers as a last straw that broke the credit market in September 2008. As mentioned in Chapter 3. Lehman Brothers was over exposed in the "subprime" mortgage market. Lehman generated a significant portion of its revenue through the issuance of mortgage-backed and asset-backed securities. When mortgage default rates began to rise and the demand for these securities began to disappear, Lehman was left with billions of dollars of rapidly depreciating securities on its balance sheet, forcing it to take large write-downs and write-offs. Eventually, the company's efforts to shed risky assets proved unsuccessful, and economic sentiment caused investors to sell off shares which rapidly depreciated faster than the mortgage failure rate. A major sell-off came (see Chapter 3) from money market managers.

**Remark 5.16:** "Today, money market funds hold $3.5 trillion in assets for a wide range of individuals and institutional investors." [105]

In this recession, money markets had concerns and fled to cash, pulling out and hoarding capital (see Remarks 3.27, 5.6). From a top-down perspective, this triggered the collapse of Lehman Brothers and almost resulted in the fall of Bear Stearns (see Remarks 3.30 and 3.31). However, from a reliability perspective, there were many top-down economic sentiment issues that perhaps are not well understood.

In February of 2009, in an article entitled, "The Man Who Made Too Much", by Gary Weiss, many interesting points were made. He talks about Hedge Fund manager John Paulson who we discussed earlier, made $3.7 billion in 2007 by effectively betting on a housing crisis.

**Remark 5.17:** Mr. Weiss questioned, "If he saw all of this coming, was it right for him to keep his own counsel…" Mr. Weiss in his article goes onto explain that Dick Fuld of Lehman Brothers and Alan Schwartz, former C.E.O. of Bear Stearns, appeared before a congressional panel and Mr. Weiss quoted Fuld as saying in the meeting, 'And I believe that unsubstantiated rumors in the marketplace caused significant harm to Lehman Brothers.' And Mr. Weiss explained that Schwartz gave similar testimony when he appeared before a Senate Banking Committee in April. As well Mr. Weiss noted that a Banking Committee chairman, Mr. Christopher Dodd also stated that 'this goes beyond rumors. This is about collusion.' However, Mr. Weiss also explain that Paulson and others were really the subject of finger pointing because of the large profits made at this time.[106]

Some articles cite this from the perspective that CEOs often blame short-sellers for their problems.

**Remark 5.18:** CEOs in particular often blame short-sellers for their company's falling prices. CEO Dick Fuld of Lehman Brothers testified before Congress that "The shorts and rumormongers succeeded in

---

[105] www.economicpolicyjournal.com/2008/09/mutual-fund-industry-group-issues.html
[106] www.portfolio.com/executives/features/2009/01/07/John-Paulson-Profits-in-Downturn, http://ayitinou.com/index.php?option=com_content&view=article&id=368:brilliant-or-evil-how-a-man-made-3-bil-betting-against-you&catid=30:general-article&Itemid=50, www.cnbc.com//id/28814840

> bringing down Bear Stearns." And Alan Schwartz, former CEO of Bear Stearns, gave similar testimony when he appeared before the Senate Banking Committee last April, saying that, "market forces continued to drive and accelerate our precipitous liquidity decline." [107]

Paulson was not the only fund manager to have profited from the banking industry's troubles.

> **Remark 5.19:** Some other Hedge Fund managers who were cited for profiting from the housing crisis were: Jim Melcher, Hedge Fund manager, Balestra Capital based in New York[108]; J. Kyle Bass, managing member and principal of the Dallas-based hedge fund Hayman Advisors LP[109]; Philip Falcone of Harbinger Capital[110]; as well as John Paulson of Harbinger Capital Partners and Paulson & Co.[111]

Goldman Sachs also successfully hedged on the housing crisis. They sold the securities and at the same time hedged against them insuring with AIG. The tax payer was a big loser as AIG received $180 billion in bailout to cover losses. Goldman's actions have drawn attention, many accusation have occurred.

> **Remark 5.19A** "McClatchy investigation found that investment bank giant Goldman Sachs made secret bets on an imminent housing crash -- while selling off billions in soon-to-be worthless securities"[112].

We encourage the reader to view all the articles to understand the issues here. Keep in mind that what's important is to value the proper role in reliability economics from both a top-down and bottom-up view. From a top-down view, mortgage-backed securities are an investment that can fluctuate in free market value. From a bottom-up view, the mortgage failure rate, while increasing in this calendar time period, did not increase with the same high failure rate (see Figure 2.4 and 2.5) as mortgage-backed securities?

We note that government oversight of a number of industries including Hedge Fund managers at times can appear difficult (see Chapter 6 on a Lobby Full of Conflicts of Interest). In November of 2008 this article was written.

---

[107] www.investorsdailyedge.com/TheLongandShortofPlayingtheStockMarket.html
[108] www.nytimes.com/2007/08/19/business/19credit.html?_r=1&scp=7&sq=2006%20credit%20mortgage&st=cse
[109] www.cnbc.com/id/31488199#bass
[110] www.bloomberg.com/apps/news?pid=20601103&sid=agHGvijV55fM&refer=us
[111] www.bloomberg.com/apps/news?pid=20601103&sid=agHGvijV55fM&refer=us
[112] www.miamiherald.com/NATION/story/1310367.html

**Remark 5.20:** "…The five hedge-fund managers who testified Thursday before the House Oversight and Government Reform Committee are more likely to find friends among Democrats, who have received 65 percent of the total $14.2 million the unregulated industry has given this election cycle to federal candidates, committees and parties. But the managers didn't appear to be asking members of Congress for protection from regulation—instead they seemed resigned to the fact that it will happen and wanted to have a hand in shaping it, according to the Washington Post. "The managers who testified—George Soros, Philip Falcone, John Paulson, James Simons and Kenneth Griffin—have themselves contributed $179,200 to Congress this election cycle, favoring Democrats with 74% of their money. Soros, however, is the only one of them to have given money to president-elect Barack Obama, who received a total of $2.6 million from the hedge fund and private equity industry this election cycle. (John McCain received about $1.6 million.) Employees from the five companies represented by these men (Soros Fund Management, Harbinger Capital, Paulson & Co., Renaissance Technologies Corp and Citadel Investment Group) gave $269,550 to Obama. Citadel employees were responsible for nearly $200,000 of that. Collectively, employees of the companies represented at Thursday's hearing have given all candidates and committees $915,900 this cycle. "Members of the Oversight Committee, who heard the managers' opinions on requiring hedge funds to register with the Securities and Exchange Commission, aren't popular targets of hedge fund money. Only three of the hedge-funds represented at the hearing had given money to members of the committee, including Reps. Paul Hodes (D-N.H.), Virginia Foxx (R-N.C.) and Paul Kanjorski (D-Pa.). Hodes and Kanjorski are also members of the House Financial Services Committee, which has more obvious jurisdiction over hedge funds. Neither the chair of the Oversight Committee, Rep. Henry Waxman of California, nor the ranking member, Virginia Rep. Tom Davis, has reported receiving any money from the hedge fund industry this election cycle."At the hearing, the hedge-fund managers approved of additional oversight for the $2 trillion industry, which has gone largely unchecked over the years."[113]

There are many reasons why the housing market remains unreliable, and why it requires strong government oversight. Top-down root cause issues (i.e. poor lending practices, allowance of mortgage backed securities subjected to economic sentiment, lack of government oversight, market regulations…) are just

[113] www.opensecrets.org/news/2008/11/hedge-fund-managers-plead-thei.html, Published by Lindsay Renick Mayer on November 14, 2008. Permission granted from opensecrets.org

as important as the bottom–up issues (i.e. unqualified buyers, job losses, people walking away from devalued properties).

### 5.7: Hoarding Commodities and Foul Play

Money is not the only asset that is hoarded. There is a tendency to hoard commodities by many investors. This is also a concern for a reliable economy.

> **Remark 5.21:** "Harmful Effects of Inflation, Tuesday, June 17th, 2008, Costantino Bresciani-Turroni, Contrarian Investors' Journal—In today's context, does a sudden fall in the price of a commodity (e.g. oil, iron, grain, wheat) mean that its underlying demand has suddenly fallen or its supply has suddenly increased? Obviously, the answer is no. "Over the years, through the developments of financial 'innovation,' commodities have become the playground of hedge funds and other money shufflers. So much so that we had to categorize demand into basic underlying demand and 'investment' demand. As we think about this issue more and more, how can commodities really be 'investments' in the first place? Is gold an investment?"But in reality, since gold is a boring, inert metal that does not have much pragmatic use and does not pay dividends, income or interests, it is unfit for 'investment.'"In the same way, commodities are tangible things valued for their pragmatic use. But they do not pay dividends, income or interests too. So, how can they be 'investments' and therefore, have 'investment' demand associated with them?" [114]

We state later that gold is really a very poor investment for job creation compared to equities or real estate (See Chapter 8). What about oil? In the energy sector, this is an area that can create havoc when hoarding occurs. The article above also points out that there are two types of demand for oil.

> **Remark 5.22:** "What makes up the demand for oil? There are basically two types of demand for oil: (1) The physical demand where the real side of the economy uses for its everyday needs and (2) The investment demand where the financial side of the economy shifts the money here and there from one asset class to the other. We need to ask ourselves the following question: Has the physical demand for oil changed? "Today, we have thought of a better way to describe those 'investment' demands: hoarding. In essence, those hedge-funds and money shufflers who 'invest'

---

[114] http://cij.inspiriting.com/?tag=hoarding, Permission from *Contrarian Investors' Journal*

in commodities are hoarding. They hoard commodities in anticipation of increased demand in the future. As their anticipation changes, they hoard and dis-hoard accordingly, resulting in irrational price movements. Worse still, some of them borrowed money to hoard, thus accentuating the violence of price changes. With central bankers like Ben Bernanke increasing the floodgates of more easy credit (see Marc Faber: Bernanke Policy Will 'Destroy' U.S. Dollar), no wonder much of these borrowed money goes into hoarding in anticipation of higher prices."All these hoarding activities distort price signals, which can even confuse the experts on the state of real underlying demand and supply. ....'"[115]

Oil of course is crucial to our economy. As the price goes up, energy-consuming businesses suffer. Businesses cut back, people get laid off, a domino effect occurs, and eventually the real estate market is affected through mortgage failure. All types of hoarding need to be stopped as much as possible.

**5.8: Summary**

In this chapter an FMEA was performed on velocity of money issues. Two main potential failure modes were identified in which velocity of money either slows suddenly or gradually. It was pointed out that there are misconceptions regarding hoarding due to the time factor. When the mass-hoarding rate increased quickly as in 2008, consequences appeared to have aggravated the unemployment and mortgage failure rates. We also discussed issues of commodity hoarding.

A historical review of hoarding was provided on the fall of the Roman Empire. Here multiple scholars have contended that root causes to its fall were wholesale hoarding of bullion, widespread looting of the Roman treasury, and a massive trade deficit. Strong U.S. parallels in our economy were provided.

We also discussed the fact that there is a wealth accumulation factor presenting strong confounding problems with hoarding. Here individuals who are able to amass millions or billions of U.S. dollars provide mathematical challenges to bringing these dollars back into economy in a timely manner.

A number of issues were also discussed regarding the housing market problems. Unreliability due to top-down issues of government deregulation, greed and economic sentiment. In an interview with Alan Greenspan, we found that he still believed in the power of the free marketplace while at the same time acknowledging the reality of greed. We asserted that economic policies should be designed to combat greed. We noted the role that money markets played which appeared to have aggravated the trigger in the collapse of Lehman Brothers and almost Bear Stearns. There are also other top-down economic sentiment issues that may not be well understood. A Bear Sterns C.E.O. before a congressional panel blamed rumormongers and short-sellers for the firm's failure.

---

[115] http://cij.inspiriting.com/?tag=hoarding, Costantino Bresciani-Turroni, Permission from Contrarian Investors' Journal. Costantino Bresciani - Turroni, hoarding, inflation, speculation Posted in Economics/Finance, Looking Forward, Market Observations

# ■ 6.0 ■
# A LOBBY FULL OF CONFLICTS OF INTEREST

### 6.1: FMEA on Tax Administration Issues

In Chapter 4, FMEA Table 4.1 indicated that a potential failure mode for implementing fair taxation was government administrative issues. In this chapter we explore this premise and also the key issue of fair representation. Table 6.1 shows the results.

**Table 6.1** FMEA Table on Key Issue of Government Tax Administration Issues

| Key Issue | Potential Failure Mode | Potential Effect of Failure | Root Cause(s) | Root Cause Rating | Design Control | Possible Corrective action |
|---|---|---|---|---|---|---|
| Govern-ment Tax Admin. Issues | Failure to implement fair tax structure | 1) Recession issues, increase in national debt.<br><br>2)High interest rate payments<br>3) Lost taxes, fiscal instability<br><br>4) Default on foreign loans | 1a) Irresponsible risk tolerance<br><br>2,3,4) Under taxation<br><br>3) Conflict of interest | 1) 9<br><br>2) 10<br><br>3) 10 | 1) Review and propose improvement<br>2) Assess government influences<br>3) Implement a reliability economics team | 1) Restrictions on lobbyists<br><br>2) Set aside tax for campaign funds to avoid lobbyist influences<br><br>3) Add a reliability economics team |
| Fair Represen-tation | Failure to provide unbiased represen-tation | Failed policies | Influence of lobbyists | 9 | 1) Review and propose improvement<br>2)Implement reliability economics | 1)Restrictions on lobbyists<br>2)Add a reliability economics team |

Chapter 4 has addressed the root cause of under-taxation while Chapter 7 will look at irresponsible risk tolerance." The 3rd root cause, conflict of interest, is now investigated.

There are numerous definitions for the term "conflict of interest." However, most of the common ones relate to public office. Here are key definitions:

1. A situation in which a public official's decisions are influenced by the official's personal interests.[116]
2. A conflict of interest is a situation in which someone in a position of trust, such as a lawyer, insurance adjuster, a politician, executive or director of a corporation or a medical research scientist or physician, has competing professional or personal interests.[117]
3. Any relationship that is or appears to be not in the best interest of the organization. A conflict of interest would prejudice an individual's ability to perform his or her duties and responsibilities objectively.[118]
4. A situation in which someone, such as an attorney or public official, has professional, personal, or financial interests or obligations and cannot take on certain new business because the prior interest or obligation would make it difficult for that person to fulfill his duties fairly.[119]
5. Conflict between the private interests and public obligations of a person in an official position.[120]

Many of these definitions, when applied, are a matter of opinion; especially when it comes to politics, since politicians are always influenced by lobbyists and self-interest. These have become integral to our system. We are not trying to finger-point in this chapter, rather to look for ways to make the economy more reliable.

**6.2: Is There A Conflict of Interest?**

The first question is do we have conflict of interest in administrating a proper estate tax or properly taxing the truly well-to-do? Here is one fact that suggests there are personal and financial reasons for such conflicts.

> **Remark 6.1:** "With a collective net worth of $3.7 billion, most of Congress's 535 members have fewer financial concerns in a recession than their constituents. U.S. senators had a median net worth of approximately $1.7 million in 2007, the most recent year for which their financial data is available, and 62 percent of the Senate's members could be considered millionaires. In the House of Representatives, the median net worth was about $684,000; with 39 percent of members having net

[116] www.wordnet.princeton.edu/perl/webwn
[117] www.en.wikipedia.org/wiki/Conflict_of_interest
[118] www.selu.edu/admin/ia/audit_terms/index.html
[119] www.millerlawinc.com/CM/Custom/Legal-Definitions.asp
[120] www.cdc.gov/hiv/topics/cba/resources/guidelines/hiv-cp/appendixD.htm

worth's estimated to be at least $1 million. By contrast, only about 1 percent of all American adults can be considered millionaires."[121]

A full list of such 2007 disclosures is provided in Appendix 6A.

**Remark 6.2:** "Financial disclosure in 2003 revealed of the 100 senators at least 40 millionaires were among them consisting of 22 Republicans and 18 Democrats."[122]

*"If the people cannot trust their government to do the job for which it exists—to protect them and to promote their common welfare—all else is lost."*

—BARACK OBAMA, speech, August 28, 2006

Another reason why we have wealthy politicians is the cost of getting elected. How much does it cost to get elected? There is a common phrase that is often mentioned in articles, in news commentaries, and actually may have started with the book entitled, *We Have the Best Congress Money Can Buy*, written about 20 years ago by P. M. Stern. Since the release of the book, not much has changed and the phrase has caught on.

**Remark 6.3:** May 29, 2008—"The Best Congress Money Can Buy…Winning an open seat in the House during the 2006 mid-terms cost an average of $1.9 million, almost four times the $500,000 that same seat cost 20 years ago. Rep. Vern Buchanan (R-Fla.) ran the election's most expensive campaign when he ran for the Florida District 13 seat, ultimately spending $11 million to secure his victory.

Gaining a seat in the Senate is even more costly, with recent campaigns in New York, Pennsylvania, and Connecticut each running more than $40 million. …. The Center for Responsive Politics reported that 85 percent of the winning Senate candidates and 94 percent of the winning House candidates in 2000 had outspent their opponents.

According to the most recent filings with the Federal Election Commission, during the 2007–8 cycle, candidates for the House of Representatives have already raised $479 million and spent $280 million. Candidates for the Senate, with far fewer races, have so far raised $210 million and spent $90 million. And most of the raising and spending are still to come….Nevertheless, money matters. According to the Center for

---

121 www.opensecrets.org/news/2008/10/as-economic-storm-brewed-congr.htm

122 www.cnn.com/2003/ALLPOLITICS/06/13/senators.finances/

> Responsive Politics, in 2006 (the most recently filed data), the average net worth of senators was around $12 million, while representatives were worth about $5 million. Is it any wonder why many voters think their representatives are out of touch?" [123]

The truth is that our politicians are under constant stress to find funds for their campaigns. Some are extremely wealthy and this may influence their views on the estate tax. Whether they have money or not, most will not wish to dig too deep into their own pockets to get elected. Although no politician enjoys having to raise funds, often they find it from big special interest groups and lobbyists who have their own agenda. Our candidates end up beholden to these groups.

> **Remark 6.4:** November 3, 2000—"OUCH! THE BEST CONGRESS MONEY CAN BUY…Of course, the special interests lobbying hard on these provisions are the same cast of characters handing out millions of dollars of campaign cash for Tuesday's election… Indeed, it is the rare Member of Congress who won't bend over backwards to help major campaign contributors on Capitol Hill at the same time his hand is out seeking last minute campaign contributions.."[124]

To say there is great deal of skepticism on how our system actually works when it comes to **conflict of interest and lobbyists** would be an understatement. Here is a conversation from *Money Talk*, America's number-one money show, airing every weekend and hosted by well respected financial expert, Bob Brinker. Below, Brinker talks to a caller named Henry. [125]

> **Remark 6.5: Henry notes**: "It's a shame that they can't address more aspects on the credit card bills in the bills they pass…"
> **Bob Brinker responds**: "Oh Henry, let's get real, when you start talking about policy in Washington and credit cards, don't you realize lobbies…lobbyists…the money flow…**We have the best government money can buy**…These policies are written by lobbyists through legislators, that's how the system works in the U.S., you know that."
> **Henry asks**: "How can we change that?"
> **Bob Brinker responds:** "The only way to change that is to get politicians in office that actually care about the people rather than care about the lobbyists. These politicians that write these bills, they're beholden to the

[123] www.flypmedia.com/content/best-congress-money-can-buy, by Matthew Schaeffer
[124] http://library.publicampaign.org/ouch/2000/11/ouch-61-best-congress-money-can-buy#
[125] *Money Talk* radio show caller, May 9, 2009

lobbyists, and the lobbyists have tremendous power because they walk around with bags of money, and they can influence policy, in a dramatic way. Compare that to the poor stiff in Boise, Idaho who's using a credit card paying 22% interest. What power does that stiff have with his congressional representative when contrasted with the moneybags lobbyist? None."

**Henry remarks**: "Throw the rascals out."

**Bob Brinker replies**: "Good luck with that one, but let's not lose sight of how this system works, tax policy, legislation, bankruptcy policy, credit card policy, the whole ball of wax is written through a process that starts with the lobbyist, lobbying the legislators, and the legislators passing the legislation. That's how the government works in the U.S. And how can you sitting there in Anyplace, USA and compete with that? And if you think you are competing with that, you're delusional."

Legislation written or influenced by special interest groups and adopted by Congress can make for an unreliable economy. Yet, such conflicts of interest are not always known or well documented. However, we cannot ignore the fact that these special interest groups flood our system of government and do so specifically to influence our politicians' every day.

**Remark 6.6:** "Since President Bush was elected the number of registered lobbyists in Washington has more than doubled. That's 16,342 lobbyists in 2000 and 34,785 last year: 65 lobbyists for every member of Congress. The total spent per month by special interests wining, dining, and seducing federal officials is now nearly $200 million."[126]

**Remark 6.7:** "From 2003 to 2008, the number of lobbyists in Washington grew from 17,000 to 22,000, many of whom have offices on K Street. Last year, lobbyists reported spending $2.8 billion to help make their voices heard. Naturally, the roster of biggest spenders reflects the key issues facing Congress. The health care industry, for example, spent $445 million, while the finance industry, which includes the real estate sector, spent $419 million. What do they get for all that money? Lobbyists work to pass—or defeat—legislation and sometimes even write the bills their clients want. They influence regulations, gather information and obtain access to government contracts."[127]

---

[126] www.washingtonspectator.org/articles/20060401cleanmoney_1.cfm, April 2006

[127] www.flypmedia.com/content/best-congress-money-can-buy, by Matthew Schaeffer

> **Remark: 6.8** "The cozy relationship between Congress and special interests has resulted in lobbying scandals... Republicans permitted a Congress in which lobbyists write the bills...."[128]

In the strictest sense this is a top-down root cause issue for our economy. The attempt by our representatives to clean-up the lobbyist problem has led to bill H.R. 2316/S.1. This bill does not go far enough.

> **Remark 6.9:** On July 31, 2007, the House passed H.R. 2316/S.1, the final House-Senate agreement on the Honest Leadership, Open Government Act.

It is really still a collective group of people conducting politics with a conflict of interest. The main problem will always be campaign funding. On the other hand, there are two sides to every issue; this is part of politics, so it is not logical to accuse representatives of breaking the law. They are hard working politicians. Nevertheless, the other side of most issues, the people's side, is typically not represented. There will be a tendency for the side that benefits business to take center stage, as legislators are strongly influenced by lobbyists. Our system of government should not be stuck in this odd unreliable situation.

**6.3: Conflicts of Interest Hampers Congress**

One does not have to look hard on the web to find information on how lobbyists have affected our mortgage crisis from a top-down perspective. It appears to have been costly. For example, stories indicate that Fannie Mae and Freddie Mac[129] did their share of lobbying to allow them to take unnecessary risks. In July of 2008 it was pointed out:

> **Remark 6.10:** "For years, critics have warned that Fannie Mae and Freddie Mac's special status as government-sponsored enterprises allowed them to shoulder risk far beyond their minimal capitalization requirements, the *Washington Post* reports. The firms have used their unique position in the financial system, and high-intensity lobbying efforts, to quash any attempt at stricter regulation."[130]

---

[128] http://speaker.house.gov/legislation?id=0002, 2007 Nancy Pelosi.

[129] Fannie Mae—the Federal National Mortgage Association—was established in the 1930s to encourage homeownership by buying mortgages from banks to freed cash for the banks so they could make new loans. Freddie Mac (Federal Home Loan Mortgage Corp.), created later but with basically the same mission, holds some of the mortgages in their own portfolio and package the rest as bonds and other securities, which they sell.

[130] www.newser.com/story/32397/fierce-lobbying-deflected-warnings-on-fannie-freddie.html

Their lobbying efforts are well documented. NPR radio news in July 2008 pointed out:

> **Remark 6.11:** "In the first three months of the year alone, Fannie Mae and Freddie Mac spent a combined total of about $3.5 million on lobbying and hired 42 outside firms. Their lobbying reports were analyzed by the Center for Responsive Politics."[131]

The conduct of Fannie and Freddie executives has extensively been covered in the media:

> **Remark 6.12:** *Mississippi Press*—Letters to the Editor—posted April 2009:
> "...the past 10 years, the personal greed at Fannie and Freddie and in Congress helped cause part of the financial crisis we're seeing today." [132]
> Here the author claims that Fannie and Freddie spent about $180 million to lobby 354 members out of the 523 politicians.

The cost for this apparent top-down failure mode appears high. In February of 2009, $200 billion in bailout funds were provided.

> **Remark 6.13:** "The Treasury Department is doubling its financial backing of mortgage giants Fannie Mae and Freddie Mac to $200 billion each, Treasury Secretary Tim Geithner announced Wednesday."[133]

*"In order to qualify for bailout funds, you need to screw somebody!"*
—Comedy Central, June 2009

This apparent "conflict of interest" top-down root cause failure mode has been extremely costly to our national debt and is a true economic reliability issue. Yet little attention has been actually given to our lobbyist problem with any reasonable proposed corrective action.

It is also possible that many manufacturing jobs have been lost in America as well due to conflict of interest with lobbyists. Both China and Japan have been cited for currency manipulation. This is described in detail in Chapter 9. By maintaining artificially weak currency, countries can increase their exports and decrease their imports. Additionally, more labor is outsourced in the U.S. with

---

[131] www.npr.org/templates/story/story.php?storyId=92540620, by Peter Overby
[132] www.gulflive.com/opinion/mississippipress/letters.ssf?/base/opinion/124074092514330.xml&coll=5, Letters to the Editor, Posted April 2009.
[133] www.bizjournals.com/sanantonio/stories/2009/02/16/daily26.html

weak currencies against the dollar providing U.S. companies with high profits by outsourcing. One bill in particular would have addressed the issue with China. This was a Schumer-Graham bill that called for a 27.5% tariff on all imports from China unless and until the yuan appreciated by an amount deemed sufficient by Congress. We do not know the exact extent to which lobbyists may have influenced this bill, but we do know they rallied against it. The bill was dropped in September of 2006. Between 2001 and 2007, 2.3 million American jobs were lost due to the China trade gap, including 366,000 last year. Now in 2009, this issue has again resurfaced and new talks with China are occurring over this issue. The reader is referred to Chapter 9, the section on currency manipulation for details.

Another key example that has created financial turmoil is related to the Medicare drug prescription program that is influencing our national debt. This pitfall was recognized by a number of members of Congress at the time the prescription drug program was passed. The writing was on the wall in the year 2000, prior to new bills on the program.

> **Remark 6.14:** Friday, September 29, 2000, McClatchy Newspapers—"Members of Congress Face Conflict of Interest When it Comes to Drug Companies—During a year when prescription drug prices and benefits are among the hottest political topics, dozens of members of Congress also have another reason to keep their eyes on pharmaceutical companies…These Senators, House members and their families own tens of millions of dollars in stock in drug manufacturers…(The article goes on to name the representatives with large holdings in these companies)."[134]

It has always been mind-boggling how such bills pass with no true concern regarding fiscal responsibility. Now flash forward to 2008 after the prescription drug program has expanded.

> **Remark 6.15:** February 26, 2008—Wamp: Rising Costs Of Prescription Drug Program Need To Be Addressed—In this article Congressman Zach Wamp states, "One of the major concerns I had about the Medicare prescription drug benefit when I opposed it in 2003 was that Medicare costs were already soaring. The legislation was too broad, favored the pharmaceutical companies over needy seniors and didn't include safeguards to keep costs down. Despite these concerns, Congress ultimately expanded the program and created new benefits that have caused Medicare costs to skyrocket even further."[135]

---

[134] www.americanchiropractic.net/general_%20interest/Conflict%20of%20Interest.pdf
[135] www.chattanoogan.com/articles/article_122808.asp, Quote by Congressman Zach Wamp

Our last example regarding lobbyist influences leading to major fiscal failure is the repeal of the Glass-Steagal Act of 1933. We discussed this and its effect on bank failures in Chapter 3.

> **Remark 6:16:** After 12 attempts in 25 years, Congress finally repeals Glass-Steagall, rewarding financial companies for more than 20 years and $300 million worth of lobbying efforts.[136]

As discussed in Chapter 3 this repeal lead to commercial banks like Citigroup and Bank Of America indulging in risky investment banking practices that lead to widespread use structured investment vehicles. Such vehicles collapsed in the mortgage meltdown. The origin is tied to this repeal.

**6.4: Summary**

If we are to be honest about these failure modes, and acknowledge the fact that they stem from conflicts of interest rather than politics as usual, then logic dictates it is unlawful. Without both sides of each issue equally represented, lobbyists and campaign funds create nothing more than potential wrong-doings in our political system and end up actually costing our nation dearly as discussed above. From a top-down perspective, there is no place for it. These are and will continue to be major failure modes for unreliability in the economy. It is unfortunately a widely accepted problem and is overdue for corrective actions. We believe that implementing a reliability economics team with individuals assigned to any proposed legislation (see Chapter 12) would provide a good check and balance. Other solutions are most likely related to finding ways for candidates to obtain campaign funds and support. This is really a governmental issue that needs to be resolved from within our system of government.

## Appendix 6A: 2007 Personal Finances of Our Representative House, Senate and Executive Branches [137]

It is difficult to gauge what a lawmaker is worth based on what they file because the disclosure forms do not require exact values. Instead, the lawmaker reports the range of value into which an asset, for example, falls. Better estimates may be available at the opensecrets.org reference.

---

[136] www.city-data.com/forum/great-debates/440049-long-demise-glass-steagall.html
[137] www.opensecrets.org/pfds/overview.php?type=W&year=2006&filter=S&sort=D

**Table 6A-1** Personal Finance of Senate Representatives

| Name | Minimum Net Worth | Maximum Net Worth |
|---|---|---|
| John Kerry (D-Mass) | $284,157,594 | $388,292,172 |
| Herb Kohl (D-Wis) | $149,443,028 | $251,647,996 |
| Edward M. Kennedy (D-Mass) | $43,821,041 | $163,298,999 |
| Jay Rockefeller (D-Wva) | $59,897,019 | $127,533,003 |
| Frank R. Lautenberg (D-NJ) | $53,326,179 | $125,692,020 |
| Dianne Feinstein (D-Calif) | $52,344,301 | $115,998,023 |
| Gordon H. Smith (R-Ore) | $28,358,029 | $63,895,999 |
| Olympia J. Snowe (R-Maine) | $15,018,074 | $51,599,001 |
| Claire McCaskill (D-Mo) | $20,419,173 | $44,437,005 |
| Elizabeth Dole (R-NC) | $14,624,035 | $48,218,910 |
| Hillary Clinton (D-NY) | $10,409,018 | $51,232,000 |
| John McCain (R-AZ) | $22,911,154 | $37,743,009 |
| Lamar Alexander (R-Tenn) | $11,811,688 | $40,536,648 |
| Johnny Isakson (R-Ga) | $8,342,077 | $24,284,999 |
| Tom Harkin (D-Iowa) | $10,499,111 | $21,938,002 |
| Ben Nelson (D-Neb) | $6,007,056 | $15,889,000 |
| Jeff Bingaman (D-NM) | $5,675,187 | $14,263,001 |
| | **Minimum** | **Maximum** |
| **Average** | $46,886,104 | $93,323,517 |

**Table 6A-2** Personal Finance of House Representatives

| Name | Minimum Net Worth | Maximum Net Worth |
|---|---|---|
| Jane Harman (D-Calif) | $236,280,153 | $558,544,002 |
| Darrell Issa (R-Calif) | $160,615,042 | $526,300,001 |
| Robin Hayes (R-NC) | $74,576,347 | $272,241,999 |
| Vernon Buchanan (R-Fla) | $69,659,542 | $401,156,971 |
| Michael McCaul (R-Texas) | $23,931,154 | $104,215,000 |
| Nancy Pelosi (D-Calif) | $19,038,894 | $143,974,989 |
| Carolyn B. Maloney (D-NY) | $17,009,100 | $83,585,994 |
| Rodney Frelinghuysen (R-NJ) | $22,414,184 | $72,286,000 |
| Nita M. Lowey (D-NY) | $16,929,476 | $70,503,415 |
| Gary Miller (R-Calif) | $14,494,042 | $65,462,000 |
| Tom Petri (R-Wis) | $10,631,037 | $66,891,999 |
| Denny Rehberg (R-Mont) | $6,896,012 | $59,814,997 |
| Kenny Ewell Marchant (R-Texas) | $9,876,624 | $53,178,582 |
| John Campbell (R-Calif) | $11,385,080 | $45,102,000 |
| F. James Sensenbrenner Jr. (R-Wis) | $19,471,684 | $28,460,630 |
| Steve Pearce (R-NM) | $8,417,014 | $38,030,000 |
| Heath Shuler (D-NC) | $3,263,026 | $41,521,996 |
| Bill Foster (D-Ill) | $7,371,012 | $35,890,000 |
| John M. Spratt Jr. (D-SC) | $6,965,022 | $33,702,995 |
| David Dreier (R-Calif) | $7,027,054 | $29,688,000 |
| Tom Price (R-Ga) | $7,072,257 | $29,270,233 |
| Fred Upton (R-Mich) | $7,218,123 | $25,871,000 |
| Rosa L. DeLauro (D-Conn) | $5,845,032 | $27,234,999 |
| John Linder (R-Ga) | $5,465,010 | $26,649,998 |
| Lloyd Doggett (D-Texas) | $8,134,096 | $21,584,999 |
| | **Minimum** | **Maximum** |
| **Average** | $31,199,441 | $114,446,512 |

**Table 6A-3** Table 6A-2 Personal Finance of Executive Branch Representatives

| Name | Minimum Net Worth | Maximum Net Worth |
|---|---|---|
| Samuel W. Bodman III | $68,717,047 | $130,708,000 |
| Dick Cheney | $20,954,025 | $99,317,000 |
| George W. Bush I | $6,364,044 | $19,374,000 |
| Rob Portman | $6,460,065 | $17,882,000 |
| Steven C. Preston | $4,804,107 | $17,464,000 |
| Elaine L. Chao | $2,858,033 | $12,720,999 |
| Robert Gates | $3,257,054 | $10,363,000 |
| Edward T. Schafer | $2,995,036 | $9,526,000 |
| James B. Peake | $1,881,262 | $7,448,000 |
| Karl C. Rove | $1,353,010 | $6,645,999 |
| Michael Chertoff | $1,970,045 | $4,852,000 |
| Joshua B. Bolten | $75,007 | $5,504,998 |
| Stephen L. Johnson | $6,006 | $90,000 |
| | **Minimum** | **Maximum** |
| **Average** | $9,361,134 | $26,299,692 |

Note: Senate, House and Executive branch rules require the disclosure of items belonging to the filer's spouse and/or dependent children. When present, those items are displayed on this page and are included.

# ■ 7.0 ■

# A SEVEN-YEAR PLAN TO ELIMINATE THE NATIONAL DEBT

## 7.1: National Debt Forcing a Potential Financial U.S. Collapse

In this chapter the potential effect of failure to administrate taxes correctly causing an increase in the national debt will be investigated. This is indicated in Table 7.1 which has been reproduced from Table 6.1 with the addition of the free trade key issue. Here the key issue of "government tax administration" with a failure mode of "failure to implement a fair tax structure" as it relates to the potential effect of failure, an "increase in the national debt" is explored. The second item on free trade and its deficit creating lost tax revenue is studied in Chapter 9, Section 9.7. This root cause issue is explored both

**Table 7.1** FMEA on Key Issue Government Tax Administration

| Key Issue | Potential Failure Mode | Potential Effect of Failure | Root Cause(s) | Root Cause Rating | Design Control | Possible Corrective Action |
|---|---|---|---|---|---|---|
| Govern-ment tax admin-istration issues | Failure to implement fair tax structure | 1) Recession issues, increase in national debt.<br><br>2) High interest rate payments<br><br>3) Lost taxes – fiscal instability.<br><br>4) Default on foreign loans | 1) Irrespon-sible risk tolerance<br><br>2,3,4) Under-taxation<br><br>3) Conflict of interest | 1) 9<br><br>2) 10<br>3) 10 | 1) Review and propose improvement<br><br>2) Assess government influences<br><br>3) Implement a reliability economics team | 1) Restrictions on lobbyists<br><br>2) Reduce lobbyist influences<br><br>3) Add a reliability economics team |
| Free trade | National debt increase | Lost tax revenue | Trade deficit tax losses | 10 | Correlation study (see 9.7) | FMEA on Trade deficit |
| Govmt. Spending | National debt increase | Requires borrowing | Excessive spending | 8 | Statutory debt limit | Reduce spending |

quantitatively and qualitatively.

Since this is an administration issue, it is clearly a top-down problem. Therefore it cannot be solved without government corrective actions.

As mentioned earlier, the national debt itself is a reliability indicator. Like other indicators discussed, such as the unemployment and mortgage failure rate, this is viewed here as a national debt failure rate. It is logical to term it this way, as the effect of failure can potentially include default on loans and financial instability. Thus, it is one of the highest reliability risks taken in the economy by our government, and its root cause rating is indicated as a 10 in the FMEA analysis (Table 6.1 and Appendix 2A, Table 2A-1). Here a 10 indicates root cause that could lead to a system (U.S.) financial failure or collapse. One key element that the reader should realize is our government is the largest employer in America. The national debt increase affects the government job market. Although there is no direct correlation, this issue funnels down from U.S. job cutbacks at the national and local level. Such job cutbacks are due to lost revenues related to the U.S. national debt. To clarify this, we review the debt situation. As of December 31, 2009 the national debt was at $12.31 trillion compared to August 2008 when it was at $9.6 trillion. Over a 2 trillion increase in one year!

The growing deficit is shown in Fig. 7.1. The latest value is $12.3 trillion (end of 2009). Later values have been estimated (see wikipedia.org reference).

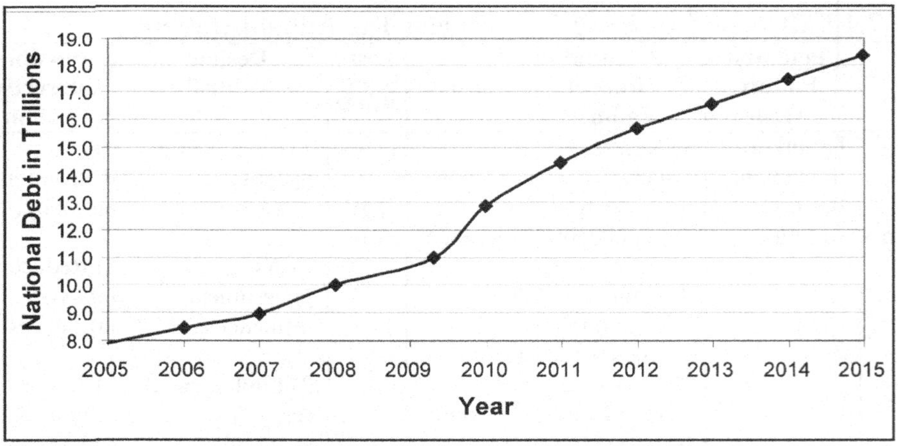


**Figure 7.1** National debt in trillions from 2005 and its projection to 2015 [138]

> **Remark 7.1:** March 17, 2009—"Treasury Department quietly reported today that the National Debt hit $11-trillion for the first time ever.... Divide it by the U.S. population and it comes up to over $36,000 in debt for every man, woman and child. It took just over 5½ months for Uncle

[138] http://en.wikipedia.org/wiki/United_States_public_debt

Sam to go another trillion dollars deeper in debt since hitting $10-trillion last September 30th. It's the fastest jump in U.S. history."[139]

In Figure 7.1, the projection after December of 2009 is somewhat aggressive. Another estimate in the news (June of 2009) for the year 2010 is an added $1.25 trillion; and for 2011 an extra $1 trillion. These are still staggering amounts! Another common indicator is the percent of the GDP now at 85%! This is shown in Table 7.1A relative to other countries and 2009 debt in Table 7.1B.

**Table 7.1A** Government Debt as Percentage of Gross Domestic Product 2009

| | | | | | | | | |
|---|---|---|---|---|---|---|---|---|
| **China** | **Indonesia** | **S. Korea** | **Malaysia** | **Taiwan** | **Vietnam** | **Philippines** | **Spain** | **Ireland** |
| **20%** | **32%** | **35%** | **40%** | **42%** | **46%** | **51%** | **57%** | **61%** |
| **Britain** | **Portugal** | **France** | **Germany** | **U.S.** | **India** | **Greece** | **Italy** | **Japan** |
| **69%** | **76%** | **77%** | **79%** | **85%** | **85%** | **108%** | **116%** | **219%** |

**Table 7.1B** 2009 Government Debt in Billions of Dollars (and Percent)

| | | | | | | |
|---|---|---|---|---|---|---|
| **Pensions** | **Medical** | **Education** | **Defense** | **Welfare** | **Protection** | **Transportation** |
| 739 (35%) | 764 (36%) | $91 (4.3%) | $794 (38%) | $407 (19%) | $52 (2.4%) | $84 (4%) |
| **Other** | **General** | **Interest** | **All Total** | **Revenue** | **Total 2009 Debt** | |
| $377 (18%) | $23 (1.1%) | $187 (9%) | **$3,517 (167%)** | $2,105 | **$1,413 Billion** | |

To put this a bit more in perspective, a rough estimate of the interest that must be paid on the national debt is about 4%. So this is said to be a reasonable value. At that rate of interest, the current U.S. government obligation is about $450 billion annually (i.e. almost a half trillion dollars). Figure 7.2 provides projections for this interest to be paid as well.

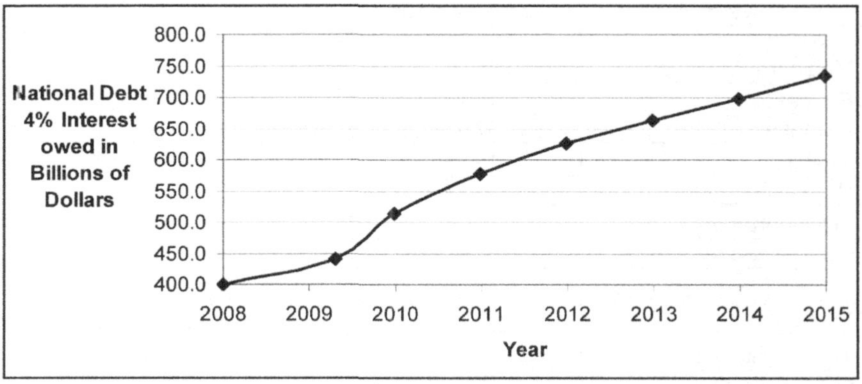


**Figure 7.2** Estimate of 4% annual interest owed on the National Debt

[139] www.cbsnews.com/blogs/2009/03/17/politics/politicalhotsheet/entry4872310.shtml

Here, the projection indicates that by 2015, the interest itself could be nearly three-quarters of a trillion dollars. Interest is a U.S. obligation and is the other part of the equation to the nation's debt that creates the actual potential for financial failure in our economy. It makes for a crippling problem since the U.S. will lack the ability to afford many of our needed programs including adopting and sustaining health care reform. And this means job cuts, which affects the Modern Recession. That is, too much of our tax dollars must go to paying off interest. This of course makes it the largest reliability economic risk facing our government.

The current Obama policy is widely recognized for its risk tolerance, an identified root cause along with excessive spending. For example, as of March 2009 the *Washington Post* reported,

> **Remark 7.2**: "...according to the Congressional Budget Office, would be an ever-expanding national debt that would exceed 82 percent of the overall economy by 2019—double last year's level—and threaten the nation's financial stability."[140]

In terms of the FMEA table, the root causes for government tax administration issues are irresponsible risk tolerance, excessive spending, under-taxation, conflicts of interest, and free trade deficit lost tax revenues.

We have addressed to this point, two of the three root cause issues:

- Under-taxation—in Chapter 4
- Conflict of interest—in Chapter 6

**Table 7.2** Government % Debt Breakdown 2009[141]

| Item | % of Revenue |
|---|---|
| Pensions | 35.1% |
| Medicare /Medicaid | 36.3% |
| Education | 4.3% |
| Defense | 37.7% |
| Welfare | 19.3% |
| Protection | 2.4% |
| Transportation | 4.0% |
| General Government | 1.1% |
| Other Spending | 17.9% |
| Interest | 8.9% |
| Total Spending | 167.1% |
| **2009 Total Debt** | About $2.3 Trillion |

[140] www.ajc.com/metro/content/printedition/2009/03/21/deficit0321.html
[141] www.usgovernmentspending.com/classic#usgs302

We will discuss a different type of conflicts of interest compared to the last chapter. Table 7.2 provides an approximate percent breakdown illustrating where U.S. debt obligations are incurred. The breakdown indicates the 2009 debt is 67% over budget. Many programs need revision. For example the federal retirement program is a clear target. With life expectancy on the rise, government programs still persist with programs like 50 years of age with just 20 years of service. And with just 5 years of service at age 62, on some federal programs[142]. The program produces huge pension problems to the national debt that equate to a 35% yearly budget problem. The government is America's largest employer. However, no congress person has yet to come forward and challenging this program. One clear possibility is that there exists a conflict of interest for a senator to address this, as most congress members look forward to early retirement benefits.

In terms of fiscal irresponsibility risk tolerance, such issues lead to excessive spending of tax dollars. It has been a bipartisan issue.

> **Remark 7.3:** It is generally accepted that there has been hypocrisy with both the Republicans and Democrats at the state and local government levels. The U.S. had broken financial policies when the Republicans were in control, and continue to have added debt in 2009 now that the Democrats are in control. During these periods, we have had each party blaming the other. Therefore, credibility of both parties is problematic.

Currently, there are few if any politicians that actually run on a platform of fiscal responsibility. Candidates appear ignorant of the tax solution as we have described. This is perceived as a conflict of interest in terms of trying to obtain campaign funds and win votes. Yet most Americans are aware of our national debt problems and might welcome such a platform. However, it is really outside the scope of this work to do finger-pointing regarding fiscal irresponsibility and the kind of risk tolerance that is occurring with our government's spending. The Modern Recession is clearly an overwhelming problem for which bailouts have been required and costly special government programs are needed. Nevertheless, we have identified national debt as the highest risk item so far in our FMEA analysis. This cannot be ignored as the reliability of the economy is at stake.

### 7.2: National Debt Corrective Actions—A Feasible Seven Year Solution

Here we provide a discussion on possible suggestions to the national debt problem, a seven year solution, and a national debt charity.

[142] http://www.opm.gov/retire/faq/pre/faq11.asp

### 7.2.1: Seven Year Declaration Of War On The National Debt

Here we would like to take the liberty to discuss an obvious but necessary corrective action. There are really only two choices to the national debt problem; they are taxation and fiscal responsibility in our spending policies. Unless the government decides to keep and run the businesses that have been bailed out, the only major source of revenues are taxes and savings on government cutbacks. As well, without a fiscal responsibility policy, no program will be of any value. Therefore, we will make two recommendations for our seven year plan:

1) Provide realistic policy that will actually declare a <u>Seven Year War On The National Debt.</u> This provides a minimal level of commitment needed. Just as in a time of war, consider enlisting civilians to provide part-time volunteer duty to help subsidize needed government programs such as Medicare, legal, social services, etc. As in a time of war, enlist doctors (such as 5 hours a week) and hospital areas to provide national health care services for the sick and needy who cannot afford health insurance in this Seven Year War period. Other professions, such as lawyers, should be required to commit some free services. This will help provide needed government cutbacks. Recognize, in the declaration of this war, that America is fighting for its future—as we can no longer afford fiscal irresponsibility.
2) Provide a new proper seven-year taxation program as discussed in Chapter 4.

At some point in time we have to ask the unthinkable question—if the U.S. becomes financially insolvent, do the foreign countries to which we owe money have a legal right to take control of our country? If the answer is yes, then the national debt and the closely linked trade deficit problems (See Chapter 9) are matters of national security. Therefore, declaring War On The National Debt makes a lot of sense. We now expand upon the taxation portion of the above suggestion with an analysis as to how a seven year solution would be financially feasible. Consider the possibility of paying off the national debt in a relatively short time. As fully supported in Chapter 4, most tax revenue is collected from the well-to-do. This is fairly well-known.

**Remark 7.4**: "It has been reported by CNBC that in 2008 about 80 percent of the taxes are paid by about 20 percent of the population."[143]

---

[143] May 2009, CNBC Cable News

This number is fairly consistent. The 2006 projected breakdown of income tax payments by income groups is shown in Table 7.3:

**Table 7.3** Individual Income and Taxes in 2006 (U.S. Treasury Estimate)

| | Top 1% | Top 5% | Top 10% | Top 25% | Top 50% | Bottom 50% |
|---|---|---|---|---|---|---|
| Percent of Income Taxes | 39.9% | 60.1% | 70.8% | 86.3% | 97.0% | 3.0% |
| Percent of Income | 22.1% | 36.7% | 47.3% | 68.2% | 87.5% | 12.5% |

The table not only estimates the percent of income tax but also the percent of income by the well-to-do. What is startling is that the top 1% make 22.1% of the income in the U.S. and the top 25% make about 86.3% of the income. This dichotomy is showing America is indeed a nation that is exhibiting an increasing separation of wealth as we mentioned earlier (also see Figure 1.1).

The reader might ask, how does one expect the federal government to have an effective bailout program without going into debt? The answer is that the federal government may not have done a thorough study of what all the issues and problems are in our economy prior to the current bailout. There are other answers to helping our financial and automotive sector besides simply spending and increasing our national debt. These are proposed in this book and on our website, www.SolutionsWithoutUSdebt.com. The website information has been sent numerous times to our representatives.

Here we suggest a solution that requires an aggressive but reasonable tax plan of the well-to-do as suggested in Chapter 4. This would entail a realistic and modified tax structure, to something like what we provided in Chapter 4 in Table 4.6 (See proposed legislation at www.SolutionsWithoutUSDebt.com). Note Table 4.6 is a continuation of the 2009 tax structure. Our new suggested brackets occur after the 35% point. We would actually recommend lower taxes for individuals making under $8,350.)

Now take a small fraction of the wealthy top 5%, say 0.33% of our total U.S. population. This is about one million people (total U.S. population is about 300 Million). For this population, it is very conceivable that they, on average, are in the million dollar income bracket range since they pay about 36.7% of the total income tax. Consider the following scenario:

> **Remark 7.5**: Under the above reasonable tax plan, we can likely pay off the national debt in under seven years. If only 0.33% of the U.S. population (approx. 1,000,000 people) make $7 million (on average) or more in salary and pay a flat tax (for simplicity) of 65%, the amount of tax

collected will be $4.55 trillion (= $7 million x 0.65 x 1 million people). In the current 2009 progressive tax scenario, they would be taxed progressively and would pay $2.43 trillion (to verify this, use one of the tax calculators on the web: www.moneyclips.com.)[144]

The increase in tax is about $2.22 trillion (= 4.55 minus 2.43 trillion). This is enough extra dollars to pay off the national debt in about five-to-seven years, taking the national debt interest into account. Additionally, with the close of tax loopholes, an improved estate tax, and a possible asset tax, the scenario is very feasible. (Note: this could be accomplished in a two-term stay by Obama in the White House). This scenario is hypothetical, but most likely a very conservative estimate when you realize how many athletes, movie stars, CEOs, and extreme-salaried individuals there are currently making more than $7 million, most likely over a million individuals. It is more likely that such an Obama policy could pay off the national debt in four years.

Other solutions are available. For example, we previously mentioned a number of good things about hoarding. Primarily, this includes deflation and the hoarding storage concept. It is possible and also important to take advantage of money hoarding/storage as part of the corrective action. The most feasible method would be an asset tax, considering that the wealthy were never taxed properly in the first place. The asset tax would recover some of those lost dollars that have compounded the national debt into what it is today. Lastly, one drastic measure would be to start collecting trade tariffs as was done earlier in the 20$^{th}$ century (see Remark 9.42-A on history of U.S. tariffs). Although free trade advocates would feel this could start a trade war if the U.S. dollar started to fall, our trading partners who are holding much of our national debt today, may surprisingly tolerate a limited time tariff plan (through negotiations). It could then be viewed in their best interest.

### 7.2.2: National Debt Charity

We briefly also suggest having a National Debt Charity Fund where the well-to-do can donate money. Currently, no such mechanism exists. Higher tax write-offs might be used as an incentive. It may not make sense initially, but when one realizes how many multi-millionaires feel indebted to this country, it would probably turn out to be helpful. Many donators know that paying off the national debt is one of the single best ways for America to be strong again. It will also help charities in the long run. The government can run more programs including being able to pay for a National Health Care Program.

---

[144] www.moneychimp.com/features/tax_brackets.htm

### 7.3 Long Term Estimated $100 Trillion Dollar National Debt

What we have not mentioned to this point is the long term entitlement programs that are an unfunded liability for Medicare, Medicaid, and Social security. These are unfounded liabilities that some have estimated are as much as $100 trillion dollars. These liabilities are currently required by law to pay out to U.S. citizens. "Estimates on the website Wikipedia have indicated that under current law, that sometime between 2030 and 2040, mandatory spending (primarily Social Security, Medicare, Medicaid, and interest on the national debt) will exceed tax revenue. In other words, all discretionary spending (e.g., defense, homeland security, law enforcement, education, etc.) will require borrowing and related deficit spending! United States must eventually choose between "bankruptcy", raising taxes, or cutting payouts."[145]

### 7.4: Summary

Here we have focused on the national debt and its importance. In so doing, we note that one of the largest problems facing our administration is the top-down responsibility of government tax administrative issues and the failure mode of failure to implement a fair tax structure. A realistic solution was provided on how the national debt could be paid off in about seven years. In light of this and the fact that there is no current realistic plan by Congress to provide something like this, then conflict of interest appears to be a reasonably supported root cause problem. As we pointed out in Chapter 6 on conflict of interest, such reliability issues are highly costly and devastating if our representatives fail to provide an administrative plan to pay off the national debt in a reasonable time frame. In light of this problem, another reasonable corrective action is to provide a reliability macroeconomic team. It is unlikely that taxing the wealthy would be a very popular concept in Congress and in the Senate. A reliability macroeconomic team would be more focused on our present and "future" financial failure modes, their effects, root causes, and corrective actions. It would be more difficult to continue having financial administrative issues with a team of economists totally focused on the reliability of the economy. Proper FMEA analysis can provide assertive solutions that cannot be continually ignored by Congress and also provide a check and balance to our country's economists. We cannot stress enough that FMEA analysis here has scored the root causes to this failure mode with a rating of 10, the highest possible rating, carrying with it a risk of U.S. financial collapse. There is little doubt that a reliability macroeconomic team would disagree with this score and its risk, which is carried forward to each generation.

[145] http://en.wikipedia.org/wiki/United_States_public_debt

## ■ 8.0 ■

# JOB CREATION AND RETENTION INVESTING

### 8.1: Job-Friendly Investing for America

Jobs are the key problem in the time of a recession. And because of this, we will look at a related key issue, namely job investing. As we have done with previous key issues, provided is a fundamental review of the failure modes, their effects, and an assessment using the FMEA approach. Table 8.1 provides an initial FMEA analysis from which to derive recommended research and actions on the problem.

**Table 8.1** FMEA on the Key Issue of Job Investing

| Key Issue | Potential Failure Mode | Potential Effect of Failure | Root Cause(s) | Root Cause Rating | Design Control | Possible Corrective action |
|---|---|---|---|---|---|---|
| Job invest-ing issues | 1) Job losses due to non friendly U.S. job investing<br><br>2) Job loss opportune-ities due to overpopula-tion problem | 1) Increase in unemployment<br>2) Slowing of velocity of money<br>3) Increases in separation of wealth<br>4) U.S. business failures and slow downs | 1) Business hoarding<br>2) Individual mass hoarding causing stock market decline<br>3) Increase job outsourcing<br>4) Increase in manufacturing outsourcing<br>5) No policy for overpopulation<br>6) Religious leaders not providing enough guidance on overpopulation. | 1) 8<br>2) 8<br>3) 8<br>4) 9<br>5) 10<br>6) 8 | 1) Assess business hoarding issues<br>2) Assess individual hoarding issues<br>3&4) Review free trade policy<br>5) Appoint committees to study overpopulation problem<br>6) Study proposals to help religious leaders | 1) Anti-hoarding legislation for individuals and corporations for job-friendly investing<br>2) Change tax structure<br>3) U.S.-mandated job quotas<br>5) Implement recommend-dations on over-population<br>6) Implement proposals with religious leaders |

The FMEA approach as we have mentioned requires a team effort. The analysis in Table 8.1 is based on our approach to this issue and on historical information. From the table, we see two dominant failure modes, job losses due to non-friendly U.S. job investing and job losses due to overpopulation. Non friendly U.S. job investing includes outsourcing as well as immigration through visas programs. Job outsourcing is addressed in Chapter 9 and we will not present an analysis for this here. Some brief comments will be provided on the U.S. visa programs and their potential effect on the U.S. job market. The overpopulation failure mode is also listed here as a job-friendly investing issue, as it requires potential government resources to address it. We will start with this key failure mode since it has an associated root cause rating of 10. The author realizes that this is a sensitive issue and does not wish to offend the reader with proposed solutions. However, since overpopulation is a Truth of the Modern Recession, the facts will minimally be discussed. It is left to government and religious leaders to find ways to best address the overpopulation problem.

**8.2: Job Loss Issues Due to Overpopulation**

The overpopulation problem is a fact both in the U.S. and around the world. It is considered by many the number one problem facing the U.S. and humankind. The U.S. population growth is close to 1% per year as shown for 2000-2009 in Table 9.5. The director of the U.S. Intelligence Agency puts it somewhat in perspective:

> **Remark 8.1:** "The director of the U.S. Central Intelligence Agency, Gen. Michael Hayden, when asked to pinpoint which issue was of most pressing concern to him, said that the most troublesome threat facing the U.S. and the world today is not terrorism or global warming, but overpopulation, especially in the poorest parts of the planet."[146]

Overpopulation is a strong reason for our recession, since the number of jobs currently available is seriously a problem compared to the number of job applicants. When this occurs, there is a serious loss of opportunity for many individuals. For example, while no official statistics are available, numerous articles constantly appear, and one specific government area found about 100 applicants per job.

> **Remark 8.2:** January 2009—"More than 350,000 resumes have been submitted online, according to the Obama transition team....Only 3,000 to 4,000 jobs are available."[147]

---

[146] www.articlesbase.com/environment-articles/overpopulation-the-biggest-threat-to-our-planets-survival-520631.html

[147] money.cnn.com/2009/01/11/news/obama_job_seekers/index.htm?postversion=2009011119

The government economists and politicians do not appear to recognize the seriousness of the studies that provide clear warning to the problem of overpopulation and its relation to an unreliable economy.

**Remark 8.3:** "In a study titled *Food, Land, Population and the U.S. Economy*, David Pimentel, professor of ecology and agriculture at Cornell University, and Mario Giampietro, senior researcher at the U.S. National Research Institute on Food and Nutrition (INRAN), estimate the maximum U.S. population for a sustainable economy at 200 million. To achieve a sustainable economy and avert disaster, the United States must reduce its population by at least one-third, and world population will have to be reduced by two-thirds, says the study."[148]

According to Remark 8.3, the recommendation for a sustainable U.S. economy is 200 million people. Currently the U.S. population is 305 million people. As indicated by Remark 8.4, this is expected to increase to 439 million by 2050.

**Remark 8.4:** "Almost all growth will take place in the less developed regions, where today's 5.3 billion population of underdeveloped countries is expected to increase to 7.8 billion in 2050. By contrast, the population of the more developed regions will remain mostly unchanged, at 1.2 billion. The world's population is expected to rise by 40% to 9.1 billion. An exception is the United States population, which is expected to increase 44% from 305 million in 2008 to 439 million in 2050."[149]

Presently with the U.S. population of 305 million, and the maximum suggested economic amount of 200 million people (Remark 8.3), the U.S. is overpopulated by 105 million. This estimate is apparently somewhat over-conservative, as the economy can accommodate more jobs during a non recession period. It is still a good reference for recessionary times considering the fact that unemployment continues to rise as of June 2009 and is now between 14.7 and 25.8 million people.

**Remark 8.5:** "The number of unemployed persons (14.7 million) and the unemployment rate (9.5 percent) were little changed in June. Since the start of the recession in December 2007, the number of unemployed

[148] http://en.wikipedia.org/wiki/Overpopulation
[149] http://en.wikipedia.org/wiki/Overpopulation

persons has increased by 7.2 million, and the unemployment rate has risen by 4.6 percentage points."[150]

Another study that includes underemployed workers as well finds the number closer to 25.8 million.

> **Remark 8.6:** "If we break down the unemployment numbers further, we see that nearly 26,000,000 American workers are either unemployed or underemployed: Unemployed = 14,500,000, Part-time workers = 9,100,000, Marginally Attached = 2,200,000, Total = 25,800,000 unemployed or underemployed workers."[151]

From the perspective of the economy, it is clear that overpopulation is a failure mode for job-friendly investing issues since the government is not applying any investing resources to this problem. With no reliability economic team available to council the White House, it appears there is no real attempt to view the issue of overpopulation in relation to a recession problem.

There are, of course, strong religious conflicts of interest amongst our politicians. It is really unavoidable, but does not play well when it comes to the separation of church and state. Since the two will forever be entangled over this issue, population control is really a responsibility of both. It would be great if the world could practice a natural family planning method, as many religious viewers seek. The magnitude of the real-world problem is larger than reliability economics; there are serious consequences that come with an overcrowded planet. We are only beginning to see the tip of the iceberg. There will always be administrative and personal choices. However, the issue currently appears as both a church and political problem. The church needs to do more to address the problem. There are other ways, for example, to stress the importance of natural family planning through an active program requiring churches around the world to heighten everyone's awareness of the overpopulation problem and to promote sermons on the issue. There are no alternatives; the solution will most likely not be resolved without both politics and the church taking full responsibility for a problem that threatens mankind. Failure is not an option. The ranking of this root cause is rated as a 10 (see Appendix 2A, Table 2A-1). Since the planet is, according to many scientists, facing catastrophic consequences economically that include the possibility of war and famine.

---

[150] www.bls.gov/news.release/empsit.nr0.htm

[151] www.mybudget360.com/real-unemployment-situation-approximately-26000000-unemployed-or-underemployed-job-growth-in-10-per-hour-jobs-while-20-per-hour-jobs-disappear/

**Remark 8.7:** "The United Nations indicates that about 850 million people are malnourished or starving, and 1.1 billion people do not have access to safe drinking water. Some argue that Earth may support 6 billion people, but only if many live in misery….the 2050 population projection is: Africa: 1.9 billion, Asia: 5.2 billion, Europe: 664 million, Latin America & Caribbean: 769 million, Northern America: 445 million. This provides a total of 8.9 billion, well over the estimated 6 billion person limit."[152]

**8.3 Job Issues through Government Sponsored Visa Programs**

The Office of Immigration Statistics reported in 2007, over 1 million people were allowed into the U.S. [153] Basically this is simply individuals having some form of work visa noted by customs (excluding green cards). The Department of Homeland Security approved about 132,000 H-1B visas in 2004 and 117,000 in 2005.[154] In 2007 the Immigration Services approved approximately 126,000 H-1B visa petitions in fiscal 2007. This ended in September with the current cap of 65,000 plus 20,000 supplemental for persons with advanced degrees from U.S. schools. The allotted time for visa is about 6 years. Companies like Microsoft, Cisco, Oracle, and Infosys are among the biggest users of the H-1B visa process. According to the Bureau of Labor Statistics, computer programming jobs dropped more than 24% from 745,000 in 2000 to 564,000 in 2004. The number of employed electrical and electronics engineers shrunk by 101,000, from 444,000 in 2000 to 343,000 last year, a drop of nearly 23%. Computer scientists and systems analysts have experienced similar losses, falling more than 16%, from 835,000 in 2000 to 700,000 in 2004. We see a number of issues from these statistics. U.S. students selecting careers now have to question their interest in these fields being outsourced. The work and expense to get a degree in computer science for example, only to find little opportunity, and lower pay due to competition, can be discouraging. We see that both the short term H-1B program and job outsourcing has severely affected not only the job market, but the future prospective students who are unable to justify these career areas. The government visa program needs a full assessment to clear these issues up. The difficulty of outsourcing is discussed in Chapter 9.

**8.4: Job Losses Due to Non-Friendly U.S. Job Investing**

The term "green economics" has a common usage; it links the financial world to Mother Nature, and to the goal that we live with our environment in a harmoniously and productive manner. Respecting our natural environment can

---

[152] http://en.wikipedia.org/wiki/Overpopulation

[153] www.dhs.gov/xlibrary/assets/statistics/publications/ois_ni_fr_2007.pdf

[154] Department of Homeland Sec., Ann. Reports on the H-1B visa program for 2004 and 2005

also be profitable, as we have seen in the area of energy, where many companies are now utilizing our ecological gifts of wind and solar power.

There are parallels with job investing and green economics. As with green economics, we should respect our economy through the corrective action of job-friendly investing for a reliable economy. This is the financing of our job environment in the hopes that we can live together harmoniously in a productive manner. Investing in America is everyone's responsibility. Job-friendly economics relies on both trickle-down and trickle-up economics. Trickle-down economics applies to large entities both government and corporate America to finance our economy. Trickle-up or bottom-up economics is the effect of every individual keeping our money flowing. However, it certainly targets the wealthy. We cannot continue to maintain an "I've Got Mine" (IGM) attitude in America. It is without a doubt problematic to our economy's reliability, as we have discussed in previous chapters. It would be helpful if we could adjust the velocity of money in a manner similar to turning a faucet and adjusting the water flow, especially in a time of recession. Here we provide practical methods for both the individual and larger entities to properly invest in America and help stimulate economic job growth. However, we will not take a totally naïve approach and expect this to occur. In fact, in a time of a recession, we feel that legislation can be implemented to require some investments to force the issue. These are provided in our website, www.SolutionsWithoutUSDebt.com.

**8.5: Hoarding Investments and Jobs**

Most hoarders do invest in some way into our economy. The problem is, the safer the investment, the fewer jobs are created. This subject is complex; we know the extreme cases are:

1. A mattress account creates no jobs.
2. Stock market and corporate and government investments create and can save the most jobs.
3. Money market investing is not well-diversified and leaves little money for corporate America.

One way to approach this issue is to divide money investments into three different groups:

**1. Active Investments** are defined here as monies invested in areas that do help job growth substantially. These can also include corporate, stock market, and real estate.

**2. Stagnant Investments** are defined here as monies in areas that do **not** help job growth substantially. These can include money markets, gold, CDs and areas of low-maintenance investing. While such areas are helpful, fleeing to such safe investments in a recession creates a stagnant cash flow, leaves certain areas with money, and deprives others.

**3. Sidelined or Uninvested Money** is defined here as monies that are removed from our economy in one way or another such as bank demand deposits that hamper job growth.

Lastly, we will also provide an assumption in order to have some terms to approach the problems. This we term as the

**Hoarding Investment Job Theory:** The safer the investments protecting the hoarding money, the fewer jobs are created.

### 8.6: Some Job Statistics by Sector

In order to understand job-friendly investing, we first look at a snap-shot of employment statistics in June of 2009 published by the Bureau of Labor Statistics[155] to understand our job sectors. Table 8.2 shows a breakdown of the two main sectors, government and private. This is then broken down by goods and services.

**Table 8.2:** Overview of U.S. Employment as of June 2009

| Category | Number in 1000s | Percent |
|---|---|---|
| **All employees** | **131,735** | **100%** |
| | | |
| **Government** | | 17% |
| Government non civilian | 20,757 | 15.8% |
| Government civilian | 1,800 | 1.4% |
| **Private** | 109,178 | 82.9% |
| | | |
| Goods sector | 18,818 | 14% |
| Service sector | 112,917 | 86% |

We see that the total workforce is about 131,735,000 people, of which the government employs 22,557,000 (=20,757,000+1,800,000) individuals, making up about 17% (about 1.4% are civilian employees) compared to the private sector's 83%. At about 1.8 million non-civilian employees, the government, according to the bureau, is said to be the nation's largest employer (excluding the post office). The table further breaks down these numbers into the production of goods and the production of services. Here we note that service sector provides the bulk of our employment according to the Bureau of Labor Statistics due to the U.S. manufacturing decline expressed in Table 8.3.

---

155 www.bls.gov/webapps/legacy/cesbtab1.htm

**Table 8.3:** Employment in Services and Manufacturing Since 1999

| | Employment In Services | | Employment In Manufacturing | |
|---|---|---|---|---|
| Year | in 1000s | Since 1999 % Change | in 1000s | Since 1999 % Change |
| **1999** | 104,416 | 0% | 17,296 | 0% |
| **2000** | 107,165 | 3% | 17,298 | 0% |
| **2001** | 108,081 | 4% | 16,516 | -5% |
| **2002** | 107,796 | 3% | 15,297 | -12% |
| **2003** | 108,051 | 3% | 14,493 | -16% |
| **2004** | 109,558 | 5% | 14,331 | -17% |
| **2005** | 111,450 | 7% | 14,220 | -18% |
| **2006** | 113,377 | 9% | 14,202 | -18% |
| **2007** | 115,356 | 10% | 13,889 | -20% |
| **2008** | 115,849 | 11% | 13,505 | -22% |
| **2009** | 112,917 | 8% | 11,869 | -31% |

Here we see that manufacturing has declined by about 31% since 1999, while service sector has grown to about 8%, with a fall-off in the service sector in the last year. We have roughly broken down the service sector in Table 8.4 from the Bureau's statistics. From this table we see that job-friendly investing must focus on both the government and the private sector.

**Table 8.4:** Breakdown of Service Sector as of June 2009

| Service Sector Breakdown | Employment in 1000s | Breakdown Percent |
|---|---|---|
| Educational & Health | 19,252 | 17% |
| Professional & Business | 16,650 | 15% |
| Retail Trade | 14,791 | 13% |
| Leisure and Hospitality | 13,177 | 12% |
| Financial | 7,755 | 7% |
| Construction | 6,224 | 6% |
| Wholesale | 5,681 | 5% |
| Transportation & warehousing | 4,221.9 | 4% |
| Information | 2,840 | 3% |
| Real Estate-related | 1,993 | 2% |
| Other | 20,332.1 | 18% |
| | **Sum** | **Sum** |
| **Total Service Sector** | **112,917** | **100%** |

## 8.7: Bottom-Up Individual Job-Friendly Investing in America

It is certainly possible to be an average or wealthy individual, invest wisely, and help your fellow man make a living. Changing your strategy to job-friendly investments and at the same time having profitability is highly possible without taking a lot of risk. It is not enough to give 1% or higher of your income away to charity each year. Individual investing is a bottom-up solution to help economic recovery and create or save jobs.

We would not discourage charity giving, but this can be somewhat more selfish than wise job-friendly investing. We reiterate the well-known saying, *"Give a person a fish and he will eat for one day, give a person a fishing pole and he will be able to eat for a lifetime."* If you have money to invest that is sidelined in a time of recession, then you are causing suffering and should feel that you are part of the problem. On the other hand, we are not proposing that anyone take huge risks and throw one's money away either.

Certainly, concern for capital preservation is not against the law, but hoarding is viewed by many religions as a selfish act that can and does cause suffering, especially in a time of an economic recession.

Economic hoarding by wealthy individuals can significantly contribute to a recession. Typically, if you are well-to-do, your money originally came from income generated by the U.S. economy and its citizens. As such your monies are privileged assets held in trust by you. We view this as a responsibility, even a requirement, to render a reasonable amount of such assets recycled back into the U.S. economy through active investments during a time of a Declared Recession. For the capitalistic system to work properly, such money cannot be sidelined or held in stagnant accounts, especially in a declared recession. Stagnant money in our economy collectively aggravates and deepens a recession, job losses, hardships, and unnecessary governmental oversight, leading to increases in the national debt.

Economic problems cannot be fixed unless the underlying root cause issues are understood and repaired. We have illustrated and supported the notion that economic hoarding is a root cause issue to the problem of velocity of money that has deepened the modern U.S. recession.

There are many ways to invest in America without hoarding cash. Wealth can be shared in a logical and meaningful way through investing, which can help the velocity of money and at the same time provide opportunities for profitability to the investor.

There are many economic advisors, including radio talk shows, who will tell you to park your money in CDs, money markets, U.S. government obligations, and savings accounts in a recessionary period. While these are safe, important investments that provide some small returns, confining investments to these main areas limits job growth, can even create job losses, and will actually limit your income. Fleeing to safe areas during a recessionary period will worsen the recession and is unnecessary. What many financial advisors fail to remind you about safe investments are key facts on dividends, for example, which are paid per share quantity, not on share value.

**Table 8.5:** Individual Responsibility Investments During a Recessionary

| Investment | Return | Comments | Recommen-ded Percent of Assets |
|---|---|---|---|
| **Ginnie Mae** Ref: www.ginniemae.gov/ | ~ 4.5% as of 4/09 Reasonably Stable | Helps make affordable housing a reality for millions of low- and moderate-income households across America by channeling global capital into the nation's housing markets. Ginnie Mae allows mortgage lenders to obtain a better price for their mortgage loans in the secondary market. This investment has not only been stable during the recession, but has generally been profitable. | 5–10% |
| **Corporate Bond Funds** Example: Vanguard High-Yield Corporate Fund Investor Shares (VWEHX) | 8.6% As of 7/09 | Supports many corporations that create jobs. Funds may fluctuate but interest income is rock-solid stable over the life of the fund. | 20–25% |
| **High Dividend Stock Funds** Example:www.kiplinger.com/columns/balance/archive/2009/balance0504.html | Monthly Income 5 to 10% | Varies by fund but typically very diversified. Dividends are dependable. | 20–25% |
| Mutual funds, Green Stock Funds Example: www.kiplinger.com/columns/value/archive/2008/va0520.htm | Good funds will beat the S&P | Mutual funds and Green economic funds are reasonably safe and will both stimulate job growth and are environmentally friendly | 20–25% |
| I-Savings bonds, Treasury bonds, U.S. government obligations, state obligations, revenue bonds, etc. | 1–4% > 2 years | Investments in the U.S. government are often backed by Uncle SAM | 5–10% |
| CD | 1–4% 3 months, 10 year | Considered safe, typically FDIC insured, provides bank with money for lending | 0–2.5% |
| Money market | 1.3% | Considered safe, money markets seek capital preservation. | |
| Gold or Silver | N/A | Is considered a hedge against a devalued dollar. Gold is low maintenance investment and is described here as not job- friendly (see Chapter 6). | |
| Cash saving accounts | 0% | | 0–2.5% |
| Buy American where possible—including real estate | N/A | Buy American cars, furniture, appliances, electronics, and real estate where possible. | 5–25% |

Therefore, unless the dividend changes you will receive the exact same interest income, no matter how low the share price falls. If you are concerned with interest income, risk is highly reduced in a dividend fund rather than in a single stock. In a stock, dividends can sometimes change. This then poses some risks that should be considered. However, in a dividend fund, the chances of any one dividend being reduced by a particular company will not hurt your overall income from the fund. Therefore, you will receive the same interest income whether the fund goes up or down in value. For example, the Vanguard High Yield Corporate Bond Fund is highly stable in share dividends over the fund's life. Even though during the recession the prices of the shares have fluctuated in value, the fund has maintained the same monthly income in 2005 as in 2008–2009. Typically, funds are much lower in risk. Table 8.5 provides a reasonably low-risk diversified investment portfolio that we feel supports job-friendly economics. The rates of return, of course, vary according to the time and date of the issue. The recommended percent of asset obligation is heavily weighted to corporate America, housing market, and government obligations. Investing in corporate America through the stock market is extremely important. When the market falls, although there is not a direct link between jobs and a stock's decline, the corporate sentiment immediately responds in order to protect their business by cutting costs. The biggest costs that most companies typically incur are in labor. Thus, jobs are hit hard during a market decline both because of the problem with sales and the need to preserve company cash.

Many jobs get permanently lost in this time as well. As we have mentioned previously, U.S. dollars are privileged assets. Everyone should act in a fiscally responsible manner. Table 8.5 should give the reader some good ideas for responsible investment during a recession.

As an interesting example, consider two very different investments, real estate versus gold. Investors would clearly have different objectives for each. Gold is typically used as a hedge against U.S. currency fluctuation. On the other hand, one typically buys a home to improve their quality of life.

However, all things being equal, such as net profit or loss in the long term, the home is more job-friendly. Homes come with electric bills, insurance, upkeep, property tax, community involvement projects, schools, and many necessities that keep our economy moving. However, gold really just sits there in a vault, waiting to be traded at a later time. If you sell your gold or your house in 30 years for the same equivalent net profit, your home has really helped the economy, while gold helped little due to its low maintenance. Typically there are two types of gold buyers, those who hoard it for future sale and the more short-term buyers for speculative trading. Speculative trading, of course, is a bit more job-friendly. Of course, gold does have some job-friendly aspects, especially when used for jewelry or industrial products. In terms of precious metals, silver would have more practical value, as it is used more commonly than gold in manufacturing.

The question is, how many individuals are willing to invest in fiscally responsible areas during a time of an economic recession? The answer is, we expect it to be low, even though we have shown that it can be relatively safe and provide excellent rates of return. Therefore, we recommend anti-hoarding legislation for wealthy individuals to be implemented during a recessionary period. This is provided in our website, www.SolutionsWithoutUSDebt.com.

This suggested legislation has some logical asset amount for investing. Forcing individuals to invest does seem like an out-of-the box proposal. However, it could potentially eliminate the need for bailout programs that increase the national debt policy. That would be significant, and worth considering, given our debt problems.

**8.8: Job-Friendly Corporate Investment in a Recessionary Period**

In this section, we will focus on corporate investing in U.S. jobs. The topic of outsourcing will be detailed in Chapter 9 on Free Trade. Here we will focus on the fact that many companies will sideline their money in cash (See Remarks 3.14 through 3.22) during a recession. This is because, as we mentioned in Chapter 3, companies feel that "Cash is King." However, this often encourages job losses, equating to negative company growth.

It is clear that the main responsibility of reliability economics should be obtaining and ensuring a healthy economy and monetary policies where **JOBS ARE REALLY KING.**

Without jobs, money becomes tight, consumption weakens, sales fall, and more layoffs occur; and then the cycle repeats. In the microscopic worldview, from a company's perspective, job layoffs, shipping jobs overseas, and manufacturing outsourcing are logically necessary for survival in today's competitive environment. However, in the macroscopic economic view, it ends up hurting U.S. companies in the long run.

The reality is, if companies reduce their sidelined cash and switch instead to job-friendly investing, it can protect their future growth and help maintain their sales. We would not pretend to be so presumptuous as to ask a company to throw away their sidelined cash, as it is necessary for many reasons. Therefore, we have proposed a corporate hoarding quota during a recessionary period in Chapter 3 in the amount of,

**$300,000 per U.S. employee.**

This proposed quota encourages job growth. Companies would more likely invest in growth opportunities and would also be encouraged to keep more employees, since each person equates to a higher amount of cash that can be saved. In terms of our suggestion regarding what companies could do with "excess" cash exceeding the quota, Table 8.6 provides possible guidelines for job-friendly investments.

**Table 8.6** Fiscal Responsibility Investments for Wealthy Corporations During Recessionary Periods

| Suggested Investment | Percentage of Money Allowed | Requirement |
|---|---|---|
| Company business | 100% | |
| Company equipment upgrade or expansion | 75% | |
| American business to business | Minimum 25%<br>Maximum 100% | This appears a bit redundant; it implies buy equipment and services from U.S. companies. |
| U.S. stock market<br><br>U.S. Stock Market Mutual Funds | Minimum 20%<br><br>Maximum 100% | Initially evenly (± 2.5%) amongst main sectors: aerospace, automotive, chemical, computer hardware, computer software, construction, consumer products, energy, financial, food & beverage, health care, manufacturing, materials, media & entertainment, metals, mining, retail, technology, telecommunications, tobacco, transportation, utilities |
| Annuities | 10% | |
| Employee executive bonuses or individuals with salary exceeding $250K/Yr. | 0% | No executive bonuses are allowed in an economic recession—no exceptions. |
| 401K matching | 25% | Non-executive (executive > $250,000) |
| U.S. charities | 50% | |
| Government obligations | 10% | |
| Personal collectables | 5% | Art, memorabilia, private planes, automobiles, sophisticated collectables, and property |
| Non-U.S. charities | 2.5% | Large sums of money (as defined by FOMC) going to overseas charities shall be the responsibility of the U.S. government during a recession and not individuals. |
| Precious metals | 2.5% | Gold and silver |
| CDs | 2.5% | Bank CDs only |
| Money markets | 2.5% | |
| Overseas investments | 2.5% | Non-U.S. businesses |

## 8.9: Summary

In this chapter an FMEA was performed on job investing issues. Overpopulation and non-friendly investing were the two failure modes identified. Root causes for non-friendly investing included individual and business hoarding, job and manufacturing outsourcing; for overpopulation, root causes showed an absence in any policy for addressing this issue.

Root causes for job losses due to overpopulation had the highest rating. It was noted that our government economist and politicians do not appear to recognize the seriousness of the studies that provide clear warning to this problem in the U.S. and its relation to an unreliable economy. It was also noted that this is a global crisis. Remark 8.3 indicated recommendations for a sustainable U.S. economy of 200 million people. Currently the U.S. population is 305 million. It was pointed out that the estimated number of unemployed individuals in the U.S. is between 14.7 and 25.8 million people. This was not out of reach for the estimates made in the study in light of a possible jobless recover (see the Chapter 11 on What the Reader Can Do). It was recommended that U.S. government invest resources into the issue of addressing the overpopulation problem which is long overdue and must be done as soon as possible. Also, religious leaders should act responsibly and address this issue.

A discussion was provided for non-friendly individual financial investing. It was noted that individual investing is a bottom-up solution to help economic recovery and create or save jobs. We have described at length that economic hoarding by the well-to-do can significantly contribute to a recession. An argument was made that indicated wealthy income and assets have been generated by the U.S. economy's citizens. These monies are privileged assets, held in trust by the well-to-do, and it is a responsibility, even a requirement, to render a reasonable amount of such assets recycled back into the U.S. economy through active investments during a time of a declared recession. Table 8.1 provided low-risk ways to invest in stocks and corporate bond funds and to gain income through dividends. It was pointed out that dividends are relatively safe, especially in a fund, even when the value of the fund fluctuates. An example of the Vanguard High Yield Corporate Bond fund showed that even though the share price dropped dramatically during the recession, the dividend remained the same and the fund's value eventually recovered.

In this chapter we did not focus on job outsourcing, as it is covered in the next chapter. Corporate investing is very important during a recession. Even though the sentiment is to sideline money, as companies feel "Cash is King," the reality is that jobs are really king. This is due to the vicious cycle of layoffs, followed by loss in consumer spending, followed by more layoffs. When companies reduce their sidelined cash, and switch to job-friendly investing, it helps to protect their future growth and to increase employment. Therefore, we have proposed a hoarding quota in Chapter 3 in the amount of $300,000 per U.S. employee. Table 8.2 provided recommendations for corporations to help in a recessionary period.

# ■ 9.0 ■

# FREE TRADE FAILURES AND RELATED JOB LOSSES

### 9.1: Free Trade FMEA Assessment

It is a terrible experience to have your job outsourced (outside the U.S.) and end up out of work. Job loss related to free trade failures are dominant key issues in the U.S. Modern Recession. The free trade deficit has accumulated to over $7.5 trillion dollars since 1971 with $6.5 trillion in just the last 20 years (see Table 9.11). Yet 93% of U.S. economists are free trade advocates! What makes this baffling is that hardly any of these economists can rationalize the U.S. trade deficit's related failure modes. Traditional economics has poorly weighed the good with the bad. Especially in light of the fact that there is no history showing any country can long sustain large trade deficits without putting its economy at risk. In reliability economics we try to be proactive and not tolerate dominant failure modes, this is a key difference compared to current economics. Here we will divide the chapter up into known dominant reliability economic failure modes and root causes; then we will discuss the key logical design controls and potential corrective actions given the current globalization that has occurred. As a reminder, we focus on failure modes, not successes. Our approach is to treat U.S. free trade and job outsourcing a bit like going to the doctor's office. The U.S. has had a love affair with free trade, but has paid a high price with known injuries. Free trade has created low-priced products, has helped control inflation, and has created much wealth for many corporations. However, in so doing, it created numerous failures wherein we have lost most of our manufacturing (see Table 8.3), outsourced jobs (causing high unemployment), observed trade violations, and have seen many other huge U.S. business failures due to foreign competition. As well in Section 9.7 we present quantitative and qualitative information on how the free trade deficit is creating tax losses that adds to each U.S. citizen's national debt credit card roughly between $2670 and $6670. This will illustrate that free trade is really not free. We also explain how such tax loss violates constitutional law and also the U.S. trade agreement. With all these issues, we now have to ask the doctor, given the abuse that we have inflicted our U.S. economy's body, what medicine and surgery might help at this point in time to try and repair it? We will discover that the best medicine appears to be equal trade (i.e. no trade deficits). Table 9.1 provides an initial FMEA analysis from which to look at the root causes of the failure modes and come up with an initial plan for corrective actions.

**Table 9.1** FMEA on the Key Issue of Free Trade – Job Issues & Tax Issues

| Economic Key Issue | Potential Failure Mode | Potential Effect of Failure | Failure Mode Root Causes | Root Cause Rating | Design Control | Possible Corrective action |
|---|---|---|---|---|---|---|
| Free trade: job issues, tax issues | 1) Job outsourcing<br><br>2) Manufacturing failure & decline<br><br>3) U.S. corporation failures<br><br>4) Lost tax revenue due to layoffs and free trade deficit<br><br>5) Trade deficit<br><br>6) Focused U.S. wealth | 1, 2, 3, 6) Increase in unemployment,<br><br>2, 3) Foreign-dominated businesses<br><br>4) Spending cutbacks or increases in national debt.<br><br>5) Increase in foreign U.S. business ownership and debt to foreigners<br><br>6) Increases in separation of wealth | 1,2,6) Cheaper labor<br><br>1–5) Foreign subsidies<br><br>1–5) Foreign currency manipulation<br><br>3) Violation of free trade policy<br><br>3, 6) Lack of government oversight<br><br>3, 4) Job outsourcing, business failures due to foreign competition, trade deficit<br><br>1, 2, 5) High- versus low-wage economies | 1) 8<br><br>2) 6<br><br>3) 6<br><br>4) 8<br><br>5) 10 | 1, 2, 4, 5) Select areas of protection ism<br><br>3) Address free trade violations<br><br>1,2,3,4,5) Assess equal trade and import certificates | 1, 2, 3, 5) Provide non–trade war protectionis m measures<br><br>3) Address issues with (WTO). Penalize foreign imports for violations, class action law suits.<br><br>1,2,3,4,5) Consider import certificates |

## 9.2: Some Background Information on Free Trade and Job Outsourcing

Here we will provide some background that looks at the benefits and historical failures of free trade as it exists today. The author would like to comment to the reader that this is an FMEA analysis. We will be mainly focusing on the failures of free trade rather than the benefits. The author is not intending to blame our free trade problems on any particular country or nationality. However, many accusations will be presented on China, Japan, India, and other countries regarding free trade violations. These are accusations by Americans and are part of the Truth of the Modern Recession. They are not meant to offend any nationality or country. They are concerns from many U.S. citizens regarding problems that plague America. As such, the author would like the reader to know that he is very fond of all nationalities and their contributions that our trading partners have made to our country. However, this research is meant to provide details that are realistic and factual to the author's best abilities. Any conclusions are based on the facts of our Modern Recession.

The basic principles of free trade from an economic theory are summarized in Remark 9.1.

> **Remark 9.1:** "The underlying economic theory of free trade agreements is that of "comparative advantage," which originated in an 1817 book entitled *On the Principles of Political Economy and Taxation* by British political economist David Ricardo…Put simply, the "theory of comparative advantage" postulates that in a free marketplace, each country/area will ultimately specialize in that activity where it has comparative advantage (i.e. natural resources, skilled artisans, agriculture-friendly weather, etc.)…. The result should be that all parties to the pact will increase their income." [156]

However, the increases in income can be narrowed down to a reduced number of individuals. This is failure mode number 6 in Table 9.1.

> **Remark 9.2:** "However, the theory refers only to aggregate wealth and says nothing about the distribution of wealth. In fact there may be significant losers, in particular among the recently protected industries with a comparative disadvantage. The proponents of free trade can, however, retort that the gains of the gainers exceed the losses of the losers."[157]

Some of the known benefits of free trade and job outsourcing are:

> **Remark 9.3:** 1) Low-priced goods, 2) reduced inflation due to maintaining low-priced products, 3) low-priced services, 4) new job opportunities in foreign-owned businesses, 5) new global opportunities in manufacturing, 6) imports/exports of agricultural and commodity, 7) export opportunities, 8) reduced likelihood of war with our trading partners due to foreign investors, and 9) manufacturing outsourcing raises the level of 3rd world countries.

> **Remark 9.4:** "In the 1980s, Milton Friedman, the Nobel Prize–winning economist and father of Monetarism, contended that some of the concerns of trade deficits are unfair criticisms in an attempt to push macroeconomic

---

[156] http://usliberals.about.com/od/theeconomyjobs/i/FreeTradeAgmts.htm
[157] http://en.wikipedia.org/wiki/Free_trade_area

policies favorable to exporting industries. In the late 1970s and early 1980s, the U.S. had experienced high inflation and Friedman's policy positions tended to defend the stronger dollar at that time. He stated his belief that these trade deficits were not necessarily harmful to the economy at the time since the currency comes back to the country (country A sells to country B, country B sells to country C who buys from country A, but the trade deficit only includes A and B)." [158]

Unfortunately, Mr. Friedman may not have realized the extent of job losses and recognize the tax consequences of the trade deficit (see Sec. 9.7).

In contrast to these benefits, there are a number of substantiated well-known current U.S. failures of free trade. From a reliability economics point of view, we have listed the main free trade and outsourcing failure modes and their effects using our FMEA approach in Table 9.1. We will briefly connect the dots to provide a bit more detail to the topics in the table. Looking then at the key six failure modes and their effects, they are:

**Remark 9.5:**

1) Significant problem for our current U.S. unemployment crisis due to job outsourcing that has occurred primarily in the manufacturing area (a decline of 31% since 1999—see Table 8.3), but is also increasing in the area of services (see Table 8.3).

2) Because of cheap foreign labor and lack of protectionism, the U.S. has lost its manufacturing base. This is well-known and a dominant challenge for America's unemployment problems and job creation problems.

3) U.S. corporation failures have occurred due to foreign competition that has had many advantages over U.S. businesses. For example, some foreign governments are accused of subsidizing products; they may pay for employee health insurance, and in general have cheaper labor. One industry that has been costly to America is the Detroit automakers. While they have had many mismanagement issues, the business structure was not able to survive the free trade competition. Japanese autos and other foreign imports have dominated our marketplace.

4) The U.S. now faces <u>lost tax revenue due to: a) layoffs (see Remark 9.6)</u> and b) excess foreign profits (<u>see Sec. 9.7</u>). The excess lost tax revenue effectively <u>adds to the national debt</u>. This will cause cutbacks, difficulties

[158] http://en.wikipedia.org/wiki/Trade_deficit

with the national debt, and problems financing U.S. government–sponsored programs.

5) Because of the trade deficit with foreign countries that have imported more goods than we export, we have also exported more dollars than we imported in foreign currency. This newfound excess of U.S. dollars held by foreigners must eventually find their way back and be reinvested into the U.S. The result is that more and more U.S. businesses are owned by foreign countries. In addition, foreign countries like China have also bought U.S. obligations, so that, increasingly, national debt is owed to foreign countries. This also makes us politically beholden to countries like China, putting us in a weaker position to seek retribution on free-trade violations as we will discuss below.

6) There is a clear focus of wealth in free trade. Outsourcing allows for U.S. companies to exist with few or no actual manufacturing workers in the States. Businessmen can find free trade highly profitable, and this increases the separation of wealth in America, along with job losses. Studies indicate that the growing cost of globalization is a continued widening of the gap between the Haves and Have-Nots.[159]

The remark on item 4 about lost tax revenue is very relevant. It is now surfacing as a main issue for U.S. financial stability in the recession and puts our economy at risk. The U.S. government appears to be its own worst enemy.

**Remark 9.6**: "Plunge in tax revenue worst since 1932—The recession is starving the government of tax revenue, just as the president and Congress are piling a major expansion of health care and other programs ....Tax receipts are on pace to drop 18 percent this year, the biggest single-year decline since the Great Depression, while the federal deficit balloons to a record $1.8 trillion. …Individual income tax receipts are down 22 percent from a year ago. Corporate income taxes are down 57 percent. Social Security tax receipts could drop for only the second time since 1940, and Medicare taxes are on pace to drop for only the third time ever." [160]

There are, of course, more failure modes and benefits of free trade. It could be a controversial long book. However, it is important to maintaining focus on the key issues. In this regard let's start by reviewing the magnitude of the trade

---

[159] www.mapcruzin.com/news/news122000b.htm, "Growing Costs of Globalization: Wider Gaps Between Haves and Have-Nots by Year 2015, Says US Intelligence Report."
[160] www.denverpost.com/nationworld/ci_12986655

deficit. Table 9.2 provides the trade deficit to China, Japan, and NAFTA (Mexico, Canada) key trading partners. Total yearly deficit (all countries) is in last column.

**Table 9.2** U.S. Trade Deficit Information in Billions of Dollars[161]

| Year | China | China % | Japan | Mexico* | Canada* | Others | Total |
|---|---|---|---|---|---|---|---|
| 2009 | $226.8 | 59.9% | $45 | $48 | $20.2 | $38.6 | $378.6 |
| 2008 | $268 | 38.5% | $74 | $65 | $78.3 | $210.6 | $695.9 |
| 2007 | $258 | 36.8% | $84 | $75 | $68 | $216.4 | $701.4 |
| 2006 | $234 | 30.8% | $90 | $65 | $72 | $299.4 | $760.4 |
| 2005 | $202 | 28.2% | $83 | $50 | $78 | $302.3 | $715.3 |
| 2004 | $162 | 26.6% | $74 | $45 | $67 | $261.9 | $609.9 |
| 2003 | $124 | 25.1% | $66 | $40 | $52 | $213 | $495 |
| 2002 | $103 | 24.5% | $70 | $37 | $48 | $163 | $421 |
| 2001 | $83 | 22.7% | $69 | $30 | $53 | $130.5 | $365.5 |
| 2000 | $84 | 22.1% | $82 | $24 | $52 | $137.8 | $379.8 |

*NAFTA Partner

Table 9.2 indicates that our biggest deficit in 2009 exists with China (59.9%), followed by Mexico (12.7%), and Japan (11.9%). Note the last column totals $5.5 trillion for 10 years compared with a $7.5 trillion total since 1971.

Warren Buffett has been quoted as saying,

> **Remark 9.7:** "The U.S trade deficit is a bigger threat to the domestic economy than either the federal budget deficit or consumer debt and could lead to political turmoil... Right now, the rest of the world owns $3 trillion more of us than we own of them." [162]

Currently many companies are now recognizing that job outsourcing has gone too far, but still are unable to resolve their apparent need.

> **Remark 9.7-A:** July 2009, "Jeffery Immelt, the CEO of General Electric, recently said that 'the United States needs to invest in American manufacturing in order to get out of our current economic crisis. Some <u>companies had gone overboard with outsourcing</u> in the past and now it was time to bring that work back into the United States to create a strong economy.... GE plans to lead this effort.' The author of the article goes on to say that at the same time GE was actually shipping more jobs overseas by cancelling U.S. orders to instead buying these parts from China."[163]

[161] www.census.gov/foreign-trade/balance/
[162] http://en.wikipedia.org/wiki/Trade_deficit#Warren_Buffett_on_trade_deficits (January 2006)
[163] www.huffingtonpost.com/mike-elk/ge-promotes-manufacturing_b_241944.html, Author Mike Elk, huffington post on line.

A historic overview of the trade deficit is depicted in Figure 9.1.

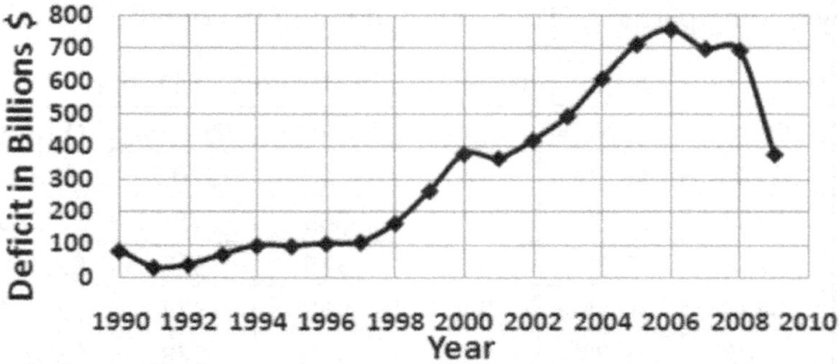


**Figure 9.1** Trade deficits in goods and services - 1991 to 2009 (see Table 9.11)

There are many economists opposing free trade including this author (see 9.7). NAFTA has been historically criticized for displacing U.S. Jobs. Now China job losses are actually much worse from our trading policies.

> **Remark 9.8:** "The High Price of "Free" Trade, November 17, 2003: Since the North American Free Trade Agreement (NAFTA) was signed in 1993, the rise in the U.S. trade deficit with Canada and Mexico through 2002 has caused the displacement of production that supported 879,280 U.S. job... Manufacturing industries were responsible for 78% of the net jobs lost under NAFTA, a total of 686,700 manufacturing jobs."[164]
> **Remark 9.8A:** An Economic Policy Institute study claiming that the trade deficit with China cost more than 2.4 million U.S. jobs between 2001 and 2008[165]
>
> **Remark 9.9**: "U.S. NAFTA Trade Deficit Surging Again Snapshot for November 5, 2003: The rise in the U.S. deficit with Canada and Mexico from 1993 to 2000 displaced production supported by 766,000 U.S. jobs. Most of those jobs would have been high-wage positions in manufacturing industries." [166]
> **Remark 9.9A** Between NAFTA and China spanning 1993 and 2008 the total job outsourcing loss is at least 3.63 million. It is hard to assess lost tax revenue. One old economic study by a Harvard economist Martin Feldstein in 1971 estimated a tax loss of $10.61 per hour on even a $15 per hour job[167]. Using this underestimated value and providing and overestimate of displaced workers for 1 year of salary, the outsourcing cost to tax payers (2000 hr. work year) is ~ $77 billion. Using a recent EPI estimate of about

[164]www.policyarchive.org/bitstream/handle/10207/8113/epi_bp147.pdf?sequence=1
[165] http://online.wsj.com/article/BT-CO-20100323-713114.html?mod=WSJ_latestheadlines
[166]/www.epi.org/economic_snapshots/entry/webfeatures_snapshots_archive_11052003/
[167] http://www.econlib.org/library/Enc/Unemployment.html

> $700 week[168] including Cobra subsidies, the taxpayer cost is $131 billion. The GDP loss from consumer spending creating less product demand and effecting other layoffs is hard to factor. The EPI estimate is 8.4 million recent jobs lost. The cascade effect may be a factor of 10 with housing and bail-out issues. This is ~$1 trillion in tax losses from the trade deficit effect.

Two recommended books criticizing Free Trade have received a lot of favorable attention.

> **Remark 9.10:** *The Myth of Free Trade: The Pooring of America*, by Ravi Batra "... The work outlines why America has become a debtor nation. The main cause is free trade. ...Moreover, poor leadership has allowed foreign nations such as Japan, South Korea, and China to sing free trade's praises while following protectionist policies as tariffs, quotas, exchange controls and the like at home...we have become an open economy, the country has become awash with red ink in trade account."[169]
>
> **Remark 9.10A:** *Free Trade Doesn't Work,* by Ian Fletcher, "Presents the failures of an unrestrained trade system and offers up a balanced discussion of what a managed trade system could accomplish in its place. His discussion of the WTO goals, and of China's open defiance of the spirit of WTO rules, is refreshingly honest and timely..."[167]

### 9.3: Free Trade Deficit, the National Debt, and U.S. Currency

Free trade deficit means foreigners increasingly own U.S. dollars. For example, when the U.S. spends $10 on imports from China and China only ends up spending $5 on imports from the U.S., China has a $5 U.S. gain. China's currency is the yuan (about 6.8 yuan equals 1 U.S. dollar as of September 2009). Therefore it has two choices: sell the dollar for the yuan, which could decrease the value of the dollar, or purchase securities such as U.S. stocks or treasury bonds. Since treasury bonds are, in essence, loans to the U.S. government, the trade deficit and the trading partners of the U.S. fund some of the national debt (also see 9.7). The vast majority of the national debt is held by Americans. However, foreigners own about $3 trillion of our $12 trillion–plus debt.

Foreigners in 2009 have been happy to hold onto U.S. securities. The concern is that at some point, foreigners may want to reduce their holdings. If this occurs rapidly, it could send the value of the dollar, U.S. stocks, and bond prices plunging, since the government will have to print money to pay back the foreign countries. This poses a risk. The current foreign holdings of the U.S. debt are listed in Table 9.3. We see there is strong correlation to the trade deficit. That is, China, Japan, and oil exporters are the largest holders of our debt and proportionately the largest countries that we have a trade deficit with. It is also a

[168] http://www.epi.org/publications/entry/jobs_crisis_fact_sheet/
[169] www.amazon.com/reviews

cause for concern that, because China and oil exporters hold so much of our debt, many consider their interests unfriendly.

> **Remark 9.11:** In February 2009—an article entitled "Did 2008's $677 Billion Trade Deficit Cause The Recession?" was posted by the economist Peter Morici, who noted that the Chinese government holds about $2 trillion in U.S. and other securities and he worries if we add that to the holdings of Middle East sovereigns and royal families, that the potential purchases of U.S. businesses by foreigners unfriendly to the U.S. is alarming. He believes the trade deficit is a root cause to the recession.[170]

To put this matter in perspective, Table 9.3 provides information on U.S. debt owed to foreigners.

**Table 9.3** U.S. Debt Owned by Foreigners and Related Trade Deficit[171]

| Nation | January 2009[172] Foreign-Owned U.S. Treasuries in Billions of Dollars | Treasuries Owned in Percentage | 2009 U.S. Trade Deficit in Billions[173] |
|---|---|---|---|
| China | 739.6 | 24.07% | 227 |
| Japan | 634.8 | 20.66% | 45 |
| Oil exporters | 186.3 | 6.06% | |
| Caribbean banks | 176.6 | 5.75% | NA |
| Brazil | 133.5 | 4.35% | |
| United Kingdom | 124.2 | 4.04% | |
| Russia | 119.6 | 3.89% | 1.3 (15.6) |
| Luxembourg | 87.2 | 2.84% | |
| Taiwan | 73.3 | 2.39% | 9 |
| Hong Kong | 71.7 | 2.33% | |
| Switzerland | 62.1 | 2.02% | |
| Germany | 56.4 | 1.84% | 19 |
| Republic of Ireland | 50 | 1.63% | 17 |
| Singapore | 38.3 | 1.25% | |
| Thailand | 37.2 | 1.21% | |
| Mexico | 34.9 | 1.14% | 48 |
| India | 32.5 | 1.06% | |
| Turkey | 31.3 | 1.02% | |
| Korea | 31.3 | 1.02% | 11 |
| All other | 351.4 | 11.43% | |
| Grand Total | 3072.2 | 100% | |

[170] http://seekingalpha.com/article/120195-did-2008-s-677-billion-trade-deficit-cause-the-recessio
[171] http://en.wikipedia.org/wiki/United_States_public_debt
[172] ttp://en.wikipedia.org/wiki/United_States_public_debt
[173] www.census.gov/foreign-trade/top/dst/current/deficit.html

Foreigners not only own U.S. debt, but buy U.S. businesses. America is now for sale to foreigners because of the trade deficit which also hurts tax revenues (see Section 9.7).

> **Remark 9.11-A** Aug. 08 - "American icons (now owned by foreigners) such as storied brewer Anheuser-Busch Companies Inc and the landmark Chrysler Building in New York....According to the Grant Thornton report...."[174]

Foreign owners often replace American workers when they buy U.S businesses. The net job increase to jobs lost is fractional[175]. Below is an except regarding a U.S company purchased by a German company. The lack of sensible reliability economics is concerning in U.S free trade policy.

> **Remark 9.11-B:** "As the American employees were leaving the company for one reason or another, they were being replaced by German employees. Also, as new positions were opened, most of the positions were filled with; who else but German individuals. 6 years after the buy-out of the American firm, the ratio of the American employees vs. German employees has increased to around 50/50...."[176]

Free trade advocates feel that foreign reinvestments create lots of job opportunities. Yet a quick investigation doesn't seem to indicate a reasonable percentage compared to what is being invested.

> **Remark 9.11C:** Aug, 2008 – "According to the Grant Thornton report, total assets at foreign-owned companies increased 15 percent to $9.2 trillion in 2005 from $8.0 trillion a year earlier and was more than three times the 1996 total of $3 trillion. Foreign-owned assets totaled just $37 billion in 1971...."[177]
> **Remark 9.11D:** "Foreign-owned companies in the United States have a work force of more than 5.3 million, or some 3.5% of all workers."[178]

According to 9.11C and D, foreigners own 15% of U.S. companies but only employ 3.5%. Extrapolating to 100%, the employment would only be 25%! Current estimate of foreign ownership is $6.9 trillion in businesses and $3 trillion in treasuries totaling $9.9 trillion. U.S. business net worth is about $50 trillion (~13.9%). The total trade deficit is $7.5 trillion. About 76% of the ownership is due to the deficit. At the mean rate of 0.55 trillion/yr. (in Table

[174] www.reuters.com/article/domesticNews/idUSN2744743020080827
[175] http://www.aflcio.org/issues/jobseconomy/jobs/outsourcing_myths.cfm
[176] www.commentaryusa.com/commentary/economy/do-foreigners-care-for-the-u.s.-economy.html
[177] http://www.reuters.com/article/idUSN2744743020080827
[178] www.nytimes.com/2009/10/18/business/18excerpt.html

9.2), half the U.S. businesses could be foreign owned in just 65 years (using 50% profit model invested in U.S. businesses); this ownership, mostly by China!

**9.4: Root Cause Discussion**
In this section we provide information on the root causes.

**9.4.1: Root Cause—High- Versus Low-Wage Economies**
We will start with the root cause of high-wage versus low-wage economies in Table 9.1, since its rating is 10. This root cause implies that whenever a low-wage country trades with a high-wage country it will create big losers and winners. One macroeconomic book explained this concept as follows:

> **Remark 9.12:** "Trade between high-wage countries tends to be a modest win for all, or almost all, concerned....By contrast, trade between countries at very different levels of economic development tends to create large classes of losers as well as winners....And the biggest growth of imports has come from countries with very low wages....South Korea, Taiwan, Hong Kong and Singapore paid wages of 25 percent of U.S. levels in 1990. Since then however, the sources of our imports have shifted to Mexico, where wages are 11 percent of the U.S. level, and China, where they're only 3 or 4 percent....[179]"

A simple theory will be provided that we will call "the law of financial free trade deficit equilibrium."

> **Remark 9.13**: **Law of Financial Free Trade Deficit Equilibrium**—Consider two containers separated by a wall, one having a high concentration of air, and one with very little air. Once the wall is removed, due to the pressure and concentration difference, after a period of time both containers will have the same amount of air, thus reaching equilibrium. In a similar manner, if two economies have free cash flow, such as China (considered a developing country) and the U.S., the currencies will flow towards financial equilibrium (from richer country to poorer). The imbalanced monetary pressure causing excess deficit is due mainly to three key trade deficit reasons: cost of wages, each country's GDP, and the value of the country's currency.

In our analogy, we might consider the point where the free trade "concentration wall" was officially removed between the U.S. and China to have occurred when President Clinton signed a bill extending permanent, normal trade status to China on October 10, 2000. This bill clearly undercut American and

---

[179] *Principles of Macroeconomics*, N. Gregory Mankiw, 5th edition, 2009 South-Western Cengage Learning, PP 192-193.

Mexican factory workers. In terms of free trade, this was a severe final attack on American factory workers. As Remark 9.12 notes, wages in China were almost a quarter of that for the Mexican worker. Since that point in time, in accordance with Remark 9.13, the high concentration of cash has flowed to the low concentration, as noted by our enormous imbalance with the trade deficit that peaked at $760 billion in 2006 (see Table 9.11). This is now magnified by the fact that, as we stated earlier, in roughly nine short years, the U.S. has ended up owing China over $800 billion through China's purchase of U.S. treasuries.

It is important to realize the relationship between GDP (Gross Domestic Product) and the population size:

> **Remark 9.14:** "In order for Americans to maintain their standard of living, GDP needs to grow at least as fast as the population!"[180]

Here, GDP is a measure of the size of our economy from everyone's total income. To put this a bit more in perspective, Tables 9.4 and 9.5 provide statistics of the population growth and GDP information from 2000 to 2008 for China and U.S.

**Table 9.4** China's Overall Population and GDP Growth from 2000 to 2008[181]

| Year | China Population (Billions) | Pop Growth Since 2000 | Adjusted Pop Growth Rate | GDP per Capita China in U.S. dollars | Real GDP* Growth Rate % | Billions GDP China |
|---|---|---|---|---|---|---|
| 2000 | 1.26183 | 0.00% | 0.9% | $3,800 | 7% | 4800 |
| 2001 | 1.27311 | 0.88% | 0.88% | $3600 | 8% | 4500 |
| 2002 | 1.28430 | 1.75% | 0.87% | $4600 | 8% | 6000 |
| 2003 | 1.28698 | 2.35% | 0.6% | $4400 | 8% | 5700 |
| 2004 | 1.29885 | 2.92% | 0.57% | $5000 | 9.1% | 6449 |
| 2005 | 1.30631 | 3.50% | 0.58% | $5600 | 9.1% | 7262 |
| 2006 | 1.31397 | 4.09% | 0.59% | $6800 | 10.2% | 8883 |
| 2007 | 1.32185 | 4.70% | 0.61% | $7700 | 10.7% | 10170 |
| 2008 | 1.33004 | 5.33% | 0.63% | $5400 | 11.9% | 7099 |
| 2009 | 1.33861 | 5.99% | 0.66% | $4900 | 9% | 6473 |

From Tables 9.4 and 9.5, our population consisted of about 304 million, while China's population consisted of 1,330 million in 2008. China, in 2008, had over four times as many consumers. Noting this, we see that China's GDP skyrocketed in this timeframe from 7 to 11.4% since the Free Trade Bill was passed between the U.S. and China. In comparison, the U.S. GDP growth rate ended down from 4.1% to 2.2% according to the source CIA World Factbook (Tables 9.4 and 9.5).

---

[180] http://truecostblog.com/2008/01/25/gdp-doesnt-matter-gdp-per-capita-does/

[181] CIA World Factbook—as of January 1, 2009, www.indexmundi.com/g/g.aspx?v=67&c=ch&l=en

**Table 9.5** U.S. Overall Population and GDP Growth from 2000 to 2008[182]

| Year | U.S. Pop (Billions) | U.S. Pop Growth Since 2000 | Adjusted Pop Growth Rate | U.S. GDP Per Capita in dollars | U.S. GDP in Billions | Real GDP* Growth Rate % |
|---|---|---|---|---|---|---|
| 2000 | 0.2756 | 0.0% | 0.91% | $33,900 | 9,255 | 4.1% |
| 2001 | 0.2781 | 0.9% | 0.9% | $36,200 | 9,963 | 5% |
| 2002 | 0.2806 | 1.79% | 0.89% | $36,300 | 10,082 | 0.3% |
| 2003 | 0.2903 | 2.71% | 0.92% | $37,600 | 10,400 | 2.45% |
| 2004 | 0.2930 | 3.63% | 0.92% | $37,800 | 10,990 | 3.1% |
| 2005 | 0.2957 | 4.55% | 0.92% | $40,100 | 11,750 | 4.4% |
| 2006 | 0.2984 | 5.46% | 0.91% | $41,600 | 12,310 | 3.2% |
| 2007 | 0.3011 | 6.35% | 0.894% | $44,000 | 13,130 | 3.2% |
| 2008 | 0.3038 | 7.24% | 0.883% | $45,800 | 13,780 | 2.1% |
| 2009 | 0.3072 | 8.21% | 0.975% | $46,300 | 13,820 | 1.1% |

One should also note that this is an inversion with our population growth compared to China. That is, China's population grew by 5.4% and their GDP by 4.4% since 2000. In contrast, the U.S. GDP growth rate contracted -1.9% while its population grew 10.3% since 2000. The World CIA Factbook defines the GDP growth on an annual basis adjusted for inflation and expressed as a percent. (The reader might note that the U.S. GDP and GDP per capita did increase from 2000 to 2008. Therefore, statistics in this regard must be reviewed from this source on the GDP growth rate.) However, it is clear that China's GDP is growing faster than the U.S., while America's population appears to be growing faster than China.

It is also important to realize that cash flow is impacted by the average income per person (this is GDP per capita). By comparison, it was $46,000 for the U.S. citizens compared to $5,300 for Chinese citizens in 2008.

> **Remark 9.15**: "While GDP measures the size of the total economy, it's GDP per capita, the slice of GDP that an "average" American has, that really matters. While GDP per capita doesn't take into account income inequality and other measures…." [183]

[182]CIA World Factbook—as of January 1, 2009, www.indexmundi.com/g/g.aspx?v=67&c=ch&l=en

[183] http://truecostblog.com/2008/01/25/gdp-doesnt-matter-gdp-per-capita-does/

So although China has four times as many consumers, we had on average a factor of 8.7 times higher incomes in 2008. This fact helps us to understand some of the trade imbalance. This is really the root cause issue; we are a high-income wage earning country trading with a low-income country. Logically, the cash flow is eventually going to get distributed. Financially, it means that the U.S. is giving up quite a bit in the name of free trade and will continue to do so until the playing field is leveled. Since China is our largest trading partner, this fact implies that the U.S. must either reduce its population, grow its GDP at a faster rate, reduce the cost of living and wage earnings, or continue to face the economic crisis that is now occurring.

On the positive side, since China's GDP is growing faster than that of the U.S., eventually the trade deficiency should come down as the value of their currency strengthens compared to the U.S. This is related to the theory of free trade, where eventually the U.S. currency will weaken; exports should then increase to bring back the trade imbalances.

> **Remark 9.16:** "As the yuan appreciates, the relative prices of Chinese-produced goods to American businesses and consumers will rise, reducing U.S. demand for Chinese imports. Simultaneously, the relative prices of U.S. products to Chinese purchasers will decrease, allowing U.S. exports to rise. At least, that is the theory."[184]

This, in theory, is how free trade should work. However, eventually when China has some measure of financial equilibrium with the U.S., the U.S. GDP per capita, according to our law of financial free trade equilibrium, must be significantly reduced simply due to the combined effect of our two populations.

So it would appear the assumption is somewhat flawed. There are also other problems with conducting free trade fairly as we have noted in the FMEA table. This has occurred with both China and Japan. Both countries have come under scrutiny for some time. This brings us to our next root cause of currency manipulation.

### 9.4.2: Root Cause—Currency Manipulation

Foreign currency manipulation is a major root cause for the first five of the six identified failure modes in Table 9.1. If the accusations are reasonable, it would require strong corrective actions. In order for free trade to work as it should, currency needs to seek its correct value. If a country's currency is weak, exports can increase since their goods are now cheaper. Eventually currency value will strengthen as its GNP increases. However, if currency is manipulated, then free trade will have strong economic reliability consequences. This is a recognized

---

[184] www.freetrade.org/node/83

violation by World Trade Organization (WTO), which was created to open up markets and promote international fair trade. The WTO creates and monitors agreements to reduce trade barriers, arbitrates in disputes over foreign market access, and watches for violations of these agreements. However, manipulation of currency is not easy to referee on the part of the WTO.

> **Remark 9.17**: "Section IV of the IMF (International Monetary Fund) charter states without reservation, that "members should avoid manipulating exchange rates in order to gain an unfair competitive advantage over other members" and defines such manipulation as "protracted, large-scale intervention in one direction in exchange market." [185, 186]

**9.4.3: The Complex Trade Violations with China**

America's history with China is bizarre. We are a capitalistic nation doing business with a Communist country. This is more to China's credit. It was not too long ago that the U.S Trade and Development Agency (TDA) prohibited any new economic activities in mainland China due to human rights violations (Tiananmen Square Massacre in 1989). Suspensions were in place from June 1989 until January 2001, after which President Bill Clinton lifted them and entered a period of free trade with China. To make matters more odd, China had, in a very short timeframe, emerged as an economic power while, in roughly the same period of time, the U.S. had fallen from its economic position. Our secretary of state, Hillary Clinton, was recently sent to China asking for loans. As of March 2009, the U.S. owed China about $800 trillion.

There have been strong accusations against China (as well as Japan, discussed below):

> **Remark 9.18:** In May of 2006, Daniel Ikenson, the author of *Currency Controversy: Surplus of Politics, Deficit of Leadership* stated that many members of Congress simply felt "China's currency is purposely undervalued to encourage Chinese exports and discourage imports and these members felt that such manipulation explains much of the bilateral trade deficit that cost U.S. jobs. Such Congress members felt an urgency for the yuan to be appreciated." He notes that these members felt that at a minimum the Schumer-Graham bill should be supported. The Schumer-Graham bill had proposed a 27.5% tariff on all imports from China until the yuan reached a fair value. However, Mr. Ikenson believes that currency manipulation would not be a key factor in the trade deficit. [187]

---

[185] http://waysandmeans.house.gov/hearings.asp?formmode=view&id=3798
[186] www.imf.org/external/np/exr/facts/imfwto.htm
[187] www.freetrade.org/node/83

In 2006 the Schumer-Graham bill although seemingly popular was heavily lobbied against.

> **Remark 9.19**: "Lobbyists tend to unite against the Schumer-Graham bill, which would levy a 27.5 percent tariff on all Chinese imports if the yuan is not revalued after 180 days of trade talks. But lobbyists do agree with the senators that the current policy is not working…"[188]

It is not well-documented to what extent lobbyists finally influenced the dropping of this bill, but in September of 2006, the bill was stopped.

> **Remark 9.20:** "Two U.S. senators said Thursday that they will abandon legislation that would have punished Chinese goods with steep tariffs. The lawmakers promised, however, to renew efforts next year meant to spur Beijing to change **currency** policies they say cost millions of American jobs." [189]

*"When special interests put their thumb on the scale, and distort the free market, the people who compete by the rules come in last."*

—BARACK OBAMA, speech, August 2, 2008

During 2007 through 2009 things did not improve. Early in 2009, the U.S. Treasury Secretary, according to CNBC, was reported as saying:

> **Remark 9.21:** January 2009–"On Thursday, Treasury Secretary designate Timothy Geithner said in a written response to questions from a U.S. Senate panel that 'President Obama—backed by the conclusions of a broad range of economists—believes China is manipulating its currency.'"[190]

Some articles started to lash out at China with other accusations.

> **Remark 9.22:** March 2009—"China's massive, prolonged, one-way and sterilized intervention in the currency market, its unprecedented foreign exchange accumulation ($1.9 trillion), and its massive current account surplus demonstrate that, once again, China is manipulating its currency, they said."[191]

In fact, once again a group of lawmakers are considering a trade tariff.

---

[188] http://thehill.com/business--lobby/pressure-gathers-for-and-against-china-tariffs-bill-2006-03-22.html

[189] www.americaneconomicalert.org/news_item.asp?NID=2275844

[190] www.cnbc.com/id/28809112

[191] http://news.alibaba.com/article/detail/markets/100077967-1-yuan-flat-vs-dollar-despite.html, See also, The Coming China Wars: Peter Navarro

> **Remark 9.23:** "In May 2009, a group of Republican and Democratic lawmakers will on Wednesday revive a bill that threatens to raise tariffs on Chinese goods to punish the country for what they call 'currency manipulation.' 'By illegally subsidizing its exports through the undervaluation of its currency by 30 per cent or more, China distorts the gains from trade, creates barriers to free and fair trade, harms U.S. industries and has destroyed millions of U.S. jobs,' those sponsoring the bill said in a statement."[192]

The problems are much worse now in 2009 compared to 2006, rendering it more difficult to act on China by raising tariffs. We cannot forget that we now owe China over $800 billion. These U.S. threats (Remark 9.23) are most likely empty, as lawmakers' hands may be tied until we can start to pay off the deficit. For example, in January, news sources reported:

> **Remark 9.24:** January 2009—"U.S. Treasury bond prices fell on worries that China might respond to Geithner's frank comments by cutting its holdings, the world's largest, of U.S. government debt."[193]

On the other hand, China is not in the best position either.

> **Remark 9.25**: The *Financial Times* quoted Mr. Ping (in February 2009) as saying—"Except for U.S. Treasuries, what can you hold? Gold? You don't hold Japanese government bonds or U.K. bonds. U.S. Treasuries are the safe-haven. For everyone, including China, it is the only option. Even if the dollar depreciates because of Washington's financial bailouts, he added, China has no other options."[194]

In China's defense, back in 2007, some articles point out that currency manipulation is costly.

> **Remark 9.26**: September 2007—"Manipulating currencies is not a costless exercise, far from it. To prevent the yuan appreciating against the dollar China's central bank (People's Bank of China) has to print more and more yuan with which to buy dollars. While this has been going on domestic credit expansion has reached dangerous levels. M2, currency and credit has been racing ahead at more than 17 per cent a year. This is akin to a runaway monetary train…" [195]

---

[192] www.freerepublic.com/focus/f-news/2249841/posts
[193] hwww.reuters.com/article/bondsNews/idUSPEK3984220090123, By Lu Jianxin and Simon Rabinovitch
[194] www.realclearworld.com/articles/2009/02/why_china_needs_us_debt.html
[195] http://marketoracle.co.uk/Article2163.html, by Gerard Jackson

Other economists believe China's government provides subsidies on certain products where low wages are not the main cost.

> **Remark 9.27**: "China's currency market intervention creates a 25 percent subsidy on its exports, and competitive advantages in industries not dependent on low-wage labor. Other Asia economies follow suit with similar industrial policies."[196]

In Table 9.6, we provide statistics on this issue.

**Table 9.6** U.S. Comparative Currency Values from 2000 to 2008 for Three Main Free Trade Partners[197]

| Year (USD=US Dollar) | 2000 | 2001 | 2002 | 2003 | 2004 | 2005 | 2006 | 2007 | 2008 | As of May 2009 |
|---|---|---|---|---|---|---|---|---|---|---|
| Yuan/USD | 8.3 | 8.3 | 8.3 | 8.3 | 8.3 | 8.2 | 8.0 | 7.6 | 6.9 | 7.0 |
| Yen/USD | 108 | 122 | 125 | 116 | 108 | 110 | 116 | 118 | 103 | 99.0 |
| Mexico Peso/USD | 9.5 | 9.3 | 9.7 | 10.8 | 11.3 | 10.9 | 10.9 | 10.9 | 11.1 | 13.2 |

In Table 9.6, we note that the yuan compared to the U.S. dollar has actually dropped in value rather than increased in the new free trade era between 2000 and 2008. This is true for Japan as well. However, Mexico has not followed suit, as its currency has strengthened against the dollar as expected.

Meanwhile, in the same time period, the public national debt of these countries shows some interesting statistics in Table 9.7.

**Table 9.7** Public Debt of the U.S. and Three Main Free Trade Partners [198]

| Public Debt % of GDP | 2004 | 2005 | 2006 | 2007 | 2008 |
|---|---|---|---|---|---|
| China | 23.1% | 23.5% | 17.4% | 20.7% | 23.1% |
| Japan | 154.6% | 164.3% | 158.0% | 176.2% | 194.4% |
| Mexico | 30.1% | 31.4% | 24.4% | 22.1% | 18.9% |
| U.S. | 62.4% | 65.0% | 64.7% | 64.7% | 70.2% |

Here we note that China has maintained its public debt from 2004 to 2008 while Japan has increased it in spite of their GDP growth. In contrast, Mexico, whose currency has strengthened, shows a decline in public debt. There are of course many reasons why China and Japan can have a high public debt. However, in view of the accusations, we cannot rule out the possibility of product subsidies.

---

[196] http://globalpolitician.com/22220-economics, Peter Morici, Univ. of Maryland, former chief economist at the U.S. International Trade Commission.

[197] http://en.wikipedia.org/wiki/U.S._dollar

[198] http://en.wikipedia.org/wiki/U.S._dollar

We can see from Table 9.3 that China's trade deficit is far worse than any other non-producing oil import country, and this has been blamed for 2.3 million U.S. job losses.

> **Remark 9.28:** July 30, 2008—"Between 2001 and 2007, 2.3 million American jobs were lost due to the China trade gap, including 366,000 last year, according to the report released today by the Economic Policy Institute (EPI).... The U.S. trade deficit with China increased from $84 billion in 2001, when China was granted entry into the World Trade Organization (WTO), to $262 billion in 2007."[199, 200]

We remind the reader that this is a failure-modes-and-effects analysis where we are looking at root cause issues at this point. As such, we are pointing out the major failure modes and root causes of free trade, specifically U.S. trade with China. We have many benefits in trading with China that are not part of this discussion. We maintain focus on this area and broaden our investigations of free trade violations with other countries as well.

**9.4.4: Other Areas of Free Trade Failures Due to WTO Violations**

Other trade accusations have occurred. For example in 2004 a letter was sent to President Bush.

> **Remark 9.29**: April 2004—"House Democrats sent a letter to the President after the release of the *National Trade Estimates* report urging President Bush to take immediate action to address the unfair trade barriers standing in the way of U.S. exports.... 'After the loss of almost three million manufacturing jobs since January 2001, and the growing problem of outsourcing in the services sector...The cases include ones involving European subsidies to Airbus, various Japanese and Korean barriers to U.S. exports of autos and auto parts, India's non-tariff barriers on textiles, lack of intellectual property protection by India, and a growing number of areas in which China is not living up to its WTO commitments, such as denial of trading rights and distribution barriers.'"[201]

Accusations continued, but no apparent penalties were imposed.

> **Remark 9.30**: April 2007—"...according to a new report from the Office of the U.S. Trade Representative (USTR).... Counterfeiting and piracy, unjustified sanitary and phytosanitary [food safety] measures, inefficient,

---

199 www.epi.org/page/-/old/newsroom/releases/2008/07/080730-release_china_trade.pdf
200 www.epi.org/publications/entry/bp219/
201 www.house.gov/apps/list/press/wm31_democrats/040401bush_admin_remove_unfair_trade.html

nontransparent customs regimes, high tariff barriers and closed services markets continue to hinder U.S. access to foreign markets," USTR General Counsel Warren Maruyama told reporters April 2 following the release of the annual National Trade Estimate on Foreign Barriers (NTE) report.... China's apparent use of prohibited export and import substitution subsidies, which USTR says harm small and medium-sized U.S. manufacturers."[202]

We are apparently unable to maintain fair trade practices or impose penalties, only tally violations.

**Remark 9.31:** April 2007—"Inadequate IPR (Intellectual Property Rights) protections reduce U.S. access to China's market and other countries' markets for such products as films, music, published materials, software, pharmaceuticals, chemicals, information technology, consumer goods, industrial goods, food products, medical devices, electrical equipment, automotive parts, clothing, and footwear, according to the release."[203]

The U.S. has been taken advantage of because of a lack of oversight. Now in 2009 with all the continued data of trade violations, business failures, and job losses, it appears things are out of control with free trade. How will violations ever stop if penalties are never imposed? It is in fact, illogical to have a free trade agreement without proper oversight and this is in itself a serious reliability free trade economic issue.

### 9.4.5: Root Cause—Job Outsourcing and Business Failures Issues with Japan

In this section, we look at the failure modes of U.S. corporation failures with root cause, job outsourcing and foreign competition. Perhaps the best example is what has happened in Detroit. It is no coincidence that our automakers are going out of business. The U.S. was badly beaten down by Japanese automaker competition. This did not happen overnight.

**Remark 9.32:** "In 2004, Japan exported to the United States over 1.7 million passenger vehicles and a substantial amount of auto parts worth a total of $46 billion. During the same time, Japan imported just 15,000 passenger vehicles and auto parts from the United States worth a total of $1.8 billion. The market share of Japanese nameplate brands reached over 30% of the total U.S. light vehicle market in 2004—including nearly 40% of passenger cars. In contrast, sales of U.S. nameplates in Japan reached

[202] http://media-newswire.com/release_1046975.html
[203] http://useu.usmission.gov/Article.asp?ID=08A0ACC7-5916-49E2-B865-0F853252FF0E

only 2% of the total market….In 2005 automotive imported $239 billion worth of cars, trucks and auto parts, and only exported $98 billion." [204]

**Remark 9.33:** "In 2008 the U.S. had a $55.8 billion trade deficit in auto and auto parts with Japan that represented about 8% of our total trade deficit. U.S. exports of autos and auto parts to Japan were almost 27% lower in 2008 than in 2000…"[205]

Many have suggested that General Motors and Chrysler's failure was a matter of quality, cost, and poor business management. These are certainly some of the issues. Nevertheless, similar to China, there have been accusations of currency manipulation with Japan that have potentially hurt Detroit auto sales. A weaker yen in competitive years (2000–2005) was described as a key issue in a 2005 in a statement by Mustafa Mohatarem, Ph.D., a chief economist for GM to the House, Ways, and Means Committee in 2005.

**Remark 9.34:** September 2005—"Japan's weak yen policy has given its exporters a huge subsidy and competitive advantage in the U.S. market, causing significant harm to U.S. manufacturers. One clear sign that a country is manipulating its currency is a substantial increase in its foreign currency reserves, which occurs as it buys and holds dollars. Japan has seen a massive increase in its foreign currency reserves since 2001, growing from $344.8 billion in July 2000 to $840 billion in July 2005… Japan's artificially weak currency provides a significant per-vehicle cost advantage that amounts to an outright annual subsidy of between $3,000 for small car to $12,000 for a luxury sedan or SUV for every vehicle exported to the United States. Cars produced here by Japanese companies also benefit heavily from this subsidy because of their high use of imported parts and components."[206]

There is little doubt in Detroit's mind that free trade has been a nightmare. Chrysler's bankruptcy and GM's turmoil is a painful occurrence that many believe is due in part to an imperfect free trade situation and a clear failure to implement reliability economics. It is another lack of oversight by the U.S. government to ignore the warning signs.

**Remark 9.35**: "From 2000–2005, subsidized by an artificially weak yen funded by $420 billion in Japanese government currency interventions, Japan's automakers have exported an annual average of 1.8 million cars

---

[204] http://waysandmeans.house.gov/hearings.asp?formmode=printfriendly&id=3798
[205] www.autotradecouncil.org/Upload/W+M%20letter.pdf
[206] waysandmeans.house.gov/hearings.asp?formmode=printfriendly&id=3798

and trucks into the United States, 13% higher than the average from 1996–2000." [207]

The automakers have had some success with Congress to make changes.

**Remark 9.36:** March 28, 2007—"Automakers Endorse Japan Currency Manipulation Act; Applaud Stabenow... "[208]

However, the yen was back down in May of 2009 to its lowest level in at least nine years (see Table 9.6). The automakers still struggle for fair trade. In a letter to President Obama, written by many representatives dated March 2009, strong problems persist:

**Remark 9.37:** "Japan also continues to block imports of U.S. auto parts using a combination of non-tariff barriers. For example Japan levies an annual automobile tax that increases by engine size, discriminating against many U.S. vehicles. Japan also continues to restrict severely the number of garages that can perform service repairs through its "certified garage and "designate garage" system. The vast majority (80%) of aftermarket parts and service sales is controlled by dealerships affiliated with Japanese OEMs which are inclined to buy and sell auto parts from closely related Japanese auto companies."[209]

Unfortunately, now much of the damage is done. The U.S. auto industry is in harsh turmoil and hundreds of thousands of jobs have been lost. Part of the problem is the difficulty the automakers have had working with a Congress that is slow to respond over the years to the warning signs. Yet in a time of crisis, in less than six months, Congress has responded with billions in taxpayer bailout money.

**Remark 9.38**: Adding the $25 billion loan program (for Car R&D) to the $85 billion in TARP funds that have already been earmarked for the auto industry brings the total in taxpayer aid going to auto companies to $110 billion.[210]

It is clear that this is a case of putting out fires with bailout funds rather than having been proactive in fighting for fair trade policies back in 2005. Auto bailouts might not have occurred if a reliability economics team existed, which would have persisted with proactive recommendations and actions.

---

[207] waysandmeans.house.gov/hearings.asp?formmode=printfriendly&id=3798
[208] www.motortrend.com/features/newswire/27417/index.html
[209] www.autotradecouncil.org/Upload/W+M%20letter.pdf
[210] www.propublica.org/ion/bailout/item/govt-begins-doling-out-25-billion-in-green-car-loans

With no such economics team available, the government continues down a path of illogical spending of taxpayer monies. One might ask for example, is it logical to have a "Cash for Clunker" 3 billion dollar program in July–August of 2009, when GM and Chrysler are not yet ready to take advantage of it since they are just coming out of bankruptcy?

> **Remark 9.39:** In a June 2009 article by Dave Admin entitled, "Cash for Clunkers Still Pathetic," Mr. Admin notes that we would be one of the few nations that provide little incentive to buy domestic cars. He believes the sale will be heavily favored for U.S. consumers to buy Toyota and Honda rather than, say, one of the big three U.S. manufacturers. He further states that the cash is simply going out of our pockets and into theirs and Japan is not even providing any help to pay for the program.[211]

A reliability economics team would not have approved of this bill. It is untimely, there was no attempt to get financial aid for it from Japan, it does not target our domestic market, or help taxpayers to recover GM and Chrysler bailout funds to assist their future growth. Additionally, if Japanese currency manipulation did occur, then this program rewards U.S. automakers' competition for apparent wrongdoings. Finally, the bill does very little in terms of reducing our gasoline consumption. For example, if a fuel-efficient car was purchased for each $4500 refund, that would amount to about 230,000 new cars ($1 billion/$4500 refund). On average, the U.S. uses about two to three gallons of gas per car per day[212]. If we are generous and assume one gallon of gas savings per day per car, that would only be 230,000 gallons of gas. America consumes about 385 million gallons of gas per day[213]. This amounts to roughly 0.00000006% gasoline energy savings per billion dollars! We point this out to illustrate the importance of implementing a reliability economics team to provide investigative FMEAs prior to implementing programs in the U.S., ensuring their value.

### 9.5: Free Trade Corrective Actions - Currency Manipulation/Government Intervention

It is clear that free trade has moved away from its original ideology and has many failure modes that have led to the harsh effects listed in Table 9.1, such as high unemployment and corporate failures. Its failure, as we have discussed, brings about potential issues of economic greed by other countries, so trade cannot work properly. Therefore, government intervention will always be present at many levels. Corrective actions and proactive economics, needs to foresee potential

---

[211] www.allpar.com/weblogs/2009/06/10/cash-for-clunkers-still-pathetic/, by Dave Admin
[212] http://lifeaftertheoilcrash.net/Research.html
[213] www.eia.doe.gov

issues such as currency manipulation, foreign competitive subsidies, and import roadblocks that may have aided in bankrupting American companies. Rather than react, it would have been better to have a signed legislation already in place that provided immediate penalties for our trading partners. Waiting is not part of reliability economic methods. Therefore, the first corrective action needs to be to pass a law that requires penalties when currency manipulation/subsidies and import blocks occur. Such legislation does two things: it forewarns our trading partners of our strong mandated required actions for free trade violation, and it ensures that actions will be taken. In this country, we have known laws for crimes. We do not wait around for someone to commit a crime and then decide what to do. The U.S. has a powerful economic team and the ability to detect foreign trade wrongdoing. Once this is proven, fines must follow just as our trading partners are doing.

> **Remark 9.40**: May 20, 2009—"Intel has been slapped with a record $1.45 billion fine…by the European Commission, which found that the California-based firm 'violated EU competition rules...'"[214]

Corrective-action fines will have consequences and require a full FMEA investigation in and of itself to understand the consequences of such well thought-out penalties. This is outside the scope of this book and would be presumptuous. Therefore, a summary of a reasonable reliability corrective-action economic plan is as follows:

Currency Manipulation Corrective Action Plan

- Provide legislation that requires actions for any country that is caught performing currency manipulation.
- Perform a FMEA on any such legislation to understand its potential failure modes and effects.
- Provide realistic legislation that can be imposed in a proactive rather than a reactive timely manner.
- Such penalties should most likely be done in test stages.
- Develop a global currency standard with stricter regulations than a simple exchange rate as suggested in Section 7.2.2

### 9.5.1: Research on Free Trade Corrective Actions for Job Outsourcing and Job Quota

Job outsourcing benefits a minority of wealthy company owners. It is well-known that for the most part, it does not benefit the majority.

---

[214] www.caltradereport.com/eWebPages/front-page-1175882866.html

> **Remark 9.41:** "According to Ravi Batra's book, *The Myth of Free Trade*, open trade in the U.S. has resulted in replacement of manufacturing jobs for service jobs, which pay less on average. The product trade deficit results in more investment money flowing into the U.S. as a trade-off. This investment money mostly ends up with wealthy investors and owners; and 'trickle down' is not sufficient to compensate for the loss of manufacturing jobs and wages. According to Batra's research, even though free trade may increase GDP, the increases do not flow to rank-and-file workers."[215]

Furthermore, according to wikipedia.org, the main benefits of free trade are:

- The wealthy own more capital which increases in value as companies are able to produce at the lowest cost in the world.
- As the world's markets merge into a single global market, the number of market-leading companies worldwide drops, with takeovers of smaller local corporations by larger multinational corporations. This process concentrates wealth in fewer corporations.
- Free trade replaces low-skilled jobs often done by the poor more easily than it replaces high-skilled jobs. This implication of the Stolper-Samuelson theorem is challenged on the basis that technology makes off-shoring high-value work feasible and more profitable than moving low-skilled jobs.

However, U.S. economists persist with free trade ideology. In the economic world, the majority of economists have strongly been in favor of free trade. They are against protectionism such as tariffs or trade quotas, and have just about hammered home the benefits. In 2007, our Federal Reserve Chairman, Ben Bernanke, concluded in a long speech on the challenges of free trade:

> **Remark 9.42:** May 1, 2007—"To sum up, international trade in goods, services, and assets, like other forms of market-based exchange, allows us to transform what we have into what we need or want under increasingly beneficial terms. Trade allows us to enjoy both a more productive economy and higher living standards....Of course, current trading arrangements are far from perfect.... Although expansion of trade makes the U.S. economy stronger...the broad benefits of trade and the associated economic change may come at a cost to some individuals, firms, and communities....We need to continue to find ways to minimize the pain of dislocation without standing in the way of economic growth and change....If we resist protectionism and isolationism while working to

---

[215] http://en.wikipedia.org/wiki/Free_trade_debate

> increase the skills and adaptability of our labor force, the forces of globalization and trade will continue to make our economy stronger and our citizens more prosperous."[216]

The ideology is, of course, not good without proper mechanisms in place to foresee the issues that have occurred not only with free trade violations, but also with high job losses and related national debt increases (see Sec. 9.7) from free trade deficit. It is foolhardy to persist without any protective policies in place to guard against violations and recessionary problems. Perhaps if we started to outsource jobs in the Senate and those held by our economists, things might improve. From a reliability economics point of view, jobs cannot endlessly keep disappearing to cheaper labor outside the U.S. Some measure of protectionism needs to kick in for issues when they occur (such as today's Modern Recession). The data is now in: the auto industry has failed, bond and stock holders for GM and Chrysler lost their investments, the government is losing tax revenue from layoffs, and it is well-documented that far too many jobs have been—and continue to be—outsourced. A reliability economic plan seeks to ensure that:

- The value of the dollar is no longer threatened
- The national debt is under control and is reduced to reasonable levels
- Companies in the U.S. can withstand foreign competition
- Unfair trade practices are under control
- Job outsourcing is less of a threat
- Government revenue returns to reasonable levels
- Bailouts are unnecessary

Lastly, we would like to cite a brief reminder that tariffs in America were at one time successful and the way the U.S. did business with foreign governments.

> **Remark 9.42-A:** In the past the U.S. has relied on Tariffs to control trade and provide protectionism. This has largely been abandoned. Historically, "Tariffs were the largest source of federal revenue from the 1790s to the eve of World War I, until it was surpassed by income taxes. Since the revenue from the tariff was considered essential and easy to collect…The GOP under Ronald Reagan and George H. W. Bush abandoned the protectionist ideology, and came out against quotas and in favor of the GATT/WTO policy of minimal economic barriers to global trade. Free trade with Canada came about as a result of the Canada-U.S. Free Trade Agreement of 1987, which led in 1994 to the North American Free Trade

[216] Chairman Ben S. Bernanke, at the Montana Economic Development Summit 2007, Butte, Montana, May 1, 2007 www.federalreserve.gov/newsevents/speech/bernanke20070501a.htm

> Agreement (NAFTA). ... some tariffs have been more resistant to change. For example, due partially to tariff pressure from the European Common Agricultural Policy, US agricultural subsidies have seen little decrease over the past few decades, even with recent pressure from the WTO.[217]

Tariffs have also been unsuccessful. The Smoot-Hawley Tariff Act of 1930 ended up increasing unemployment due to retaliation by U.S. trading partners. However this occurred when the U.S. had a trade surplus. With today's deficit, the U.S. can win most tariff wars. However, unemployment issues then were also confounded by the great depression and a poor consumer marketplace. Tariffs can be problematic for our current free trade environment. Trading partners sometimes can understand that a tariff is appropriate, such as a penalty issue or perhaps a war tariff. We might suggest this to help pay for U.S. missions like Afghanistan.

**9.5.2: Research for Corrective Action for Jobs in the Service Sector**

To this extent, we review the trade deficit situation a little closer to understand our strengths and weaknesses, and where it might be possible to help our position by ensuring our economic reliability growth. Table 9.8 breaks down the trade deficit from 2000 to 2009.

**Table 9.8** U.S. Service & Good Trade Imbalance Broken Out [218]

| Year | Export Services | Import Services | Service Trade Surplus | Import goods | Export Goods | Goods Deficit | Overall Deficit |
|---|---|---|---|---|---|---|---|
| 2000 | 311.9 | 232.3 | 79.6 | 1,243.5 | 784.3 | -459.2 | -379.6 |
| 2001 | 301.6 | 231.9 | 69.7 | 1,167.9 | 731.2 | -436.7 | -367.0 |
| 2002 | 308.4 | 241 | 67.4 | 1,189.3 | 697.6 | -491.7 | -424.3 |
| 2003 | 316.4 | 256.2 | 60.2 | 1,283.9 | 724.4 | -559.5 | -499.3 |
| 2004 | 364.1 | 298.3 | 65.8 | 1,499.5 | 818.3 | -681.2 | -615.4 |
| 2005 | 403.1 | 319.8 | 83.3 | 1,705.3 | 908.4 | -796.9 | -713.6 |
| 2006 | 448.7 | 355.4 | 93.3 | 1,882.7 | 1,032.1 | -850.6 | -757.3 |
| 2007 | 513.2 | 385.1 | 128.1 | 1,985.2 | 1,149.2 | -836.0 | -707.9 |
| 2008 | 576.3 | 413.4 | 162.9 | 2,115.2 | 1,283.1 | -832.1 | -669.2 |
| 2009 | 509.2 | 370.8 | 138.4 | 1,933.35 | 1,045.5 | -517.05 | -378.6 |

From Table 9.8, we see that the service industry is currently the main source of health for our trade deficit. It is also a great area where jobs can be more easily protected compared to our manufacturing goods sector.

> **Remark 9.43:** "The United States leads the world as the premier producer and exporter of services. As the largest component of the U.S. economy,

---

[217] http://en.wikipedia.org/wiki/Tariff_in_American_history

[218] 1. U.S. Bureau of Labor Statistics , 2. U.S. Department of Commerce, www.blogmybrain.com/stock_apps/graphical_economy

the services sector includes all economic activity other than agriculture, mining and manufacturing. The service sector accounts for about 80 percent of GDP and private nonfarm employment (over 81 million jobs)."[219]

**Remark 9.44**: "(2008) GDP by sector—agriculture (0.9%), industry (20.6%), services (78.5%)"[220]

Additionally, one of the old arguments for free trade was that America should focus on skilled labor while outsourcing more unskilled jobs. This was one philosophy by free trade advocates. However, our highly skilled jobs are currently under attack to be outsourced by CEOs, predominantly by India.

**Remark 9.45:** "Stronger India After Global Recession—China has shown its superiority in manufacturing and exporting goods at rock bottom prices to Americans and others and India is doing the same by selling the services of its English speaking talented young adults in business and knowledge process outsourcing sectors. ..."[221]

Losing millions more jobs to India in the service sector and going from a trade surplus to a deficit now threatens more jobs and leaves the U.S. government with lost tax revenue from unemployed skilled laborers.

**Remark 9.46**: "Bangalore—In a year when outsourcing of application development and maintenance projects has slowed down, top customers such as Bank of America, JPMorgan and Citibank continue to send more back office projects to India, as they seek to lower their cost of operations by up to 40%...According to Nasscom, India's back office outsourcing industry will grow at 18.4% this year to reach $14.8 billion. Outsourcing of IT services will clock a lower growth at around 13.5% this year, and could even decline to single digit growth if the situation does not improve. ...The current recession is forcing companies from other verticals such as media, entertainment, healthcare, energy and utilities to consider outsourcing of back office work."[222]

Even in the entertainment industry, CEOs have chosen to start outsourcing jobs.

---

[219] www.unzco.com/basicguide/c8.html
[220] http://en.wikipedia.org/wiki/Economy_of_the_United_States
[221] http://ezinearticles.com/?Stronger-India-After-Global-Recession&id=2224188, By Kanti Mohan Pandit
[222] http://economictimes.indiatimes.com/Recession-proves-good-for-Indian-outsourcing-firms/articleshow/4774575.cms

**Remark 9.47**: January 2009—"Warner Bros., the 90-year-old film studio in Burbank, California, is preparing to outsource jobs to India and Poland as part of a studio-wide cost-cutting move."[223]

This outsourcing is taking place in spite of great profits in this industry.

**Remark 9.48**: November 2008—"Time Warner: profit from the content business is up 14% from last quarter. Another entertainment powerhouse, Activision Blizzard, reported incredible earnings yesterday: revenue more than doubled. The CEO, Bobby Kotick, went on to state that 'there's nothing that would suggest to us today that our business isn't going to continue to perform well." [224]

Studies now show that this sector is starting to follow a devastating pursuit to the manufacturing area. This is somewhat indicated in Table 8.3, which shows a decline in the service sector of 3% in the last year. This number is of course confounded by the recession job losses, making it a difficult statistic to assess.

**Remark 9.49:** March 2, 2009—"A study done by a team of scholars in Duke, Harvard and Berkeley University reveal that the loss of about 1,000,000 skilled migrant workers to nations like India and China will affect the U.S. economy like a catastrophe which will take decades to recover."[225]

### 9.5.3: Corrective Action—Job Quotas and Service Outsourcing

In the world of free trade, protectionism in the form of tariffs or trade quotas is frowned on by many economists especially in our global economy. A more logical requirement is perhaps a minimum level of American job quotas for importing companies. Here we mean by quotas is to require any company (foreign or domestic) that imports goods or services into the U.S. which employs foreign workers should also be required to employ a certain minimum number of American citizens (especially when the unemployment rate is greater than 8%). If they have an inability to do so, than we would suggest a certain tariff. The ratio of required American workers to the number of foreign workers should be determined by the government. Alternately, the number of American workers required for any company could be based on gross profits. This is our main suggestion for corrective action. Government free trade advocates must realize that it does not serve the common good for a multibillion dollar international corporation to simply import goods or services and provide limited job creation in America. Some will argue that the value of a company's stock serves the common good in of itself and the employment picture is not as important. The only

[223] www.employmentspectator.com/2009/01/warner-bros-to-outsource-us-jobs-to-india-poland/
[224] http://current.com/items/89499290_movie-business-is-recession-proof.htm
[225] http:// news.oneindia.in/2009/03/02/us-job-loss-boon-to-india-and-china-report.html

realistic answer is that there are necessary trade-offs. Companies must be profitable, but they also should provide a reasonable level of employment to the U.S community that they are selling items to. If not, these CEOs only increase the separation of wealth that contributes to a reduction in the velocity of money and hence retards true economic growth.

Job quotas in the service industry are probably the quickest and best place to start bringing back employment and making sense out of our free trade job problem. The concept of mandated U.S. job quotas is less likely to start a trade war, especially in the service sector. The following would be the method that we suggest.

1) Provide a multidisciplinary team to make recommendations for job quotas and how it would be implemented to any company selling in the U.S.
2) The concept is a bit simpler than tariffs or product quotas which appear threatening to free trade policy. Here a U.S. policy would be put in place to issue a statement that when U.S. unemployment rate reaches a critical level, say 8% or greater, U.S. service industry job quota will be a requirement to protect the nation's financial stability.
3) Then, in the spirit of job quotas, either require a certain level of jobs per number of foreign employees working for each company or base the number of required U.S. job on gross profit level. Negotiate with our foreign competitors regarding U.S. job quota needs. Negotiations should be part of the free trade solutions. These can better be viewed as requirements and not an arbitrary protectionism act by the U.S. If a company cannot meet the requirement for U.S. jobs, than consider a tariff on their services as a possible alternative. We do anticipate trade war issues, but starting in a deficit service sector area, should allow for successful negotiations. Additionally, America can win most any trade war as we usually dominate the consumer side especially in the area of importing goods and many service sectors.
4) As we mentioned in Chapter 1, test verification is part of any reliability economic requirement. We suggest starting with the service sector (compared to goods) as it is less threatening for a stress test. A narrow area like entertainment movie industry, Information Technology, or transportation.
5) Require U.S. job quotas for the industry over a period of three to six months. Expand the program to other areas including goods with continued monitoring to see how well the success of the program turns out.

### 9.5.4: A Junk Tax Corrective Action on Goods

Lastly, one needs to realize that every item imported into the United States eventually ends up as junk. This is certainly a reliability economic issue of future concern. The current cost of running a dump in the U.S. ranges between $25 to $100 per ton. It might be difficult to assess our trade deficit in weight, but in terms of automobiles, the statistic for the weight of cars in more recent years is provided by Table 9.9.

**Table 9.9** Average Weight of New Cars and Light Trucks, 1975-2006 (Pounds)[226]

| Year | Cars (Tons) | Trucks (Tons) |
|---|---|---|
| 2000 | 3,369 | 4,375 |
| 2001 | 3,380 | 4,463 |
| 2002 | 3,391 | 4,546 |
| 2003 | 3,421 | 4,586 |
| 2004 | 3,462 | 4,710 |
| 2005 | 3,490 | 4,711 |
| 2006 | 3,563 | 4,712 |

With our trade imbalance, we should not lose sight of the fact that we are importing JUNK. As such, it is logical to impose a junk tax on imports. This may appear as a tricky way to provide a measure of protectionism, but recycling and dumping TVs, automobiles, batteries and so forth is an expensive proposition. For example, according to Table 9.9, the average car was about 1.75 tons in 2006, and a truck was 2.4 tons. If we incurred a tax of $100 per ton, the assessment would be about $175 per car and $240 per truck. For example, Japan exported 1.7 million passenger vehicles to the U.S. in 2004. All these aging cars will end up in the dump in roughly 20 years. The cost will probably be well over $0.3 billion dollars per year. Recycling requires more sophisticated estimates. Note that the U.S. tax savings would really be doubled. For example, if junk were to cost the U.S. $1 billion a year in taxes, citizens would gain $1 billion, a net $2 billion. Finally, one should expect some level of trade war retaliation with foreign junk tax. However, as we mentioned before, American can win most any trade war as we are such a large consumer of goods.

### 9.5.5: Bottom-Up Corrective Action for Labor Unions

Although it is not appropriate for us to suggest legal battles, it appears that some accusations that we have found in the news appear to warrant strong action. Soaring job losses in Detroit have cost United Auto Workers (UAWs) a high price. It seems that the UAW should respond directly with international legal action in response to the alleged free trade violations by Japan and China. This action should be taken rather than depend on our legislature and economists to take action, which has apparently never occurred. For example, in the remark above, we noted Intel was fined $1.45 billion by the European Commission. Such lawsuits may be warranted on our competitors. There are apparently a lot of facts

---

[226] Source: U.S. Environmental Protection Agency, *Light-Duty Automotive Technology and Fuel Economy Trends: 1975 Through 2006*, Appendix D, July 2006.

regarding trade violations that we have pointed out. It would be logical to seek retribution if these charges are accurate.

**9.5.6: Equal Trade Corrective Action– Warren Buffet's Plan**

Warren Buffett proposed an idea to fix the trade deficit using import certificates. The idea was introduced into legislation in the Balanced Trade Restoration Act of 2006. This equal trade plan was dismissed. We fully supported this proposal.

> **Remark 9.49A:** "Buffett's plan proposes creating a market for *import certificates* that would represent the right to import a certain dollar amount of goods into the United States from other countries. These certificates would be issued to US exporters in an amount equal to the dollar amount of the goods they export, and can be sold to importers, who must purchase them in order to legally import goods." [227, 228]

**9.6: Trade Deficit for Oil versus All Goods and Energy Policy Issues**

The OPEC oil U.S. trade imbalance has varied over the years and is a constant issue. In 2008 OPEC trade imbalance was about 22% compared to China that total 33%. Table 9.10 illustrates the issue in 2008.

**Table 9.10** U.S. Trade Deficit Comparison to OPEC in 2008

| Country/Area | Deficit in Percent |
|---|---|
| China | 33% |
| NAFTA | 18% |
| OPEC Nations | 22% |
| Others | 28% |
| TOTAL | 100% |

We rightfully seek energy independence, OPEC issues are a sizeable part of America's free trade deficit problems. Here, we briefly comment on energy policy especially with regard to wind and solar solutions, since there is much controversy that policy makers are putting too much emphasis on this compared to the needs of other more traditional energy sector solutions. The remark below puts this somewhat in perspective in terms of job creation, its relative projected impact on energy consumption, and our recession.

> **Remark 9.50:** "The Bias Against Oil And Gas, By Robert J. Samuelson – In 2007, wind and solar generated less than 1 percent of U.S. electricity. Even a tenfold expansion will leave their contribution small. By contrast, oil and natural gas now provide two-thirds of Americans' energy. They will dominate consumption for decades….. Consider: In 2008, the oil and gas industries employed 1.8 million people.

[227] http://en.wikipedia.org/wiki/Import_Certificates

[228] http://money.cnn.com/magazines/fortune/fortune_archive/2003/11/10/352872/index.htm

> Jobs in the solar and wind industries are reckoned (by their trade associations) to be 35,000 and 85,000, respectively. A 5% rise in oil jobs (90,000) approaches a doubling for wind and solar (120,000)…oil will swamp 'green' jobs."[229]

It light of such comments that are widely discussed by numerous other articles, it appears a bit illogical that our government seems to have a bias against supporting natural gas and oil development. The president of ExxonMobile, Rex Tillerson, back in 2004 even then provided similar insight.

> **Remark 9.51:** "However, even with this very high growth rate, by 2030 the share of energy supply from wind and solar will amount to less than 1% of the world's total energy demand….The enormity of what our petroleum industry delivers day in and day out is not well understood by the public and, regrettably, by many policy-makers.."[230]

Actually, other sources suggest wind and solar are between 1 and 2%. Nevertheless, efficiency, sustainability, renewability, and clean energy are the key issues. Solar is least efficient, 50 -60 cents per kW/hr, wind about 10-15 cents kW/hr, while nuclear and coal are 3-4 cents per kW/hr. Many now feel nuclear meets all these key requirements. Many articles by energy experts agree with these facts. Some even argue that we are supporting OPEC through the lack of a proper long term energy policy where we are importing 12 million barrels a day. Reducing the trade deficit, like the national debt, needs to be a priority for the U.S. It is not the intent of this book to go further in trying to resolve our energy policy. The author supports alternative energy as it certainly has its place in America. However, this is another case for Reliability Economics. Proper root cause failure analysis of our energy policy would lead to a better decision process.

### 9.7 Free Trade Deficit Related Tax Losses

We conclude this chapter by investigating the FMEA effect in Table 9.1, "loss of tax revenue" due to the free trade deficit. There are a number of reasons why we might expect tax losses from the free trade deficit. First we would like to mention that the explosion of the free trade deficit has become of the same order of magnitude as the national debt. In fact, the two show somewhat of a similar time series as displayed in Figure 9.2. This graph is simply the data from the U.S. government website listed in Table 9.11 for Columns 2 and 4. Figure 9.2 shows the trade deficit has exceeded the national debt in certain years. The trade deficit appears correlated, influencing the national debt, after 2001.

---

[229] http://loga.la/loganews/?p=37, The Bias Against Oil And Gas, By Robert J. Samuelson, May 4, 2009

[230] www.energybulletin.net/node/3624, Published Dec 12 2004 by Oil and Gas Journal, Archived Dec 12 2004, Exxon president predicts non-OPEC peak in 10 years by Sam Fletcher

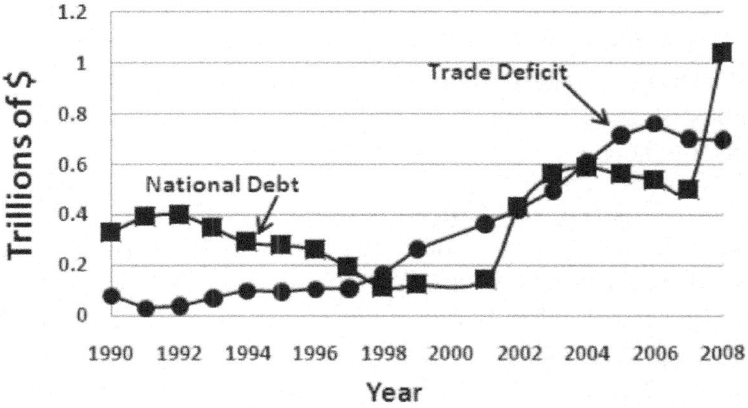


**Figure 9.2** Comparison between trade deficit and national debt.

It is instructive to actually look at the mathematical correlation. Although we are making no claims as to how influential the trade deficit might be on U.S. tax losses, we will show that it is reason for concern. There are budgetary reasons why after the period from 1990 to 2001 the national debt increased from 2003 to 2008. In fact the main government expenses: defense and military, health & services and social security all increased by a total of 89% on average between these periods[219]! Therefore, we are not claiming that the free trade deficit is the main reason for the increase in Figure 9.2, but our investigation will show there are serious tax revenue concerns.

The concern is a trade imbalance also provides tax consequences representing a combination of ways in which taxes are collected depending on the type of trade (import vs. export) for goods and services. As a simple example, the U.S. collects tax revenues on U.S. worker salaries for exported services compared to imported services for which no salary taxes are collected from foreign workers. This illustrates one simple difference in Trade Deficit Tax (TDT) consequences that can occur depending on the type of trade imbalance.

The U.S. Free Trade Deficit has accumulated to $6.57 trillion dollars over the last 20 years and $7.5 trillion since 1971. The National Debt now totals around $12.1 trillion. In fact, from 1990 to 2007, the trade deficit totaled $5.51 trillion, which was fairly close to the national debt in those years that totaled $6.1 trillion. From a bird's eye view, we see two very explosive amounts.

The question is then, are there excessive TDT losses due to the trade deficit, and is it effecting the national debt? Unfortunately, we will only be able to provide simple quantitative and qualitative information to demonstrate concern. First let's look at some more qualitative reasons.

One basic concern of a trade deficit is that more money leaves the U.S. in trade than comes in, and can contribute to the national debt. Free trade advocates argue that such U.S. dollars must be reinvested back in the U.S., and while this is true, it leaves one unanswered question, what about related TDT loss consequences that have incurred in the trading transition? As well deficit reinvestments mean foreigners own more and more of the U.S. Here we provide simple examples of what we mean by trade transitions being associated with tax collection consequences from a U.S. trade deficit.

**U.S. Import Related Tax Consequences:**

1) Imports create decreases in federal tax revenues for various reasons, such as products made by non U.S. citizens who do not pay federal tax compared to products or services that would have created tax revenues if the products were not imported. Thus as U.S. made goods are replaced with foreign imports, so too are U.S. jobs and lost taxed wages in addition to unemployment benefits. Seemingly temporary, yet U.S. displaced workers occur frequently enough that the U.S. taxes burden is yearly (see Remark 9.9A estimate of $77 billion).
2) U.S. trade deficit enables foreigners to buy numerous American businesses and own more and more of the U.S. IRS data show that foreign-owned corporations doing business here typically pay far less in U.S. income taxes than do purely American firms with comparable sales and assets. This is because it's hard to determine how much of a corporation's worldwide earnings relate to its U.S. activities and therefore are subject to U.S. tax. There are many other tax issues that create serious tax problems.[231]
3) Many U.S. CEOs outsource jobs creating service TDT losses, these "imported services" decrease potential tax revenues of the company's workforce compared to non outsourcing. This also creates higher unemployment. Unemployment causes more lost tax dollars due to U.S. government subsidies until workers can recover. Profits of U.S. companies abroad may end up abroad decreasing tax revenues.
4) U.S. companies' off-shoring manufacturing find as much as a 15% tax reduction due to both tax loopholes and lower tax in other countries.
5) Foreign profits from the trade deficit that are reinvested typically do not provide the tax revenue that U.S. citizen reinvestments may provide. For example, currently foreign reinvestments are considerable in U.S. government obligations for the U.S. national debt and now total about $3 trillion. This provides tax liability as the U.S. has to pay interest on this money to foreigners. On the other hand, U.S. citizens pay taxes on many of their reinvestments when owning U.S. business and equities. Foreigners who reinvest in buying U.S. business also find ways to avoid U.S. taxes. Job outsourcing often occurs once a U.S. business is taken over.

---

[231] www.ctj.org/hid_ent/part-2/part2-3.htm, "Tax breaks for multinational corporations"

6) There is a national debt, trade deficit cyclic effect (Sec. 9.3) when foreigners reinvest in U.S. treasuries, the interest obligation creates ***negative*** economic growth or jobs potential reducing taxes.

**U.S. Export Related Tax Revenue:**

7) Exports create federal tax revenue gains for various reasons (products more likely made by U.S. citizens who pay income tax, U.S. companies pay taxes on profits, we export services to foreign companies and these creates tax revenue through income tax, etc.)

These are basic examples, but serve to help in understanding the reasons for reliability economic concerns.

**9.71 Correlation Analysis – Free Trade Deficit and National Debt**

Next we provide a quantitative assessment. Here we use a simple mathematical correlation assessment that should be helpful as part of our initial reliability economic investigation. Correlations are sought all the time in many areas. For example in health, we know that being overweight is correlated to diabetes, smoking has been correlated to lung cancer and emphysema, and so forth.

In a similar manner, according to our FMEA work in Chapter 7 and here, we suspect that the U.S. free trade deficit may be linked to America's national debt due to related TDT losses.

Despite the complex nature in interpreting the data, mathematically we simply will look at the raw data. Results show below that a correlation exists of about 84% in select time periods between 1990 and 2008. First we mention that it is clear the two can be unrelated in certain time periods. For example, we know that the trade deficit in 1990 to about 1995 was minimal compared to the national debt (see Table 9.11 and Figure 9.2). At this point in time where the free trade deficit was just starting to accumulate, tax losses would be minimal. Similarly, one would anticipate a weaker correlation in 2008 and 2009, since the U.S. expenditures have been highly irregular due to the modern recession compared to the free trade deficit which has dropped dramatically due to the recession.

To perform this simple assessment, we provide the trade deficit data (from the U.S. Census.gov website. This is listed in Table 9.11. Column 2 provides the free trade deficit data in trillions of dollars. Columns 3 and 5 reflect the cumulative results and the running totals of each.

First we will look at the raw data in select years that make sense where we expect a correlation to occur. In order to identify the possibility of a mathematical correlation, logically certain years are able to reveal the underlining relation better than other periods in the historical data set. Then the select year assumptions are:

**1)** Select a reasonable sequential time period within the normal 20 year time frame of interest. We stated earlier that from 1990 to 1995, there was a minor trade deficit and there was little correlation. We also noted

that 2008 and 2009 were highly irregular in government spending. These years will be ignored in the correlation analysis.
**2)** We use values M1 in Table 9.11, a set of 11 years from 1996 -2007 to look for a correlation. We ignore an irregular point, the year 2000.

**Table 9.11** National Debt and Free Trade Deficit Data (1990-2009)[232]

| Year | Annual Trade Deficit in Trillions $ | Cumulative Trade Deficit in Trillions $ | National Debt in Trillions $ | Cumulative National Debt in Trillions $ |
|---|---|---|---|---|
| 1990 | 0.081 | 1.01+ | 0.33 | 3.21 |
| 1991 | 0.031 | 1.04 | 0.39 | 3.6 |
| 1992 | 0.039 | 1.08 | 0.4 | 4 |
| 1993 | 0.070 | 1.15 | 0.35 | 4.35 |
| 1994 | 0.098 | 1.25 | 0.29 | 4.64 |
| 1995 | 0.096 | 1.35 | 0.28 | 4.92 |
| 1996 | 0.104 M1 | 1.45 | 0.26 | 5.18 |
| 1997 | 0.108 M1 | 1.56 | 0.19 | 5.37 |
| 1998 | 0.166 M1 | 1.73 | 0.11 | 5.48 |
| 1999 | 0.265 M1 | 1.99 | 0.12 | 5.6 |
| 2000 | 0.380 | 2.37 | 0.03** | 5.63 |
| 2001 | 0.366 M1 | 2.74 | 0.14 | 5.77 |
| 2002 | 0.422 M1 | 3.16 | 0.43 | 6.2 |
| 2003 | 0.495 M1 | 3.65 | 0.56 | 6.76 |
| 2004 | 0.610 M1 | 4.26 | 0.59 | 7.35 |
| 2005 | 0.715 M1 | 4.98 | 0.56 | 7.91 |
| 2006 | 0.760 M1 | 5.74 | 0.54 | 8.45 |
| 2007 | 0.701 M1 | 6.44 | 0.5 | 8.95 |
| 2008 | 0.696 | 7.14 | 1.04 | 9.99 |
| 2009 | 0.379 | 7.52 | 2.3 | 12.3 |

Next we look at the raw data by performing a regression analysis of Col. 2 and Col. 4 shown in Figure 9.3. This provides an estimate of how well the national debt and trade deficit correlate. This is obtained from $R^2$ of 0.711. The square root of this values is the correlation coefficient of 0.84 (R-value), indicating an 84% correlation, in this select period from 1996 to 2007. Figure 9.3 also shows the 95% confidence bounds about the regression line. The P-value found of 0.001 (Figure 9.3) indicate a probability of 1 in a 1000 that the correlation is by chance. A "Durbin-Watson" statistics for Model 1 was found to be 0.96. This large value (> 0.8) indicates an unlikely autocorrelation.

[232] Trade Def. Ref. http://www.census.gov/foreign-trade/statistics/historical/gands.pdf,
National Debt Ref: www.whitehouse.gov/omb/budget/fy2010/assets/hist.pdf (may be revised)
** Outlier point - an irregular data point. +Accumulated trade deficit since 1971

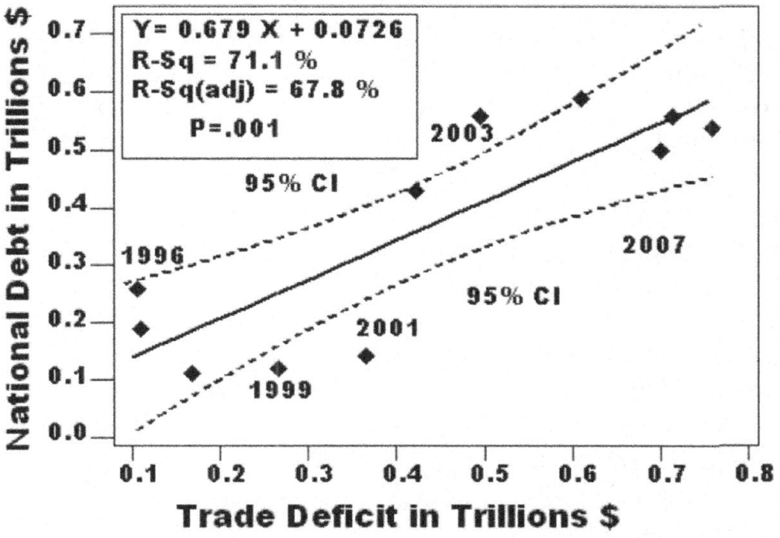


**Figure 9.3** Model 1 of the national debt versus the trade deficit, 1996 to 2007

The actual dollar relationship is potentially challenging. To understand this, we note the slope in Figure 9.3 is given by the X-Y relationship on the graph (i.e. Y=0.679X -.0726). First note the Y intercept (.0726) is relatively small compared to values in Column 3 from 1996-2007. This implies there would be little or no tax consequence to the national debt if the trade deficit were zero. It also means we can approximate Y(National Debt) ~ 0.68 X(Trade Def.).

This implies 68% of some trade deficit X-quantity is linked in our model to lost tax revenue and effectively adds to the national debt. We now assert a 3rd model assumption that: this mathematical relationship is valid for any time period. That is, we have been able to identify an underlying relationship using select years; the relationship should still be reasonably valid for other time periods. The question is now, what is the X-quantity? The reason we do not take the entire trade deficit of $7.5 trillion as the X-quantity is that we know excess government spending is complex and also some of the trade deficit reinvestment actually creates tax revenue. Foreigners reinvest trade deficit dollars in businesses and treasuries and both can help GDP growth and tax revenue through businesses and job creation. This indicates the need for a more complex (multiple regression) model. While this is outside our scope we provide an alternate model that will not change the correlation coefficient. The model is Y=(0.679X -.0726)f where f is a fractional estimate or Y ~ 0.679 Xf. This equation will be realized by multiplying Column 4 (national debt) by f then fitting the M1 data in the same way. As an example, we take f=40%. First note that 40% of $7.5 trillion equates to $3 trillion (the X-quantity) that coincides with foreigner investment into U.S. Treasury (see Table 9.3). Note this quantity of foreign reinvestment would not be there if it was not for the trade deficit, providing some f=0.4 justification for our model. We now multiply \$3 trillion by 0.68 giving \$2 trillion of effective trade deficit that is added to the national debt. The 95% confidence lower bound in Fig. 9.3 was estimated (not shown) to be \$0.8 trillion. The \$2 trillion seems high in light of Remark 9.9A for example. The \$0.8 and \$2 trillion values of \$12.3 trillion total national debt imply since 1971 roughly 6.5% to 16.3% of the national debt is due to the trade deficit. This is also between 10.7 and 26.7 cents of every trade deficit dollar adds to the national debt. With the U.S. population of about 300 million, this equates to between \$2667 to \$6667 added to each citizen's national debt credit card! We see that free trade is not really free due to this *reverse tariff* effect! ***That is a reverse tariff is defined here as a tax on imports paid on trade deficit goods and/or services, by the importing country's citizens due to trade deficit tax loss consequences. This presents an economic flaw of free trade.*** This model is crude. However the range is likely to be reasonable and the model illustrates the correlation. Trade deficit tax loss issues are highly complex, and providing an accurate assessment is most likely a Ph.D. thesis. However, we have now provided reasonable quantitative and qualitative assessment. From our results, we are baffled by a trade policy in which ordinary taxpayers end up subsidizing the deficit through the national debt and now question its legality.

### 9.8: Free Trade Deficit Ethical and Legal Constitutional Law Questions – Concluding Remarks

We would like to conclude with remarks regarding the ethical and possible legal ramifications surrounding the free trade deficit. In this chapter we have seen a number of related free trade accusations that relate to ethical greed issues:

1) Currency manipulation by U.S. trading partners, 2) Excessive Job outsourcing, 3) Product subsidies by foreign governments, 4) Unfair non tariff trade barriers by our trading partners, 5) Lack of intellectual property rights protection, and 6) Product counterfeiting.

We also assessed qualitatively and quantitatively that the free trade deficit creates tax losses in Section 9.7, which were estimated in a crude model to have a lower bound estimate of \$0.8 trillion since 1971 effectively adding to the national debt.

This problem of tax related consequences seems to imply strong legal issues. It means that U.S. citizens are in part funding the ethical problems, and the free trade deficit itself. In effect, U.S. citizens are enabling job outsourcing, currency manipulation, and so forth. One interesting thing observed in our correlation analysis was that if the free trade deficit went to zero, the tax consequences would also diminish. This indicates that equal (i.e., balanced trade) would in fact be an excellent corrective action. However, we noted that Warren Buffet's equal trade proposal (Sec. 9.5.6) using import certificates was dropped.

At this point we ask the legal question, is it a violation of law for U.S. tax payers to be put in a position of funding the trade deficit. As a taxpayer, it is certainly aggravating to realize that we are partially paying for the trade deficit and all the related greed issues. We address this in two ways, 1) does it violate free trade policy itself, and 2) does it violate a constitutional law.

***Does it violate constitutional law?*** We have identified and verified with a constitutional lawyer[233], a violation on tax of interstate commerce. This constitutional law states (Article 1, Section 9, Clause 5): "No Tax or Duty shall be laid on articles exported from any State." The argument is then, U.S. tax payers are actually paying a "reverse tariff" tax on moving imported trade deficit goods from state to state through tax losses due to the trade deficit (that we discussed in this chapter). In other words, U.S. citizens are paying an interstate tax since the import trade deficit goods have tax consequences that increase our National debt. Therefore, it is a violation of constitutional law that tax payers are subsidizing the free trade deficit on imported deficit goods that are moved from state to state across America. From our graph in Figure 9.3, tax losses diminish to zero if trade deficit approaches zero. Therefore, only equal trade will not violate this law.

***Does it violate free trade agreement?*** The agreement between our trading partners requires elimination of tariffs and quotas on most (if not all) goods and services traded between them. Our argument is similar to that above, U.S. tax payers are actually paying a "reverse tariff" on imported trade deficit goods through trade deficit tax losses (that we discussed). Since the trade deficit is partially funded by U.S. tax payers, then this is a self-imposed tax on trade surplus of imports and is a reverse tariff that U.S. citizens are paying on deficit imports. Therefore, a trade deficit violates free trade policy itself!

For the reader's interest, legal council agrees with the above arguments[231]. However, legal council has also cautioned, when constitutional law is violated that the courts may choose not to rule citing a "Political Question Doctrine," if the court feels "it is prudent not to interfere". The final counter argument is, mathematically we show there is a solution, that of equal trade which does not have tax consequence (Figure 9.3). The constitution is here to protect us. The court should not ignore that any country cannot sustain large, trade deficits.

We see that free trade deficit has created ethical and legal issues. Economics appears to weigh the good with the bad as has been done with our free trade policy. This is a key difference with our approach. In reliability economics, we would not tolerate and seek to resolve such failure modes as the trade deficit and its related issues[234, 235]. We feel if equal trade was implement it would create millions of U.S. jobs, help pay off the National Debt, reduce separation of wealth, reduce housing and business failure rate, stop foreigners (dominated by China) from buying up the U.S. and help assure America's future.

---

[233] Private communications with Wesley Oliver, Professor of Constitutional law, Widener University, March 2010

[234] www.CitizensForEqualTrade.Org, Author is founder of this website.
Free Trade Deficit Violation of Constitutional Law, submitted: Center of Constitutional Rights (3/29/10)

[235] www.modernrecession.com (see authors other references therein with slide presentations )

# ■ 10.0 ■

# MIDDLE EAST LONG-TERM SOLUTION

### 10.1: Iraq War

The cost of any unfunded war will increase our national debt. And this can equate to job losses. In the short-run, war increases jobs due to military spending. However, in the long run, the costs will hurt our government's funding programs and eventually create more job cuts. The U.S. should not fight unfunded wars and drive up the national debt. Any foreign war also effectively increases the U.S. trade deficit as well due to the maintenance cost overseas. There should be creative logic in the way we spend when possible. If necessary, as we have said before, we might try war tariffs to get some of our trading partners to help fund our efforts. We present cheaper methods in this chapter. The notion that war is good for the economy is known to be faulty (see Remark 10.2) especially with our national debt. As described in Chapter 7, the larger the national debt, the more government jobs will eventually be lost on both the state and national level. This is a key issue since the government is our largest civilian employer and the cost of war is becoming more problematic in the Modern Recession.

Everyone knows about the Bush administration's faulty justifications for the Iraq war. It is not the intent of the book to belabor the point. Unfortunately, nuclear proliferation is the number-one issue in the free world. So there was an apparent appalling attempt to solve a root cause problem: "Find Weapons of Mass Destruction." The big problem is there are always political agendas that create complex motives.

> **Remark 10.1:** Alan Greenspan, September 16, 2007—"I am saddened that it is politically inconvenient to acknowledge what everyone knows: the Iraq war is largely about oil.[236]"

### 10.2: Middle East Conflict

However, rather than belabor the endless known points, from a reliability economics perspective, it is best to ask root cause questions: What is the real cause of the Middle East crisis? What possible cost effective corrective actions

[236] www.timesonline.co.uk/tol/news/world/article2461214.ece

may exist now? What are the true costs incurred by our economy? What will the Middle East crisis continue to cost us and mankind?

> **Remark 10.2:** Apparently, the true cost of the Iraq war to Americans is seriously underestimated. Nobel prize–winning economist Joseph Stiglitz and co-author Linda Bilmes explained in their book, *The Three Trillion Dollar War*. "Figuring in macroeconomic costs (including veteran's post war health care for example) and interest-the war has been funded with much borrowed money-the cost rises to $4.5 trillion; add Afghanistan, and the bill tops $7 trillion".[237]
> "It used to be thought that wars are good for the economy. No economist really believes that anymore", Stiglitz said in an interview. Stiglitz and Bilmes argue the true costs are at least $3 trillion under what they call an ultraconservative estimate…[238]"

The cost effects of this conflict are of course not just in dollar amounts, but also with American lives lost. It hurts our new position in the world; we are now perceived to be an aggressor. It is also a strategy by our enemies to force us to fight a costly war and is thus a monetary victory for their side including the maintenance costs. If the costs of this and other Middle East wars are going to be so enormous, perhaps it's time to perform a stronger root cause analysis to look for ideas to improve the Middle East situation with less costs.

### 10.3: Root cause Analysis of the Middle East War

In this case we require a human or behavioral FMEA. This is not so different from a product reliability analysis. In this case, it is a bit like reverse-engineering a product, by seeing how it is made from a competitor to understand the competition's strengths and weaknesses. Similarly, we have to look into the mindset, or human engineering, that is occurring within our enemy. How is our enemy built? What is their mindset? What is their background? How does it compare to our mindset? How do they arrive at their religious aggressiveness?

> **Remark 10.3:** In an article by Dr. Sami Alrabaa entitled, "Middle East Mired in a Culture of Hatred," Dr. Alrabaa states that a Palestinian presenter at Hamas's Al-Aqsa television asked a little girl what she wanted to be when she grew up. The girl replied she wanted to be a fighter

---

[237] www.amazon.com/gp/product/product-description/0393334171/ref=dp_proddesc_0?ie=UTF8&n=283155&s=books, from *Publishers Weekly*.

[238] www.reuters.com/article/topNews/idUSN2921527420080302

and liberate Palestine and "throw all the Jews out of Palestine." She added that she wanted to kill as many Israelis as possible like Reem Riyashi.[239]

Here's a child getting this kind of education at such a young age, while a typical U.S. child is learning about normal life and perhaps sports or cartoons!

**Remark 10.4:** In the same article above Dr. Alrabaa stated that in 2007, Hamas's Al-Aqsa TV aired a weekly show that featured a Mickey Mouse look-alike. The Mickey Mouse-like character Dr. Alrabaa urged children to support armed resistance against Israel. Then the article stated that the character was beaten to death by a character portraying an Israeli…later Dr. Alrabaa noted that school textbooks depict an aggressive image of Israel.[240]

There are many articles regarding children in the Middle East who are being taught to hate Jews.

**Remark 10.5:** In an article by Alan Gray entitled "Mothers for Peace Challenge The Brainwashing of Middle East Children (*NewsBlaze)*… Alan Gray listened to a Muslim woman who he quoted as saying that as a child she was taught to hate Jews both at home and in school. The woman went on to say that the Palestinian schools have pictures of suicide bombers on the walls. …"[241]

This human analysis allows one to understand the root cause problem of a trained education in hatred; this is a reality for many Middle Eastern children. Yet there is no counter educational measures taken on the U.S. part. Where is our counter war on education?

**10.4: Corrective Actions for the Middle East Problems**

There are, then, two choices about the Middle East crisis in terms of seeking a corrective action:

**War**
**And/or**
**Education.**

Education is a long-term solution. On the other hand, relative to the time frame of this conflict and its growing involvement by the Western and Eastern

---

[239] http://islam-watch.org/Sami/Middle-East-Mired-in-Culture-of-Hatred.htm
[240] http://islam-watch.org/Sami/Middle-East-Mired-in-Culture-of-Hatred.htm
[241] http://newsblaze.com/story/20060216080217nnnn.nb/topstory.html

worlds, the educational approach should not be discarded. The actual violence in the Middle East between Israel and Arabs really began around 1920 and is approaching a status as a 100-year-old unresolved conflict.

> **Remark 10.6:** By the 1920s, the Jewish and Arab populations had grown hostile to each other and acts of violence persisted from both sides of the conflict. ...Eventually, violence between Arab and Jews had begun a vicious cycle which continues to this day.[242]

The vicious cycle persist especially in light of the fact that war has yet to resolve the root cause problem of the best acceptable U.N. resolution to date for Israel's land boundary, known as the green line.

> **Remark 10.7:** "The War came to an end with the signing of the 1949 Armistice Agreements between Israel and each of its Arab neighbors. This 1949 armistice line, the so-called **green line**, is to this day the internationally-recognized border of the state of Israel. It is often referred to as the 'pre-1967' border."[243]

This is the strongest root cause issue now between Israel and a number of Arab factions. Many countries are being dragged into this conflict, as these small factions refuse to respect this agreement. Education must work to give all concerned the chance to understand the difficulty of not accepting this resolve. Human engineering by the small factions is preventing peace.

> **Remark 10.8:** Dr. Sami Alrabaa (Remarks 10.3 and 10.4) states that Western governments needs to pressure Arab countries to use genuine freedom of speech. Currently the Arab journalists and writers who wish to provide balanced articles on Arab-Israeli conflict are banned from publishing.[244]

However, while freedom of the press would certainly go a long way, this is also about schools and education. Knowledge of the final agreement and an understanding of the consequence of not accepting this resolve for Israel, the Arab nations, and generally all countries, really should be the focus. There is also a major need to counter the educational propaganda war. Educational propaganda is a part of our enemy's tactic used by terrorists and therefore should be part of

---

[242] http://en.wikipedia.org/wiki/Arab%E2%80%93Israeli_conflict
[243] http://en.wikipedia.org/wiki/Arab%E2%80%93Israeli_conflict
[244] http://islam-watch.org/Sami/Middle-East-Mired-in-Culture-of-Hatred.htm

our battle plan as well. Counter educational methods should not be underestimated, it is the key to terrorist tactics, why not combat it?

We should not lose sight of the fact that solutions should be cost-effective. The Iraq war has been estimated at $12 billion per month. The U.S. and our allies would be better off spending much of that money to help evolve education in the Middle East upon the acceptance of the agreed-upon green line boundary to fight hate education that is occurring. This would combat the human engineering of mistrust that is ingrained in our enemies; it likely would catch on and avalanche a higher acceptance in the Middle East. It is clear we cannot abandon arms, but we cannot continue to discard education and the need for freedom of speech in the Middle East. Education is the only long-term answer. Otherwise this problem will only escalate.

> **Remark 10.9:** May 20, 2009, Tehran, Iran—"Iran test-fired a missile capable of striking Israel, U.S. Mideast bases and Europe on Wednesday—a show of strength touted by President Mahmoud Ahmadinejad as he battles for re-election next month against more moderate opponents."[245]

**10.5: Summary**

Here we have determined a corrective-action cost-effective education approach would be preferable to war in the Middle East. There seems to be little work for a bottom-up plan to educate young Arabs on the importance of the UN green line Middle East resolution. There is no effort to counter the hate educational that is occurring in middle-eastern children at a young age. This reliability economics plan is long-term but will more likely secure a better future when compared to drawn-out war. Although it is not America's job to school our enemy, we have pointed out that educational propaganda is a part of our enemy's tactic. Education is actively being used by terrorists and therefore should be part of our battle plan as well. Education and freedom of speech should not be underestimated in helping to fight nuclear proliferation and promoting a lasting peace.

*"With the magnitude of the challenges we face right now, what we need in Washington are not more political tactics—we need more good ideas. We don't need more point-scoring—we need more problem-solving."*

—BARACK OBAMA, press conference, March 17, 2009

[245] http://news.yahoo.com/s/ap/20090520/ap_on_re_mi_ea/ml_iran_missile_test

# ■ 11.0 ■

# IMPLEMENTING RELIABILITY ECONOMICS

Here we will discuss how to implement a reliability economic corporate approach in government without interfering in the traditional legislation voting process. Although not interfering, a reliability corporate model could still be powerful and influential in problem solving just as it is in industry. This is not a Keynesian (government intervention) approach, but a government self-assurance program. The strong parallels between government and industry need to be understood to why this is practical. The government is like a business, it is our largest employer. It's legislatures like in industry are the engineers, the designers. Their product is legislation. In the corporate model a team of quality and reliability economists would be employed to assure their product is reliable. Legislatures could learn to depend on an Office of Quality and Reliability Economics as they do the Congressional Budget Office (CBO). The consumer demands customer satisfaction which means highly reliable products with good quality. In industry any good company uses a reliability and quality team that independently provides design assurance. They use a number of tools to help the design engineers (legislatures) assess and find potential failure modes in the proposed product (legislation) that could prevent millions of dollars if potential failure mode(s) would otherwise escape to the consumer. In the same sense potential failure modes in a legislation bill will be highly costly. The design engineer (legislature) does not have to implement their recommendations in industry if they feel it will hurt the design (legislation). However, they then may put their product (legislation) at risk. The recommendations are reported, and management (congress) becomes aware of what safeguards are built into the design (legislation) or not. This then can influence the vote on the legislation but does not interfere with the legislative voting process. The objective is to fill the ***existing reliability legislation gap*** not reviewed in the design (legislation) idea phase. In the same way that a reliability engineer does not design products, the reliability economist would not be responsible for the original legislative design. Without training, an economist would not be qualified as a reliability economist. This established reliability science should not be ignored in economics due to the high cost of failure modes. Analogous to industry, we believe in a mindset of designing it right the first time for reliability through historical understanding of the current environment, root cause investigations, and often a team approach. Classical economics may provide valuable tools but falls far short of these goals. Reliability economics provides a different set of tools such as FMEA. This tool allows for team participation. Given the difficult partisan political environment in the U.S., one of the foreseen strengths in our FMEA examples is the logical progression of root cause analysis, which is basic to problem solving, and should allow for a high level of agreement for bipartisan corrective action solutions. The key philosophy is that only when understanding root causes can solutions be found, only when fixing failure modes can reliability growth be achieved. *People in industry can understand the need for a reliability economic corporate model in government. Politicians with no industrial experience, who have not observed the benefits, lack this foresight and understanding. This sadly presents a barrier.*

In this book we have focused on the well-known FMEA technique and applied it to the economy. However, to meet the challenge of today's economy we envision it will require developing a reliability economic team with a mindset to design-in reliability into the economy. Just as in industry, it is one thing to make a product; it is another to make it reliable – so to in the economy, each policy must have a reliability economist that is responsible to ensure it will be written to design for reliability. We anticipate that this team would perform three basic activities described in Chapter 1 (adapted from industry):[1]

- Design for reliability economics
- Reliability economic verification
- Root cause fiscal analyses

Similar to industry, these activities would be the building block to a sound reliability program for the economy that sits on a foundation of concurrent economic engineering. Just as economists are needed in government, so too is a Design for Reliability-Economic (DfR-E) team needed that would be responsible for these three basic activities:

1. The first reliability economic activity is to support new policy to help design for reliability. This starts with the idea phase of the policy development cycle and continues until its obsolescence. Each policy should be required to have a reliability economist assigned to the project to assure it contains a positive policy for reliability improvement by utilizing known fiscal-of-failure knowledge (discussed more below) to design out potential fiscal problems. The reliability economist would help spearhead the FMEA effort ensuring that a multi-disciplinary team made up of democrats, republicans, reliability economists, and other expert participants in the area of interest, maintain a bipartisan atmosphere with a reliability mindset. The reliability economist can use a full set of DfR-E tools that might include:

- Fiscal of Failure Analysis
- FMEA and Benchmarking
- Risk Mitigation Studies
- Economic Design Studies
- Modeling
- Design Rules

**2.** The second activity is reliability economic verification. Here verification studies and demonstration tests ensure meeting the challenges of a consumer economy. Reliability verification should take place in three phases – through a historical review of known similar data, early field data tracking with small scale testing, followed by long term maturity tracking. Reliability validation techniques can include:

- Economic Processes
- Reliability Monitoring
- Field Data Analysis
- Reliability Screening
- Design Validation

**3.** The third activity, fiscal analysis, would be critical to a reliability economist's ability to affect the design process. This should include "Fiscal-of-Failure" analysis that is defined as understanding the nature of how and why a policy can fail when it interacts with the real economy during the design's full life cycle. This includes current CBO analysis. The reliability economist should understand the consumer's use and misuse conditions and the policy's interactions to assist the design team in working around limitations inherent in the selected design approach. This would be a key to designing and building any future policy that will meet consumer expectations. These tools include:

- Design Analysis
- Policy interactions
- Reverse Engineering of Similar Policies
- Policy Construction Breakdown
- Process Analysis

Reliability economics with the three proposed major activities can support a phased economic design development cycle that in industry we call ***Stage-Gate***.

**Table 11.1** Stage-Gate Reliability Economic Approach

| Phase | Stage-Gate | Task | Description |
|---|---|---|---|
| 1 | **Idea** | Designing-in Reliability | Concurrent engineering approach tools such as Failure Modes and Effects Analysis (FMEA) and benchmarking to other policies. Ensure that consumer requirements are met. |
| 2 | **Evaluate** | Design Assessment Reliability Testing, Fiscal of Failure Analysis | Risk mitigation studies and reliability growth efforts focus on finding and fixing failure modes/ root causes, concurrent with the design process. Using the techniques of reliability growth, life testing with Test Analyze and Fix (TAAF) and others as necessary for the economic design. |
| 3 | **Develop** | Design Maturity Testing | Demonstrate that a design is reliably meeting the consumers' expectation. Perform statistically significant tests, usually on a small scale. |
| 4 | **Transition** | Screening | Ensure early design is robust. Check for infant mortality problems in the field. |
| 5 | **Production** (implementation) | Monitoring | Ensure continual design reliability and quality to design obsolesces. |

The Stage-Gate method is shown in the Table 11.1. The Stage-Gate effort would underpin economic design development, starting with design conception and continue through final design obsolescence. The Stage-Gate method is essential in designing-in reliability capable of meeting consumers' expectations. In reliability economics it should ensure that a design will meet the consumers' needs as it starts with an understanding of the full design requirements, economic environments "hazardous condition" (such as use and misuse, economic greed problems) to full design life, potential design use and misuse, total design cost goals, and reliability service life needs.

Finally, to determine the level of effort associated with any policy, it typically should depend on whether it is a modification of a working policy, if it is a revolutionary one, or if it is a working policy with failure modes. The measure of risk needs to be explored to understand the policy development effort and cost. In general, there are different goals depending on if the policy is an existing one or a new design:

- Major goal of an existing design is
  - Reliability growth
  - Ensure reliability growth by finding and fixing failure modes through root cause analysis, design controls and corrective actions
- Major goal of a New Design
  - Ensure the design is reliable
  - Design-in reliability
  - Be proactive not reactive

In order to facilitate the proposed DfR-E science, we suggest some initial basic economic reliability design rules (modified from reliability in industry):

- **Design Rule 1:** A reliability economic design should be able to withstand risky conditions, such as consumer use and abuse, economic greed, and terrorism to a reasonable extent.
- **Design Rule 2:** In order to fix fiscal failure modes of a design, root causes must first be properly identified and substantiated.
- **Design Rule 3:** Finding and fixing fiscal failure modes in an economic design is the only way to achieve reliability economic growth.
- **Design Rule 4:** Every economic design should require a FMEA be performed with a multi-disciplinary team in order to properly identify the FMEA factors and achieve agreement amongst the owners of the policy. Then design controls need investigation prior to corrective actions.

Reliability also has a complete set of statistical tools for predictive analysis. For example, a statistical Weibull analysis was demonstrated in the Appendix of Chapter 2 on the unemployment failure rate.

# ■ 12.0 ■

# WHAT THE READER CAN DO

As of March 2010, there is talk of a jobless recovery. This is a sustained period of jobless growth during our recovery. This could occur in spite of a recovered stock market and possibly positive GDP growth.

However, the U.S. as of March 2010 has done little in the area of structural economic changes that plague our recession to remedy such problems. Bailout is not a solution to the problems that have caused our recession. Many of the changes suggested in our book have certainly not been addressed. The key economic indicators as of March 2010 are 10% unemployment rate, $12.5 trillion national debt, $350 billion projected free trade deficit, and a high housing failure rate all still dismal problems.

We recommend each reader write their representatives to promote real changes. On the next 2 pages is a proposed letter. Please cut the letter out, copy it, and mail it to your government officials. (Mayor, Governor, State and Federal Representatives and President Obama.)

**Dear**
As an American citizen, I would like to see real economic change to the root cause problems that plague our Modern Recession. Bailouts have not addressed these.

These proposed economic changes I am recommending are provided in the book, *The Truth to the Modern Recession* or on the website www.solutionsWithoutUSDebt.com. I agree with the author for the following suggestions:

1) Congress Should Declare a Seven Year of War on the National Debt that Includes:

   - A Seven year commitment by Congress
   - Draft professionals like lawyers, engineers, doctors, and nurses to provide free part time help for the sick and needy during this declared war
   - Pay off the National Debt with
     - An equitable change in the tax structure – "A One Hundred Percent Equitable Progressive Income Tax Structure with a Salary Cap"
     - A higher estate tax policy on the wealthy
     - An asset tax on the wealthy
     - A life time wealth cap for the wealthy
     - A bill to close tax loopholes on the wealthy such as 15% long term capital gains tax allowed for hedge-fund profiteers
     - Stop the trade deficit which is responsible for ½ of our national debt

2) Stop the Continual Separation of Wealth and Consequential Money Hoarding by the Wealthy Through
   - An annual income salary cap
   - A lifetime estate cap

3) Improved Restrictions on Lobbyists Including Prohibiting Them to Write Any Legislation
   - Require all campaign funds to be taken out of our income taxes

4) New Free Trade Policies:
   - Does not violate the Article 1, Sec. 9, Clause 5 of the constitution in which U.S. tax payers are actually paying a tax on moving

imported trade deficit goods from state to state through tax losses due to the trade deficit. Does not violate free trade agreement, where U.S. citizens are paying trade deficit tariffs from tax losses.
- Requires any company that imports goods or services into the U.S. that employs foreign workers should also be required to employ a certain minimum number of American citizens (especially when the unemployment rate is greater than 8%)
- U.S. policy on foreign governments for immediate penalties for currency manipulation
- U.S. policy on foreign world trade violations
- Junk tax on all imports by weight
- Require Import Certificates as suggested by Warren Buffett

5) Anti-hoarding Legislation in a Time of a Declared Recession for
    - Wealthy individuals
    - Wealthy corporations

6) Restore a New Version of the "Glass-Steagall Act" to Help Regulate Large Financial Institutions that Have Become too Big to Fail.

7) A New Proactive Reliability Macroeconomics Team
    - To help build reliability into our economic policies
    - To help design test verification for all new economic policies
    - To investigate root causes of economic failed policies

8) A Website That Provides Full Root Cause Analysis and Corrective Actions for Any New Legislation or Economic Policy
    - Preferably adopting the industry standard Failure Modes Effects Analysis method for our government

9) An Educational Campaign in the Middle East to Stop Hate Against the U.S.
    - Counter education propaganda used by terrorists on young children
    - Educational solutions are less expensive than war and needed.

10) Perform Impartial Investigation of Hedge Fund Managers and Their Role in Influencing the Stock Market and the Modern Recession

Sincerely,
Name:
Address:

## List of Tables

## List of Figures

## List of Remarks

## Dedication

This book is dedicated to my daughters and to their generation who are likely to be faced with a terrible financial burden and repercussions from the national debt. It is the hope that work may help spark the needed fiscal responsibility to alleviate this problem.

## Acknowledgements

I would like to thank and acknowledge my family for their patience and review of much of this material. I am especially grateful to my wife Linda for her ideas.

I would like to thank my editors, Lou Rosenberg and Collin Tracy.

The author also appreciates all the contributions from the literature, and websites, for their data, copyright permissions, and available information. This helps in providing a healthy perspective of how America feels on many issues.

## About the Author

Dr. Feinberg is a reliability economist and engineer. He has a unique multi-disciplined background that includes a M.S. and Ph.D. in physics, 30 years of industrial reliability engineering, an exceptional background in mathematics and finance, and is an avid scholar and attentive researcher on the economy. He is also the author of the book, *Design for Reliability.* Dr. Feinberg uses his diverse expertise to provide a novel approach in researching facts for uncovering the *Truth to the Modern Recession* and seeking the root causes that lead to credible reliable solutions. He introduces a new method termed Reliability Economics for the layman to provide a friendly and understandable approach. He is also the founder of www.CitizensForEqualTrade.org. You may contact Dr. Feinberg through the book website, www.modernrecession.com. All author profits are donated (see www.modernrecession.com for details).

## Disclaimer and Legal Statements

**Legal Information on References**
All references cited in this book are from facts and ideas in the public domain, government studies, or respectfully done by using the method of 'fair use' exemption. The author believe he has maintained 'fair use' of any fractional quotes as provided for in section 107 of the U.S. Copyright Law. In accordance with Title 17 U.S.C. Section 107. The purpose of these quotes is strictly educational and informational (i.e. the dissemination of published facts or information to benefit the reader). The author respects and appreciates, these helpful sources and has done his best to maintain accurate quotes, references, and not to abuse the 'fair use' exemption allowance. As such the author has provided clear credit to the references with indentations and quotation marks.

**Legal Information on Accuracy of Material**
While every care has been taken in the preparation of this publication, the author cannot be held legally responsible for the accuracy of the information contained throughout this book. The author will not accept any responsibilities for personal opinions presented in references and expressed in the reference articles, or any other form. Such facts are presented as informative and only to aid in analysis to help address reliability issues in our economy. As such these are in no way meant to find blame with any particular individual or organization whose name may appear from news stories. Facts presented are only partially quoted by newspapers, radio, TV and/or websites for informational purposes and are restricted in length by the fair use exemption allowance. The accuracy of these references has not been substantiated, and the author cannot take responsibility for their information. Although all the findings and facts presented in this book are believed to be accurate, the author cannot be held responsible for the material or its outcome of the recommendations, or any liability associated with the material presented and makes no representation about its quality. Links and references to this material are made to facilitate access to information.

The term "Remark" appears throughout the novel to signify an information source. The term is meant to indicate it is a REMARK; that this source provides partial information; not that the information itself has been determined as an accurate source. By reading this book, the reader accepts full responsibility to determine the accuracy of what is presented and the Remarks provided.

## Index

Made in United States
North Haven, CT
10 November 2026

22096534R00109